Ethical Dilemmas in Genealogy

Penny Walters, PhD.

Sincere thanks are due to:

- my parents
- my six children
- in alphabetical order: Peggy Clemens Lauritzen, Ivor Disney, Mark Fletcher, Nathan Dylan Goodwin, Julie Hahn, D. P. Lindegaard, Pat Marley, Thomas MacEntee, Tom Murray, Andrew Nash, Sharon Parnham, Joana Saahirah, Mike Slucutt, Toni Sutton, Serena Williams, Ruth Wood.

Note from the author:

This book contains my thoughts on genealogical issues; they are intended to hopefully inspire people to consider the issues. Please feel free to contact me with any of the ethical dilemmas that you have experienced within genealogy.

'There are no clear cut rights and wrongs, and the debate about issues can be more informative and enlightening than any notion of a fixed answer.'

Contents

Chapter 1: What are ethical dilemmas?

'I'm just researching my family, what possible problems could there be?'

"Someone has taken some of my photos from my online tree and put them on their tree, without asking me"

"I've done a DNA test specifically to find out who my birth mother is"

"My cousin is really angry that I've put his wife and children's names on my online tree, and demanded that they be removed from the tree"

"When I was in a museum recently, I saw some mummies in glass cabinets, they were really eerie"

"I don't understand how my DNA has come back as Ghanaian, when my grandfather came from Jamaica"

"I've noticed that some of my family are on someone else's tree and they have loads of wrong information on there, but I'm not sure if I should I tell them, they might think I'm being rude"

"I've discovered some very sensitive information on my client's tree about living relatives, but they have only contracted me to devise a simple pedigree chart"

"I've looked at my great grandparents' marriage certificate, and I'm not sure if I should tell my grandfather that his mother was seven months' pregnant when she got married"

These are some examples of issues that can arise when researching family history. Have you had similar situations arise when investigating your family history? If you have, then finding the right solution isn't always easy. When we have difficult decisions, choosing the best solution becomes an ethical dilemma, which can be defined as *'a situation in which there are genuine reasons pointing toward two different courses of action'*[1] or a *'challenging situation that involves competing sets of values.'*[2]

Genealogy has now become a popular hobby

Genealogy is now a hugely popular hobby and it has been reported as being placed second only to gardening, followed by fishing, then bowling, biking, photography, collecting, reading, music, hiking and sports.[3] However, it could be argued that the wording of questions about genealogy being a hobby can alter the answers, for example, the question, *'are you interested in your ancestors?'* would result in many yes's, but there would probably be a different answer to the question, *'would you devote time and resources to finding your ancestors?'* which would probably be mostly no's. Maybe *'Genealogy is not like other pastimes. In fact, it is not really a pastime at all. Genealogy is a field of study that is integral to the human condition. As a result, it is perhaps more relevant to talk about levels of interests rather than just a single interest when discussing genealogy.'*[4] Gordon, 2017, observed that, *'Billions of people find at least a part of their sense of personal identity intricately linked to family history and genetics. Rare indeed are those individuals who have no such interest.'*[5] If each family has one person dedicated to compiling the family tree, then, although other family members know about and have access to their tree, they wouldn't actively be undertaking any research. 'Genealogy In Time' magazine calculated that probably only one out of forty people in their definition of the 'average' extended family would be conducting genealogy research. They felt that this translates into about 2.5% of the world population, which they estimated to be about eleven million people worldwide, during 2013. The 'actively researching' figures could well be more now, because of the surge in DNA testing. Intensive DNA test advertising could be seen as 'hooking' casual genealogists into being more serious ones, who would potentially engage more with the various DNA companies' services. Have we got a genuine interest in compiling our family history, or have we been encouraged into it through the lure of being told our ethnicity estimates?

Hobby or duty

There are many hobbies that can be enjoyed, but is genealogy 'just' a hobby, or does it feel like it is your 'duty' to research the family tree, especially when nobody else within the family is doing it? The International Association of Jewish Genealogical Societies (IAJGS) explained that, *'It can be argued that the study of genealogy itself, if not an 'ethical' activity as such, is a mitzvah* (commandment or obligation) *in accordance with the Torah principle of teaching knowledge of the people, their tribes, and remembering the days of old.'*[6] For the Mormon Church, it's very important, if not vital, that people know their biological relatives.[7] Jackson pointed out that you will ideally meet deceased ancestors in heaven.[8] Cardinal Sean O'Malley mentioned DNA testing and the fascination to find our origins in his 2018 Christmas sermon, quipping, *'You might get a robot, or someone might buy you a MyHeritage DNA test.'*[9] The Cardinal's point for his audience seemed to imply that Christmas is an opportunity to discover 'why we are here.' Founder of MyHeritage DNA company, Gilad Japhet, explained in his 'MyHeritage Live 2018' keynote conference address that his *'hobby became his passion.'*[10] I spend hours (and hours) on my tree, and get so excited when I find a 'new' person (even though they aren't 'new', they were always there, but I didn't know about them yet). It feels really important to people, including me, to document all these relatives.

Accessibility

Doing family tree research is quite an accessible hobby, with many 'entry points.' Some relatives have left intriguing and interesting photographs, some even have lots of detail on the back of the photographs. People used to write a little summary of what the photo was about, which is invaluable years later. Some ancestors have devised their tree already, which covers a lot of ground work for descendants. However, because an ancestor researched their tree and devised a beautiful hand written version doesn't actually make it correct. Some people have even been accused of fabrication,[11] some by error, and some with a more sinister motive with their deception.

The internet has revolutionised family history research, as many records and archives are online, and those that aren't online can be more readily accessed by looking through searchable indexes, which explain where the records are. Websites can host your tree, and you can print pedigrees; and when you enter names, dates and addresses, the websites send 'hints' that seem to match with the information that you included. Many basic records are online, including birth, marriage, death records, censuses, and many newspapers. People can look at maps, and locate where ancestors lived, and even calculate distances to and from work, or how far an ancestor had to walk to visit a sweetheart, or more sadly, we can look at maps to view diaspora routes. You can zoom in on an online map, and even see the property you were investigating. People can undertake this research at home on a personal computer, or on their mobile, tablet or laptop. Those who don't have enough money for that technology can access many records online at libraries or related institutions, and often the staff will help. Potential access to all this information has meant that many different people are now undertaking research into their family history. Potentially, everyone could get involved.

The increase in the number of 'searching' format television programmes has made researching family history look easy and enjoyable. The programmes result in positive outcomes, and lots of nice overseas travel for celebrities. People at home probably don't realise there has been a team of researchers working for months behind the scenes. The tone is usually very positive and successful; it wouldn't make for 'good television' if people's searches ended in a disaster. The UK's 'Long Lost Families' programme helps adoptees search for family, and one of the presenters, Davina McCall remarked, *'It's how the story is told of people's situations and problems they face, or feelings they have carried around for their whole life. Watching those bad feelings disappear in one single instant is miraculous. That's what I think is so lovely.'*[12] Whilst the stories are usually so positive, it can give many viewers a false hope, although others will get positive inspiration to undertake their own search.

Relationship between ethics and genealogy

In its new accessible online based format, many new ethical dilemmas are emerging within family history and genealogy. One scenario that has affected many people is, for example, that some people simply add relatives to their tree from suggested matches, without verifying the information, and then others subsequently add those unverified people to their tree, as if the information were fact. If it isn't referenced, it should be checked[13] before it is added to the tree. On some trees, people have someone marrying two people who are, in fact, the same person, but with a slightly different name (for example, Jane Smith married two men, Jerry Reilly and Jeremiah O'Reilly); there are people who have supposedly had children when they were toddlers, or even women who had children years after they were dead. Should these things be pointed out to the person whose tree it is? It's a bit of an awkward situation, but adding people without checking the sources can make people's trees go completely awry. It can be easy when you're new to genealogy to just add people, assuming that the other person whose tree you are potentially related to, has researched their tree information. How this issue can be resolved can become a dilemma. Some people could be really grateful that someone has pointed out an inconsistency or an error, as it helps them get their tree as accurate as possible, but others may feel cross that their tree has been criticised, and that the pointing out of potential errors has ultimately criticised them and their research skills.

We are searching into people's private lives, and although it seems fine for us to do this investigating of deceased ancestors, we may well be offended by those methods of searching being used on us, now or in the future. Over a period of many years, I have taken time and used my research skills to (what I would consider) thoroughly investigate my ancestors' lives. However, people can now utilise social media networks such as Facebook or Instagram, for example, to locate living relatives, and therefore have very quick access to a variety of personal information. It might seem fine to contact someone via social media, because we have good intentions, but on reflection, we might be quite shocked that someone had approached us that way, as we don't know what their intentions are. Many people on online forums say that as soon as they have contacted a potential 'match' or 'relative' via social media, that they get 'blocked.' Being approached by a potential previously unknown match may be scary or even confrontational for some people, who may have researched their tree for completely different reasons to the new match.

A commonly reported genealogy gripe involves people taking photographs from your tree. I was quite upset that someone 'took' some of my photographs from my online tree and added them to their tree, without asking first. I politely messaged the person and asked why they had downloaded and saved my photographs from my tree as I couldn't see an obvious familial relationship between us, and I wasn't happy with their reply. I couldn't initially work out what the next step was, as the person said my photographs were 'in the public domain' on a public tree, and I felt the person wasn't as understanding as I'd hoped for, in their response. On reflection, was there a right, wrong or better way to deal with this issue? My tree is public because I feel that there's no point in other people having to spend the years I've spent researching my relatives and ancestors, and 're-invent the wheel,' but I did feel cross about the specific photo being used. I wasn't sure why I was so cross though? It played on my mind, and a dilemma developed.

When people are at a wedding, for example, they can probably expect other people to take photographs of the group, and maybe a 'lifted' wedding photo could end up on someone else's tree on a website, but my picture of four generations of ladies, sitting on my mum's sofa isn't a photo that I'd expected someone would want to add to their tree. The lady sounded shocked that I was asking her to justify her actions. *I thought she was brusque; she maybe thought I was being silly.* So, who was right? If someone is 'right', it implies that someone with the opposite or a very different opinion is 'wrong.' Should we have corresponded a bit differently? Realistically, this was someone that I would never expect to meet. The people and the photograph that she'd added from my tree were linked through the marriage of a very distant relative, and not a blood relative. However, maybe we could have collaborated and established some links, and perhaps even broken through a brick wall. We could have developed a relationship, and maybe become friends. The messaging thread made us both feel uncomfortable, and we didn't message again after she said she'd take down 'my' photographs. This was an ethical dilemma, presumably for both of us. I was left wondering why I was so possessive over old photographs, and she was probably wondering why I objected to her adding them without asking first. The use of someone else's photographs without asking seems to be a common complaint on a message board forum in Ancestry.[14] I also debated making my tree private, so my ethical dilemma had a further 'ripple effect.' It could also be the case that because you've had photographs taken from your tree, that you start taking photographs from other people's trees.

Another example of a genealogy ethical dilemma is that some friends say that they aren't really interested in their family history. I then start excitedly persuading them to research their tree, as if it's their 'duty' to know about their history; and, on reflection, I have maybe 'forced' my opinion onto them. Most of my friends have somewhat dutifully started a tree, and many have then done DNA tests because of my exuberant encouragement. I also have friends who say that they haven't been in touch, for example, with their sister or father for many years, because of an unrepaired rift, and that bothers me as well, because I feel that they should try and fix the problem. I assume that families want to stay connected, but maybe this is an idealistic and somewhat 'romantic' notion. I'd 'looked' for biological relatives for many years. *But, who am I to persuade (maybe coerce) friends into researching their family history?*

I'm also surprised when people say they have ancestors from another country, but that they've never visited that country or any remaining relatives. Suddenly I start consulting maps for them, and looking at airfares and the weather. *Why do I start encouraging friends to save up and travel there, and re-connect with their 'homeland'?* They don't consider that country to be a homeland, as they see it as just a country that their ancestors left many generations ago, not a homeland. The debates we have reveal to me that these issues are our own personal opinions. They present as ethical dilemmas because I encourage friends to research their family tree, and maybe they just plain don't want to? My zest for researching family history could perhaps be upsetting for some people because I could potentially 'open a can of worms.' Maybe I could encourage a friend to do her tree, and undertake a DNA test, and it's then revealed that her dad isn't biologically related to her? What have I started there? I'm sure we have joked to friends that, as a genealogist, we can find information about someone within minutes. Is that a good thing? My altruistic, but maybe naïve hope, is that people will research their tree, meet long lost relatives, travel to lovely places, and have positive outcomes. At the reunion, there would be lovely music playing in the background and the people would skip through fields.

A crucial point is that each of us thinks we're 'nice,' and we probably wouldn't want to intentionally hurt anyone with anything we said or did. However, what happens when our opinions about whether something is right or wrong differ from someone else's, to the extent where we feel that their opinion is not reconcilable with ours? For example, some people consider that a baby born to parents who weren't married would be a terrible situation and cause shame on the family, but for others, whether the parents were married is not an issue; some people find a new relative's contact information and simply send an email, but for others it's days, months, even years of painfully wondering what is the 'best' way to approach him or her; finding some ethnicities within DNA test results is a source of great joy for some people, whereas for others it's a shock; some family historians spend more time researching an ancestral tree than spending quality time with family and friends; some people would be shocked that females aren't included in some cultures' family trees; mixed race marriages were banned or are even still frowned upon in some cultures; for many people, being adopted isn't an issue at all, for others being adopted is a source of great angst; and some people tell tales with some amusement of criminal ancestors in the family, when that situation would have caused major problems for the family at the time. These examples show a variety of potential debates and dilemmas within genealogy.

Traditionally, researching family history involved listening to relatives telling stories, then undertaking a paper trail, telling children a long held oral history, or asking relatives about specific points; and 'digging through' a box of photographs or memorabilia. Maybe the shape of society is changing? Dunaway and Baum suggested that people aren't gathering family stories any more, '... *archives and formal histories have long replaced oral chronicles as official history.*'[15] Now, researching family history involves people dealing with others via the internet, and these are often strangers that you will never even meet in person. An unspoken internet etiquette ('netiquette') has developed, but some people will approach 'matches' with a lack of sensitivity, and may verge on being impolite, or it could be felt that they asked shocking questions. Messages can vary from a bit of a summary of the potential relative's enquiry, through to messages along the somewhat irritating lines of *'we overlap, do you know how?'* and onto more shocking and life-changing messages which may say, *'I think I'm your daughter; did you know my mum in 1967?'* Some people assert that it is their tree, so they can do what they like with it, add who they like, omit who they like. People are therefore finding many situations within recording their family history that they're not entirely happy with, nor are they sure what to do about resolving these ethical dilemmas.

What does the word 'ethics' mean?

It feels like the word 'ethics' means 'right *versus* wrong', but, in fact, all ethical issues are on a continuum. *'Ethics is a notoriously difficult subject because everyone has subjective judgments about what is right and what is wrong.*'[16] Ethics deals with values relating to conduct, with respect to the apparent rightness and wrongness of actions, and to the goodness and badness of the motives and ends of actions. Ethics is related to our conscience, an inner sense of right and wrong; but can also be affected by cultural norms, etiquette, laws, religion, and the period of time that people were living in. Singer argued that, *'Ethics is about how we ought to live,*'[17] which could mean 'how we would ideally live,' or it can mean 'prescribing how we should live', by defining rules. Descriptive ethics aims to describe people's behaviour, examining the choices that people make, and the values that are held by communities and societies. Normative ethics examines the norms by which people make moral decisions, assuming that there are norms in place, and questions the rights and wrongs of decisions, looking at the motives and justifications of behaviour. *'Ethics and morals ... are sometimes used interchangeably, they are different: ethics refer to rules provided by an external source, for example, codes of conduct in workplaces or principles in religions. Morals refer to an individual's own principles regarding right and wrong.*'[18]

Morality

The term 'morality' can be used either descriptively, to refer to codes of conduct put forward by a society or a group (such as a religion), or accepted by an individual for his/her own behaviour; or normatively, to refer to a code of conduct that, given specified conditions, would be put forward by all rational persons.[19] Ethics involves, *'Moral principles that govern a person's behaviour or the conducting of an activity.*'[20] However, it could be concluded that, *'There does not seem to be much reason to think that a single definition of morality will be applicable to all moral discussions.*'[21]

Philosophy

Philosophy (from the Greek φιλοσοφια or *'philosophía'*, meaning *'the love of wisdom'*) is the study of knowledge, or *'thinking about thinking'*[22] or *'the study of the fundamental nature of knowledge, reality, and existence, especially when considered as an academic discipline.'*[23] It can be simply stated that, *'The task of philosophical analysis is to consider alternative* answers.'[24]

Western philosophy can be divided into three main schools of thought, *'The first, drawing on the work of Aristotle, holds that the virtues (such as justice, charity, and generosity) are dispositions to act in ways that benefit both the person possessing them and that person's society. The second, defended particularly by Kant, makes the concept of duty central to morality: humans are bound, from a knowledge of their duty as rational beings, to obey the categorical imperative to respect other rational beings. Thirdly, utilitarianism asserts that the guiding principle of conduct should be the greatest happiness or benefit of the greatest number.'*[25] Academic philosophy is traditionally divided into four major areas of study: 'Metaphysics,' 'Epistemology,' 'Logic' and 'Ethics.' There are a number of useful 'introduction to philosophy' texts,[26,27,28,29,30] which expand upon the theories of established 'great thinkers', such as Aristotle, Sophocles, Plato, Kant, Kierkegaard, Nietzsche and Bentham. *'Those who study philosophy are perpetually engaged in asking, answering, and arguing for their answers to life's most basic questions.'*[31]

Ethical issues can be observed, discussed and commented on through many disciplines other than philosophy, such as history, anthropology (the study of humans and human behaviour and societies in the past and present), ethology (the scientific and objective study of animal behaviour, usually with a focus on behaviour under natural conditions), evolutionary theory (the process by which organisms change over time as a result of changes in heritable physical or behavioural traits), psychology, sociology, and religion. It has been stated that, *'Even among those who believe they know ethics, there is not total agreement on the meaning of the terms that are used.'*[32] There are, therefore, no clear-cut rights and wrongs, and the **debate** about issues can be more informative and enlightening than any notion of a fixed answer.

Here is a simple example of an everyday type of ethical dilemma

If I find a £10 note on the ground what could/ should I do?

My options could be:
- keep it
- buy a lottery ticket, as I'm feeling lucky now
- buy a treat for my children
- give it to the next homeless person I see

- tear it in half and give one piece to my best friend (although this essentially 'breaks' it; unless we meet another time and tape it back together)

My parents would probably have advised me to:
- ask around if anyone has dropped it
- take it to the local lost property at a police station, where they can wait for the owner to claim it
- give it to a charity, for them to distribute altruistically
- give it to a local religious group, or a church, mosque, synagogue
- invest it in my bank savings account, to earn interest
- buy some materials to start a small business

My elderly grandparents would have probably advised me to:
- hide the money, until I can make an informed decision
- bury the money, to access it later
- leave it where I found it, for someone else to make the decision
- don't get involved, it could be a trick

I'm assuming that we will all have different ideas of what to do in this imaginary scenario. However, if I suggest keeping it, and you suggest giving it to a homeless person, I may think you're *silly*, you should have kept it; and you may think I'm *selfish* as I have other money and the homeless person probably doesn't have any.

Perhaps finding £10 isn't enough to form an impression, so, what if you found a £50 note? What about finding £1,000? Would your response to what you would do if you found £10 differ from finding £1000, and why?

These decisions then have consequences. On reflection:

- who is **right**?
- who has better **morals**?

- who had a better thought process and **reasoning** behind the decision?
- who was **kinder**?
- who felt **nicer** afterwards?
- if we repeat the story, what is the **role of the new person** hearing this story?
- should a third person have to **agree** with me?
- is there a difference between what we **ought** to ideally do, and what we **actually** do?
- if one of us is **right**, is the other person **wrong**?
- should we each try to **persuade** the other person of our correct opinion?
- what were your **thought processes** behind your decision?
- what would you do in **future**?

An example of another ethical dilemma is given here:

> *'A group of children were playing near two railway tracks, one still in use, while the other not. Only one child played on the unused track, the rest on the operational track. A train is coming, and you are just beside the track interchange. You can make the train change its course to the unused track and save most of the children. However, that would also mean the lone child playing by the unused track would be sacrificed. Or should you let the train go its way?'*

Srivastava pondered, *'Let's take a pause to think what kind of decision we could make.'*[33] He argued that, 'Most people would probably choose to divert the course of the train, and sacrifice only one child. Saving most of the children at the expense of only one child was a rational decision most people would make, morally and emotionally. But, have you thought that the child who chose to play on the unused track had, in fact, made the right decision to play at a safe place? Nevertheless, he had to be sacrificed because of other children who chose to play in a more dangerous place. You might not try to change the course of the train because you may believe that the children playing on the operational track were aware that the track was still in use, and that they would run away when they hear the train's sirens. If the train was diverted, that lone child would probably die because he would never have expected that a train could come over on the unused track. Further, the track that was not in use was probably not in use, because it was not safe. If the train was diverted to such a track, we may put the lives of all passengers on board at stake. And in our attempt to save a few children, thinking that the train may run over them, we might end up sacrificing hundreds of people. While we are all aware that life is full of tough decisions that need to be made, we may not realise that a hasty decision may not always be the 'right' one. What's 'right' isn't always popular, and what's popular isn't always right.' Interesting conclusion.

MacDonald pointed out that, *'An ethical dilemma is any situation in which there are genuine ethical reasons pointing toward two different courses of action. Technically, the* word 'dilemma' means that there are precisely two options. In casual usage, though, we might use the word 'dilemma' even when we see three or four options.'[34]

If you now take the following genealogical scenario, you can see a variety of dilemmas and decisions emerging:

~ if you were adopted, what would you do about searching
for your biological family? ~

- nothing, you've had a happy upbringing and are not interested in biological family
- get your original birth certificate and study the information on it
- look for your birth mother, but not anyone else
- begin searching when you're eighteen
- leave well alone, it's a potential 'can of worms' or Pandora's box
- ask your adoptive parents' advice about potentially searching, and see if they're ok with it
- ask your friends or partner, to get a range of opinions
- hope for a positive outcome and reunion
- look for your birth father, as it was your birth mother who gave you away
- contact an intermediary to help with the contact and reunion process
- join a self-help group and see what others have done
- go for counselling to discuss all the issues
- distract yourself from thinking about these issues, and keep busy
- wait until your adoptive parents pass away, out of respect for them
- look on Facebook or other social media, for people with the same name and send them a private message
- do a DNA test to look for matches
- build a mirror tree on your DNA testing site, to look for hints and clues
- focus on constructing an ancestral tree rather than looking for living relatives
- contact a television programme, to get some help

All of these are potentially good options, and, when you look at them and maybe add what you would do into that list, then you can see that some scenarios are conflicting. Some people will say you've had a good life so far, why 'rock the boat'; others may say that it's really important that you try to find your biological mother, as maybe her baby was taken from her, and she had no choice. Situations such as this one can make you feel confused or uneasy, and therefore have produced an ethical dilemma for you to ponder.

The next chapter looks at the concept of ethical dilemmas within genealogy.

Chapter 2: Ethical dilemmas in genealogy

Bust of Plato[35]
who was a philosopher in Classical Greece, and widely considered a pivotal figure in the development of Western philosophy

****

Some common dilemmas within genealogy

Ancestry has a Message Board forum of users' dilemmas, *'Ethics in Genealogy'*[36] which included the following topics raised by users:

- others 'poaching' information from their tree (80 comments)
- people downloading and re-uploading photographs as their own (42 comments)
- people not amending older incorrect pedigrees, just uploading new versions (17 comments)
- requests for people to be removed from trees (12 comments)
- relatives asking for living people's information to be removed from a tree (11 comments)
- including offensive labels from censuses, for example, 'insane', 'idiot' (10 comments) see an interesting book about this topic[37]
- people refusing to collaborate (10 comments)
- users demanding help (5 comments)
- strange attitudes (5 comments)

Because it is a message board forum for users, not a complaints system, Ancestry encourages people who post to read the Community Guidelines[38] which include advice under the following five subject headings, and each guideline has an explanation as to what is meant by it.

- be nice
- respect people's privacy
- think before you post
- learn to collaborate effectively
- report issues

Schneider, observed that, within a genealogy group she used to belong to, *'The two areas with the hottest debates were issues dealing with 1) sharing data and 2) what kind of data should we share - if we could agree on the issue of sharing in the first place.'*[39] 'Smart Steps For Savy Genealogists' has a section entitled *'Minding Your Manners in Family History: Rules of the Road for All Genealogists,'* which commented that, for example, when collaborating, *'For you to assume you have the right to ask and receive an entire collection is a tad presumptuous and bad taste.'*[40]

I have gathered a selection of issues and scenarios that I have pondered over. What are your thoughts about the following situations?

Privacy and confidentiality

Ancestry explained in their section 'Privacy for Your Family Tree' that, *'We want you to feel comfortable creating and sharing your online family tree so we allow you to choose between three levels of privacy: public, private, or unindexed (hidden).'*[41] This implies that customers have previously raised questions about privacy concerns. But, how private can we realistically be with modern technology? *'Due to the digital revolution, people no longer have a high level of control over what is public information, leading to a tension between the values of transparency and privacy.'*[42] The International Association of Jewish Genealogical Societies (IAJGS)[43] pointed out that the 'right to privacy' versus 'freedom of information' is an area of potential conflict, suggesting that data should be evaluated in the light of sensitivities of the living, versus the importance of disseminating information.[44]

It is exciting to find records for ancestors, so we feel justified in doing a thorough search, because they are 'ours,' but 'does the end justify the means'? Many people have been asked by a relative to remove their information from their tree, as they weren't happy to find this information on the internet. If a relative asks to be removed from your tree because of their privacy and confidentiality issues, what should you do? You might explain to the person that the information is factual, and it will remain on the tree, or you could do as they asked and remove the information, which will distort your tree, or you could ensure that living people are 'hidden.'

Adorno explained that, *'According to Aristotle 'all men by nature desire to know' and this desire is one of the features that distinguishes humans from other animals.'*[45] There is a current trend for the need for 'transparency,' but has this gone too far? Transparency implies openness, good communication and accountability. Brin[46] asked whether technology would force us to choose between privacy and freedom. Han[47] warned that transparency is a cultural norm created by neoliberal market forces, which he explained as the insatiable drive toward voluntary disclosure, arguing that the dictates of transparency enforce a totalitarian system of openness, at the expense of other social values such as shame, secrecy, and trust. *'Considered crucial to democracy, transparency touches our political and economic lives as well as our private lives. Anyone can obtain information about anything. Everything, and everyone, has become transparent: unveiled or exposed by the apparatuses that exert a kind of collective control over the post-capitalist world.'*[48] Han warned that, *'Transparency has a dark side... Behind the apparent accessibility of knowledge lies the disappearance of privacy, homogenization, and the collapse of trust... Technology creates the illusion of total containment and the constant monitoring of information, but what we lack is adequate interpretation of the information.'*[49] Freud and Nietzsche would have argued that transparency is not possible, because of the blocking function of the unconscious. Sanders and West[50] suggested that not only do the realms of the revealed and concealed require each other, but also that transparency, in practice, produces the very opacities it claims to obviate. Cryptographer and privacy specialist Schneier[51] argued that the 'transparent society' concept is a myth, claiming it ignores wide differences in the relative power of those who access information.

The volume of accessible information on the internet has meant that people are finding information much more quickly and easily now, than when people had to undertake a slower paper trail. You can type in a name on a searching site, and often quickly get someone's life information via a wealth of records: birth, marriage and death records, addresses from censuses, and occupations from trade directories. In the British 1939 register, you can see who people lived with, their exact date of birth and jobs, even their middle name. Travel or emigration records can reveal where people travelled to, on what dates, and sometimes who with and who they were intending to visit. You can also find stories on grave websites, in newspaper articles, and view photographs of criminals.

Because of the speed of finding information now, people may not have taken the time to process new information carefully. As soon as you have a DNA match, the testing company gives an indication of the potential relationship. It can therefore be very exciting to notice a new DNA match who is labelled as 'first cousin', and we may send a message, but not realise the implications of contacting this previously unknown relative. If someone is labelled as first cousin, then one of your two parents are related to one of the other person's two parents. This could potentially mean that, if you haven't already met or know about this person, then there could be a secret being uncovered.

Is it justifiable that we have so much information about people on our trees? Fruit, ready to be picked by others.

Sharing, collaborating and inspiring others

It can be very enjoyable to share and inspire others, and sharing without any obvious 'returns' is a nice altruistic feeling, for example putting a GEDcom onto the DNA collaboration website GEDmatch[52] where you're not sure who has been helped by your visible pedigree, but presumably those who consult it will get some help with new information, or by verifying what they already know. On reflection, it's sad that some families pass down more stories than others, and that we have to ask strangers for information from their tree. However, whilst we may feel that we have shared our information, and are open to collaboration, there are those who don't seem to want to share their family history knowledge.

There is always devastation when you get matches on DNA testing sites and see this, for example, a recent screen shot of my 'new' cousin DNA matches on Ancestry: 'no tree,' 'no tree,' 'no tree,' 'no tree'…

The genealogists' classic gripe … why don't people have a public tree? …

Scott quipped, *'These are the matches that can send you out looking for consolation in the bottom of a bowl of ice cream, but when you've finished your ice cream, get started on figuring out who this cousin is.'*[53]

There are many reasons why people may not share their trees:

- people might not know how to devise a tree
- some people have only just started their tree research and haven't filled in many people yet
- some people aren't yet sure that their information is correct
- a great deal of time and effort is involved in researching family history and some may feel that it is 'their' research, and don't want to share any of their hard work
- many people only wanted DNA ethnicity estimates, not any other information
- some are not sure about whether they have correctly filled in specific ancestors, because they were fragmented from biological family, for example, adoptees
- many people don't have a subscription to a DNA testing site
- people haven't linked their tree and DNA together
- some have an offline tree, constructed by software
- some may have had a public tree and others used the information without asking, so they subsequently made their tree private
- people can be suspicious of where this family information is going, and who could potentially be accessing it
- and actually, *it is not compulsory to share your tree*

Some people's approach to collaborating could be seen as somewhat irritating, however, and it may feel like they are asking you to solve their family tree mysteries. A post on an Ancestry message board summed it up well, *'You get a message from a user with a cryptic username. Without preamble, it says "I saw such-and-such in your tree, and I have some kind of problem with it, and how do you explain it?" No 'my name is,' no 'please,' no 'thank you,' no closing or signature. In other words, a message from a person demanding free use of your time and attention. My inclination is to help others in this hobby I enjoy, and I think it's rude to ignore inquiries, but I'm also not here as anyone's unpaid servant... Do you answer the question, ignore it, chide him or her for bad manners, or what? H.'*[54] Some people haven't thought through how to approach people online, and lack 'netiquette.' Schneider commented that, disappointingly, *'In all the years I've been helping people find their Catudal roots I have only had five responses where the person actually not only thanked me, but offered some information that I was missing. Each time I've experienced this phenomenon I swear I'll never ever share again.'*[55]

Legacy Tree Genealogists' online blog summed it up that, *'You see you have new DNA cousin matches, and you get excited... You do a genealogy happy dance, and you send them a message. And then you wait. And wait. And wait. And nothing happens. It's frustrating, isn't it? You need these cousins, and you just can't reach them. You don't know what went wrong, or whether they even received the messages...'* [56] The post provided the following tips to enable people to get more replies:

- use email whenever you can
- use a g-mail account
- make your subject line sing
- be very specific
- share who you are and what you know
- come bearing gifts
- don't fixate on trees
- remember that this is a job application
- be open to multiple ways of working together
- consider your digital footprint
- try another path
- don't take it personally
- be patient

An interesting post by Rachel Fountain gave some ideas for altruistically sharing your family history. Her five useful sharing tips[57] included:

- donate your research - donate copies of your research to libraries, genealogical societies, family history societies
- help your family learn about their history - a number of family members will have different interests in different parts of your research, older folk may enjoy reminiscing, some will feel inspired to do own research, some will feel a new sense of pride in their history
- plan a trip - your research can provide the itinerary for a family history road trip or day trip to explore the places your ancestors lived; this could be quite locally or longer distances, even abroad
- create a story - your research can create various narratives about ancestors, which can be turned into a story, which often resembles national history
- get creative - you can produce digital memories such as memorial sites or movies, or produce physical memories such as photo books

Dick Eastman, who has been writing a genealogy newsletter[58] for more than twenty years has a really altruistic approach to sharing, announcing in a section about 'copyright and other legal things,' *'Steal these articles! Yes, you may copy and republish most of the articles in this newsletter elsewhere, with a very few exceptions.'*[59]

A fantastic example of sharing, was the opportunity to attend a free workshop, *'Sharing stories about your ancestors'*, facilitated by Cathy Scuffil, Historian in Residence at Dublin City Library and Archive[60] Ireland.

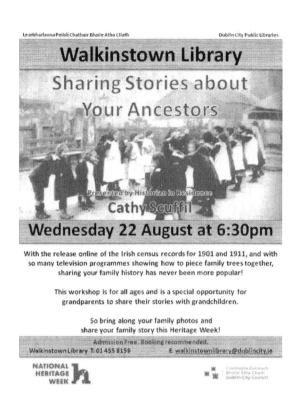

Poster reproduced with permission of Cathy Scuffil

Dublin City Council's team of Historians in Residence[61] *'bring history to communities across the city with talks, walks, workshops, research and all things history, and it's all free. The historians are available to meet schools, history clubs, residents' groups, retirement groups, and community groups to talk about history and to give help and advice on historical research, so get in touch.'*[62]

Another idea for sharing and collaborating in family history, is a project[63] which linked Dallas, USA school children with elderly folk from a local senior living community (housing) scheme. They physically met and then continued as pen pals, with the focus on both young and elderly sharing stories and also for the children to develop their hand writing skills. Both youngsters and elders reportedly enjoyed receiving mail from each other, and the children got to hear reminiscences from the elders. Bettinger and Woodbury urged us to get younger people involved, explaining that, *'... the results of a DNA test reveal the random tendrils through time that physically connect us to our ancestors and family history. Younger test-takers often benefit more from the results of testing, more than older generations. DNA is taught in biology class from a young age, and students have extensive experience with computers, so there is a minimal learning curve. Additionally, younger test-takers typically have more living ancestors (parents, grandparents, maybe even great-grandparents) and older relatives they can test in order* to reveal even more information about their family history.'[64] Bettinger and Woodbury included the nice family relationship botanical metaphor of 'tendril,' which is defined as, 'a threadlike, leafless organ of climbing plants, often growing in spiral form, which attaches itself to or twines round some other body, so as to support the plant.'[65]

Finding errors in other people's trees

A common irritation for family historians is finding a tree that looks really interesting and useful for matches, but then you find a huge number of situations where they have clear errors. For example, a woman being the mother of a baby when she would have been about three years of age, or a marriage of more than a hundred years' duration, or people being married to the same person twice but their name was spelled slightly differently in one instance and they've made it look like someone married two different people, and then added different children to the two marriages. 'Who Do You Think You Are?' magazine editor, Sarah Williams, remarked in reply to readers' letters that, '...it seems that this is a bugbear for many of you.'[66] Scott wryly observed that, 'We know to look for babies born to toddler moms, zombies who died in 1909 but show up in the 1920 census, and other tell-tale signs.'[67] If something is an error, then it could potentially be corrected. Some people will amend information or delete people from their tree if it's found that there was a genuine error, others may plough ahead regardless.

Ethical dilemmas in this situation include whether or not to point out these errors to the owner of the tree. Many errors can be duplicated by people getting hints from other people's incorrect trees, but not checking the accuracy of the information. Some people state that some of their ancestor's information is recorded 'wrongly' on a specific record, for example a man was seventy four on a census, but ten years earlier he was forty nine; or his name was John James Smythe on some records, but George John Smith on others. Descendants say that this is the same person but that they are incorrectly reported on the records. However, it may be that they have accessed and then included an incorrect record, and it isn't that ancestors lied or gave incorrect information to an enumerator.

Errors in your own tree

I was alerted to new 'tools' that I could utilise, which I was overjoyed to see, one of which is termed 'consistency issues.'[68] However, I was horrified to be alerted to 298 consistency issues in my tree (that I thought I had carefully researched for over thirty years), which includes 2,205 people! 298 errors? I've become one of those people with lots of errors in their tree! The list included some obviously basic errors that I could then investigate and potentially change. However, some 'errors' could perhaps be seen as 'culturally bound' situations, such as: siblings with same first name (that was common when children died young); large spouse age difference of more than thirty five years (this might be uncommon, but there is nothing essentially 'wrong' with this); person had a child when they were less than sixteen years old (many people have a teenage pregnancy), sixteen is a legal age in specific countries, but pregnancy can occur before; same sex spouses (legalised now in many countries); siblings with close age, two siblings who are not twins were born too close in time to be biological siblings (but one could be a biological child, the other could be adopted, for example).

On the whole, however, the 'consistency issues' which were pointed out were valid, and were silly mistakes on my behalf. MyHeritage also provides links to view your tree statistics, some of which are in the form of pie charts and some in bar charts.

Age distribution

Age range	Number of people	Percentage
0-9	42	4%
10-19	60	5%
20-29	66	6%
30-39	69	6%
40-49	99	9%
50-59	124	11%
60-69	102	9%
70-79	102	9%
80-89	105	9%
90+	351	31%

My tree looks like a healthy place to be, as nearly a third are aged over ninety! When I looked more closely, about one third of my tree appeared to be over ninety years of age. So this is another error, as I haven't put deceased people down as such. If I don't know when someone died, I have often left that section blank. My tree's gender distribution seemed to be half males and half females, but 2% (one hundred and twenty people) were 'unassigned' so these are my careless mistakes of not including genders, (although a few were babies who were noted in the 1911 Census according to mothers reporting how many of their children had died, but names or birth dates weren't provided). About two thirds of my inclusions were single and about one third were married; and about two thirds were dead and one third were alive. This last figure sounded too high. These pointers are therefore useful for amending and correcting your tree.

A key dilemma with finding errors in our tree, however, is should we point out our own errors to people that we know rely on our tree, or who we collaborate a lot with? I have some people that I regularly collaborate with and they often utilise new information from my tree, and I 'grab' new information from theirs, as their information has always been reliable, but maybe I don't check their new information as thoroughly as I should, and maybe we are potentially perpetuating errors.

Utilising automatic additions to a tree from a website hint

A relative in my biological tree, Eileen Clifford (reportedly the wife of my great uncle), was recorded as the head of the house's 'granddaughter' but didn't automatically get added to my tree through Ancestry. However, when noticing her name, surname and relationship to the head of family, after some further investigation, revealed a whole new line.

1911 Wales Census: 2 April, 1911	
Registration district: Bridgend Registration District Number: 591 Sub-registration district: Cowbridge ED, institution, or vessel: 11 Household schedule number: 7 Piece: 32565	7, Chapel Road, Llanharan, Glamorgan, Wales
Harry North, age 57	Head
Ann North, age 55	Wife
Ivor North, age 21	Son
Henry North, age 18	Son
Jacob North, age 16	Son
Guladys North, age 14 (name transcribed incorrectly)	Daughter
Eileen Clifford, age 6	Grand daughter
Hatie North, age 19 (name transcribed incorrectly)	Daughter

Ancestry has automatic additions for a family in a census for example, but doesn't currently have an automatic addition for grandchildren or other relationships, other than spouses, and parent-child, and some vital people may therefore be overlooked. Grandchildren, nephews, nieces or mothers in law, for example, usually have different surnames, but you can infer or investigate relationships further. If there appears to be an elderly or widowed person living with the family you could investigate if this person is a mother in law who is living with her daughter and son in law.

Spelling variations

The advent of standard or 'correct' spelling is relatively new; probably only since officials wanted to record events, and then when printing was invented. If people couldn't read or write, they would say their name or address to an official, who was then responsible for recording this information. Sometimes the official language was different to the spoken language, for example, many old records in the UK were written in Latin. This can make searching for an ancestor difficult sometimes, especially when pet or nicknames got included in official documents. Heritage explains this succinctly in her response to a reader's question asking, 'which surname should I follow?' She points out that, *'Names can be misheard or copied out incorrectly in record sources too, and this can lead to real mistakes rather than just variant spellings.'*[69]

For example, a surname held to be O'Reilly could be spelled:

- O'Reilly
- Reilly
- Reiley
- Reilley
- Reily
- O Reilly
- O'Rahilly

And so on.

A useful dictionary has been produced, which, *'...includes family names of the UK, covering English, Scottish, Welsh, Irish, Cornish, and immigrant surnames. It includes every surname that currently has more than 100 bearers, and those that had more than 20 bearers in the 1881 census. Each entry contains lists of variant spellings of the name, an explanation of its origins (including the etymology)...'*[70] This is useful to consult, when you don't know many variations for the name you are searching for.

The dictionary includes surnames such as:

Davies
- Variants: Davys, Daviss, Davis, Daves
- Current frequencies: GB 21,5074; Ireland 782
- GB frequency in 1881: 152,045

Jack
- Variants: Jacka, Jagg, Jacks, Geake
- Current frequencies: GB 7,268; Ireland 201
- GB frequency in 1881: 6,332

It can be difficult to imagine that, previously, people didn't strictly adhere to specific spellings of a word, and we can feel frustrated at the many variations. People state that things are spelled 'wrong' when they were just spelled differently. People who travelled to another country may have had to give their details to someone speaking a different language, different dialect or had a different accent. We perhaps can't guess how a word would sound with an accent. For example, during the Famine, Irish emigrants would have had to give their details to Welsh, Scottish, English, Canadian or American officials. In addition, some people Anglicised or even completely changed their name when travelling, to avoid any confrontation, or to 'blend in.' It can therefore be difficult for a descendent to work out whether a record contains different spellings of a person's name, or whether it's a different person to the one you're searching for. Some spelling variations are clerical or transcription errors, rather than just variations. It can be a dilemma which spelling to include on your tree.

Intrusion of some civil records

The 1911 UK census, taken on the 2nd April, contained more questions and information than previous censuses and is also the first available census to view which was filled in by those in the household, so people can now see their ancestors' handwriting and signature. The UK Census Online website reveals that, *'The 1911 Census is thought to be one of the most important record sets, as it shows family records in detail before WW1... Additional pieces of information included for the first time are nationality, duration of current marriage, number of children born within that marriage, number of living children and the number of any children who had died...'*[71]

The Government could have perhaps more sensitively worded the questions about how many children had been born, and how many had died within the marriage. Some may have felt embarrassed about the number of children born within the marriage, as maybe they had children before they were married, and this would possibly be a secret to the children. Many people would have probably felt upset at the time to record how many of their children had died, and descendants many years later would feel upset to read that their ancestor had babies and children who died (often very young). However, statisticians can now note the number of women and trends for child mortality. Sadly, it can be difficult to locate a name for the children who died before 1911, but were born after the 1901 census.

UK 1939 Register

Find My Past usefully explained that, *'In December 1938, it was announced... that, in the event of war, a National Register would be taken that listed the personal details of every civilian in Great Britain and Northern Ireland...The identity cards issued were essential items from the point the Register was taken right up until 1952, when the legal requirement to carry them ceased.'*[72] The National Records of Scotland[73] explained that, on 29 September 1939, the Government carried out an enumeration of the population. The Second World War had started nearly one month earlier and the enumeration was required for providing the necessary information for: issuing national identity cards, issuing food and clothing ration books, identifying children eligible for evacuation from areas vulnerable to bombing, and identifying adults eligible for call up into the Armed Forces. In Scotland, the enumeration was carried out by the National Records of Scotland (NRS), because of its responsibility for the Census, and people can now consult the National Health Service Central Register (NHSCR) and order an official extract.[74] The 1939 Register was made available for viewing online on the Find My Past website on 2nd November, 2015.[75] Other website have subsequently acquired the 1939 Register, such as My Heritage,[76] and Ancestry,[77] whose 1939 strapline asks, *'What was life really like for your grandparents?'* This strapline assumes that you know who your grandparents were, that they were living in the UK in 1939, and that a few details: name, address, date of birth, job title, and other members of the household constitute a description of what their life was *'really like.'* The Ancestry version of the 1939 Register usefully includes information from Column 5 of the original form, which marks individuals who were resident in hospitals, asylums or prisons, with the letters O, V, S, P and I, standing for Officer, Visitor, Servant, Patient or Inmate.[78]

The 1939 Register includes people who perhaps feel a bit closer in time to us than those outside the one hundred year privacy laws for opening up the Censuses. The 1939 Register includes information about people who were the parents, grand-parents and some great-grandparents of people currently alive, and it bridges the gap between the published 1911 Census, and the present day. People can search by a number of routes, including someone's name, street, map, or through an advanced search. The 1939 Register continued to be updated until 1991, which is relatively recent, so some information may be confidential. The exact given date of birth for people is revealed, which is fantastic when discovering relatives' birth dates, as the censuses just have ages, and year of birth has to be calculated; however, it may be that some sensitive information is revealed if people had not been honest about or concealed their exact date of birth. If women got married, their new surname was handwritten above their maiden names, by National Health Service (NHS) clerks, men's information wasn't changed. The 1939 Register also reveals how much women's lives changed during the Second World War. The most popular occupations listed for women were domestic duties, with other jobs such as 'housekeeper', 'shop assistant' and 'dressmaker'. By 1943, almost 90% of single women and 80% of married women were working in factories, on the land or in the armed forces, because they were recruited into traditionally male spheres in order to help with the war effort.[79] Quirkily, Ancestry pointed out that some famous peoples' names and addresses[80] are available on the 1939 Register, for example, Winston Churchill (1st Lord of the Admiralty at the time); authors George Orwell (Eric Arthur Blair), Virginia Woolf and A. A. Milne; former suffragette and political campaigner Sylvia Pankhurst, and (future) Bletchley Park codebreakers Alan Turing and Alfred Dillwyn Knox.

A dilemma is that some people's records have been opened erroneously; some people, for example, currently alive and in their nineties, have been noticed as an open record. On the other hand, their birth certificate could be purchased to reveal the same information (and more).[81] Because the Register only includes the UK and Northern Ireland, not southern Ireland, this could raise some resentment about the separation between northern and southern Ireland.

Surnames

The expectation that women adopt their husband's surname at marriage is fundamentally rooted in patriarchal marital traditions.[82] The modern expectation that women adopt their husband's surname at marriage began in the 9th century 'doctrine of coverture' in English common law. *'Prior to marriage a woman could freely execute a will, enter into contracts, sue or be sued in her own name, and sell or give away her real estate or personal property as she wished. Once she married, however, her legal existence as an individual was suspended under 'marital unity,' a legal fiction in which the husband and wife were considered a single entity: the husband.'*[83] At birth, women received their father's surname; when they were 'given away'[84] at marriage, they automatically took their husband's surname. *'This is the strongest gendered social norm that we enforce and expect.'*[85] The phrase 'giving away the bride' was therefore literal, as women were considered to be property, transferred from husband to father.

Many women, and traditionally in some specific countries, don't want or don't have to change their surname when they get married.[86] The term 'double-barrelled name' first became popular in Victorian times, referring to two-part last names. *'A double-barrelled name comes about when two different family names are joined together, usually after a marriage... These days, though, taking two surnames is no longer a class signifier. Instead, many couples now choose to double-barrel their surnames after marriage when the woman doesn't fancy forgoing her name entirely but wants to nod to her new marital status, or when the man wants to take his wife's name, too.'*[87] It has become a popular option for civil partnerships and same-sex marriages.

Different countries' traditions[88] include, for example, in Britain, a double surname is heritable, and often taken in order to preserve a family name which would have become extinct, due to the absence of male descendants bearing the name, connected to the inheritance of a family estate. In Hispanic tradition, double surnames are the norm, and not an indication of social status. A person will take the (first) surname of their father, followed by the (first) surname of their mother (that is, their maternal grandfather's surname). The double surname itself is not heritable. These names are combined without a hyphen, but there are heritable double surnames which are combined with a hyphen. In German tradition, double surnames are taken upon marriage, written with or without hyphen, combining the husband's surname with the wife's; more recently the sequence has become optional under some legislations. These double surnames are 'alliance names' and, as such, not heritable.

A dilemma here is that women who choose not to take their husband's surname upon getting married are often perceived as having very different relationship dynamics to those who do change their name. *'A woman's choice of surname can influence how outsiders view the balance of power in her marriage, with women who kept their maiden name generally seen as having more authority in the relationship. A woman's decision about her marital surname may also affect how people see her husband.'*[89] The lack of conventions regarding which surname to use after same-sex marriage has created a dilemma for some, *'...who would take whose name? Many people did not want to entirely give up their name, thus a hyphenated last name was the most popular option for those contemplating a name change.'*[90] Many family historians are used to looking for surname changes after marriage, and this may add another line of searching to trees, with women who have chosen not to change their surname. In the future, it may be more difficult to search via naming traditions for same-sex marriages.

Secrets, lies

People are often interested in other people's secrets. Many magazines and newspapers sell well because of the reported stories of celebrities, for example, sales of women's magazines in the UK, for the first half of 2018 totalled 167,904 for 'Hello!' magazine, 162,338 for 'Closer', and 155,044 for 'New!'[91] It could be seen that there is vicarious pleasure in researching ancestors; we can look somewhat voyeuristically into other people's lives, with the added benefit that they are related to us, and we're not too far on the 'outside' for it to be considered intrusive 'snooping.' We hear some family historians saying, with an element of amusement, that they have discovered that their ancestor was, for example, a bigamist, a renowned criminal, or a prostitute; however, those situations would have caused a lot of problems or been a major ordeal for that person at the time. If it was a secret then and has been forgotten over time, or was concealed, then the research involves detective work, but, if it involves detective work, should you be doing it? *'Genealogy is a fascinating and compelling activity that demands the same kind of persistence and deductive reasoning as detective work. Tracing ancestors is really about solving a series of mysteries.'*[92]

For example, seen on Facebook in a Genealogy group,[93] the following question was posed:

What were the darkest things you've uncovered in your family tree?

Many people had then described an anecdotal story of an uncovered secret or lie, often in great detail. Each person who replied had a visible name which is clickable to their home page, which anyone who joined that group could read about. It probably wouldn't take too long to identify who the secrets were about if they mentioned relationships, such as stating, *'I was devastated to find out that my grandfather was married to two women at the same time.'* Someone noticing this comment on social media may be surprised or hurt by this. Finding a bigamous ancestor may also imply that there are not-too-distant relatives 'out there.'

Lents explained that, *'We think of our identities as relatively fixed now because we have traceable identification cards, birth certificates, and social security numbers from a very early age. But none of that existed until recently. Many families had secrets covered up with lies. Troubles with the law or social scandal often led families to relocate, change names, and invent a past. Forging records was much easier in the past, especially when moving to a different region or country.'*[94]

A huge dilemma here is that once you have uncovered a family or an individual's secret, should you reveal that information to other family members? For example, what would be the benefit of telling or discussing with your mother that her mother got married when she was pregnant? Some people may be really upset to hear such revelations. Imber-Black, pointed out that, *'As a family therapist, I'm a professional secret-keeper. I'm often the very first person with whom someone risks telling a long held secret. Several decades of guiding people struggling with secrets have taught me that they have an awesome if paradoxical power to unite people - and to divide them.'*[95] An experienced family historian may decide beforehand what uncovered potential secrets or lies to put (or not) on a tree, or in a report. Schneider, for example, explained that, *'I have not documented stories of child abuse, sexual abuse, spousal abuse, incest, suicide, adoption, sexual orientation, mental illness, drug and alcohol abuse or addiction and criminal activity.'*[96]

Imber-Black warned that, *'If family members keep secrets from each other, or from the outside world, the emotional fallout can last a lifetime.'*[97] Revealing secrets and exposing people can shape and scar, and potentially divide relationships between family members, and even result in permanent estrangement. Those people can then be scared who to trust, which can change the way they form intimate relationships. Some people's development could be 'frozen' at crucial points in life, theoretically preventing the growth of self-identity. Revealing secrets can lead to painful miscommunication within a family, causing much unnecessary guilt and doubt. Schneider warned that, *'People don't want to share the very types of information they are so hungry to know about others... People don't want to divulge their dark truths but they sure want to know someone else's.'*[98] For example, if sisters found that they were, in fact, biologically half-sisters, this could lead some daughters to challenge and confront their mother, and this can create enormous rifts in the family. The father may well not know, and suddenly the relationship has fragmented, and some cracks can't be repaired.

People can appear in television programmes to discuss these family issues. 'The Secrets in My Family' television series featured members of the public, using Ancestry's DNA test, to potentially solve family mysteries and uncover secret family members. Moncur explained that, *'Ancestry uses family history and the science of genomics to help people better understand themselves and how we are all connected, so a show like The Secrets in My Family is the perfect platform for us to demonstrate how we solve mysteries and bring people together.'*[99] Wyatt added that the series would, *"shine a light on some long-kept secrets and hopefully create new starts for all the families involved."* However, these are very positive assumptions of the outcomes, and the practical reality can be far from ideal.

Case study: Zak, 2018, published a fascinating account of a long held secret (or lie) about Jeanne Louise Calment's universally accepted record of a reputed lifespan of 122 years and 164 days, reportedly living from 21 February, 1875 to 4 August, 1997. He explained that the plausibility of the record was based on the lifespans of other centenarians, the hereditary longevity of her ancestors, and that she had always lived in a specific small town (Arles, France). Zak revealed that he had found multiple contradictions in her interviews, biographies, photos, and documents. He put forward the argument that Jeanne's daughter acquired her mother's identity after her death. Zak pointed out that the case he researched could be used as *'an example of the vulnerability of seemingly well-established facts.'*[100] Since his revelations, others[101] have reported Zak's claims.

Criminal ancestors

For some people, it's quirky to find a 'criminal' in the family. It's often one of the first tales people tell you about their family tree. But, what is a criminal? Over the years, what has been considered a crime, has changed, and you're only labelled a criminal when you're caught. Silver explained that, *'The difference between 'serious' and 'not-so-serious' is often in the eye of the beholder... 'Larceny' (theft) is simply the wrongful taking of property with the intent to permanently deprive the owner - it doesn't have to be jewelry or a laptop. Ever pop a few grapes in your mouth while grocery shopping? Sure, probably no one cares about any of those things because they are small potatoes, but potatoes they are, nonetheless.'*[102]

The National Archives UK has seventeen guides[103] to specifically help you search for criminals and convicts, and related records, such as: Old Bailey trials;[104] prisoners and prison staff; legal disputes; bankrupts and insolvent debtors; coroners' inquests;[105] administrations of probate; death duties; wills; Court martial and desertions in the British Army; Criminal courts in England and Wales from 1972; divorce; annulment of marriage; inquisitions; post mortems; military service appeal tribunals; conscientious objectors; outlaws; War crimes 1939-1945. The Victorian prisoners' photograph albums[106] contain photographs and details of prisoners in Wandsworth prison from 1872 to 1873.

Taking a photograph of a prisoner made it easier to identify criminals who had been convicted, or offenders who went on to commit further crimes. The prisoners' photograph albums (in volumes PCOM 2/290[107] and PCOM 2/291[108]) contain a photograph and each entry also includes: prisoner's physical description, date and place of birth, the crime they committed, sentence, place of conviction, prisoner's intended residence after release from prison, and often give the prisoner's place of residence before imprisonment. *'Photographing of criminals began in the 1840s only a few years after the invention of photography, but it was not until 1888 that French police officer and biometrics researcher Alphonse Bertillon[109] standardized the process...'*[110]

Baynes reported that, *'An era when stealing some sweets will earn you four months' hard labour and sacrilege will see you hauled before a judge.'* [111] Cardiff Borough Police Force Records' Crimes and Photographs collection show individuals, their crime and punishment, for example:

Name	Crime	Punishment
George Gibson	Fake pretences, stealing a pair of shoes	One month hard labour
James Graut	Wilful damage	5/- costs or seven days imprisonment
William Jones	Sacrilege	Bound over
William Harris	Travelling on GWR without paying a fare	11/- fine and costs or seven days hard labour
Gwen Evans	Obtaining food by false pretences	Nine calendar months hard labour
Mary Hetherington	Stealing a shawl	Seven days imprisonment
Lily Morgan	Abandoning her child	Bound over on £5 good behaviour over twelve months
James Thomas	Shop breaking and stealing sweets	Four months hard labour

West Glamorgan Archive Service, Swansea, Wales[112] has digitised records, including Swansea and Surrounding Area, Wales, Gaol Records, 1877-1922 (including Nominal Gaol Registers for the years 1877-1922 for Swansea, Brecon and Carmarthen prisons, and photograph albums of prisoners). Who Do You Think You Are? magazine reported that Fife Family History Society had released a 'Kalendar of Convicts'[113] which, *'contains over 45,000 Fife court records from 1790-1880, accompanied by more information about the individuals in birth, marriage and death records, census returns, newspaper articles, transported convict records and photographs.'*[114]

Why are people interested in finding records of their ancestors' crimes, and what are the benefits of finding these records? It would be so upsetting if someone found that their ancestor was convicted for an offence that society may not consider a crime now, or that they were later found to be innocent of the crime. The wealth of information given in that record would be useful in other circumstances. It's a great joy finding a photograph of an ancestor, but if the photograph is from when they were arrested, it was presumably a very low point or one of the worst days of their life. Ancestors may not necessarily have understood the reasoning behind the police taking their photograph, especially when the process was a new one. Did anyone arrested know that their photo would be revealed for anyone to see, many years later? Some 'mugshots'[115] (headshots) include those from the early 1900s, so these people could potentially be living people's parents or grandparents. It would be mixed feelings indeed to find a criminal ancestor, and these photographs may be the only photo we could see of that ancestor.

Many convicts were transported for what we would now probably consider petty crimes.[116] More serious crimes, such as rape and murder, were not transportable offences, as they were punishable by death. Between 1788 and 1868, about 162,000 convicts were transported by the British government to various penal colonies in Australia.[117] It was reported that, *'More than 2 million Britons and an estimated 4 million Australians are related to convicts deported from Britain to Australia in the 18th and 19th centuries… the vast majority, 87% of men and 91% of women, were convicted of minor offences, particularly property crimes. They included stealing fish from a river or pond, embezzlement, receiving or buying stolen goods, setting fire to underwood or petty theft.'*[118] Some people may well feel that the crime was really insignificant and be interested in the ancestors' physical and emotional journey, but there may also be people who feel ashamed of that piece of their history because of the 'criminal' label. In any instance, it would have been a life changing move, from the UK to Australia. How do Australian descendants feel about this now?

Mummies that have been removed from tombs, and transferred to museums

In some countries, people, and especially royalty, spent a long time, and in some cases, most of their adult life, carefully preparing for their afterlife. Egyptian pharaohs took the greatest care in being preserved, potentially forever. So, is it acceptable to excavate these people many years later, investigate the remains, transfer the bodies to museums or laboratories, and disseminate some aspects of the information found?

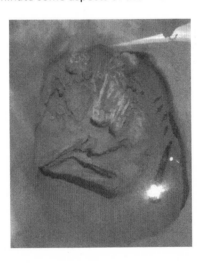

Photograph taken by Penny Walters, August 2018

These two people are on display in a glass cabinet in a museum, who are buried together, and who looked like they were buried cuddling. People may think it's gory or even funny, and take a photograph and walk by. The notice below the exhibit is in Arabic, and the English translation reads, *'Two skeletons were cut into sections and then tied together, beside them is a group of arrowheads. Al Qusais[119] (1500-1200 BC).'[120]*

In a different museum, there are two mummies on display in two cabinets, in a very quiet and serene part of a museum. However, they are not in their own country any more. The top of the sarcophagus is raised, so visitors can see the embalmed bodies. They were people, and now they are exposed. It is informatively explained that, *'The Egyptian objects in the Museum of Cultural History arrived as donations... The mummy Dismutenibtes came from Thebes. It was acquired by the Armenian Giovanni Anastasi, who was the consul general of Norway-Sweden in Alexandria. The mummy was donated to the Royal Frederick University (now the University of Oslo) in 1838. The mummy we call "Nofret" came from Akhmin. In 1889, it was presented to King Oscar II by German Egyptologist Heinrich Karl Brugsch. The king gave the mummy to the University's ethnographic collection.'[121]*

Photograph taken by Penny Walters, November 2018

The mummies were donations and were acquired by dignitaries or Egyptologists, and it is useful for visitors to get a glimpse into how Egyptians used to bury their dead. The website explains that artefacts were distributed among several European countries, as gifts from Khediv Abbas II of Egypt, because it was impossible for the museum in Cairo to take care of so many. Therefore, these mummified people were not taken, they were given to the Museum. The Museum of Cultural History does not actively acquire antiquities, 'The 1970 UNESCO Convention regulates the trade of cultural heritage. Norway ratified the convention in 2007, and Norwegian legislation complies with its recommendations.'[122]

In a separate cabinet are a number of 'shabti', little statuette figures which ancient Egyptians often placed in their tombs, and which would theoretically perform tasks for the deceased in the afterlife. 'There is some evidence of the sacrificial burial of servants with the deceased. However, this practice was quickly seen as unnecessary and wasteful, and instead symbolic images of servants were painted inside tombs to aid the deceased in the afterworld. This practice developed into the use of small statuettes known as Shabti.'[123] Whilst these figurines would have provided some comfort for the deceased at the time, they are now a few metres away in a separate cabinet.

A sensational headline describes a mummified young teenager in Peru, 'The must-see attraction for visitors to Museo Santuarios Andinos (Museum of Andean Sanctuaries) in Arequipa, Peru is without a doubt the Mummy Juanita, one of the world's best-preserved corpses.'[124] Flowers explained that a positive aspect of displaying skeletons is that, '... Mummies from around the world offer people a glimpse into the literal, tangible past, bringing history to life in a way no written chronicle can... Mummy Juanita... was discovered in the Andes in 1995. Uncannily well-preserved (even her organs and the contents of her stomach were intact) she immediately captivated researchers... Today, Juanita has been relocated from her icy tomb. She sits on display at the Museum of Andean Sanctuaries in Arequipa, Peru, where she seems to greet visitors from across the centuries.'[125] Whilst this teenager offers a 'fantastic glimpse into the past,' the child is on display for all to see.

This photograph is of a man's skeleton which was found in the Gokstad ship (a 9th century Viking ship found in a burial mound at Gokstad in Norway), and he was reportedly[126] a tall and sturdy, approximately forty year old man, killed by sword wounds, in battle c900AD. He had been buried with a tent, kitchen utensils, a sleigh, beds, three small boats, sixty four shields, twelve horses, eight dogs, falcons and two peacocks, but is now sadly, alone preserved in a glass cabinet in the amazing Viking Ship Museum.[127]

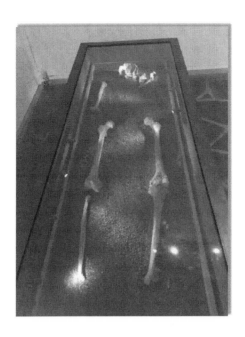

These people described have been removed from their burial place and displayed, usually in a see-through glass cabinet, and are often called a mummy or corpse, not human beings. Whilst their appearance is often intact, and the artefacts found with them are very informative, their artefacts were removed from them, which may have been some comfort at the time. All the information gleaned from them has informed researchers, and visitors pay to go into museums, which gives income generation to the museum, and allows access to more visitors in the future.

It was reported[128] that a variety of mummies, including thousand-year-old crocodiles and a 20th century pneumonia victim, explaining that a great benefit is that these preserved remains tell 'remarkable stories' about life and death. Tragically, some mummies were murder victims. With the advent of DNA testing, the mystery over the identity of some people has been discovered, for example, an Egyptian mummy's 4,000-year-old severed head discovered in a tomb in Deit el-Bersha was solved; the head belonged to the governor Djehutynakht; the FBI spokesperson said that they were trying to develop criminal procedures using historical items.[129]

There is a notice on the display board at Bristol Museum[130] in the Egyptian section, which poignantly reminds people that, *'This mummy is a person and not just an item on display.'*

Unmarked graves

Carol and Luis Garrido, two admirers of William Blake,[131] English mystic, poet, artist and engraver, were upset to find only a stone saying that the remains of Blake and his wife Catherine Sophia lay 'nearby'. They spent two years researching and eventually pinpointed the exact site, and '... *after years of fundraising, the Blake Society has been able to mark the spot with an official memorial.*'[132] This was obviously a really important issue for those people to pay respect to someone they admired, but why do people need to know the exact spot for a burial? If you find an ancestor's grave was unmarked, should you pay for a headstone? Paying homage seems important for many people, but do people have responsibilities to tend to graves many years or generations later? How long for?

Families used to visit the deceased, and make it a family event, so knowing the exact location was vital. '*Up until the early 20th century, cemeteries were a popular place to relax, picnic and get together near a loved one's grave... Cemeteries are no longer used for recreation, and many have come to regard children playing in a cemetery as disrespectful. Cemeteries have become "creepy" places and are rarely visited except by family members or vandals. Some are abandoned altogether.*'[133]

Offensive obituaries

A newspaper removed a paid obituary from its website, which, although it was in the Obituaries section, it detailed a deceased woman's affair with her husband's brother and accused her of abandoning her two children. '*The newspaper took down the obituary amid an outcry from readers who felt it was in poor taste... She passed away on May 31, 2018, in Springfield and will now face judgment. She will not be missed by Gina and Jay, and they understand that this world is a better place without her.*'[134] A dilemma here is that, essentially, anything can be said in an obituary, but it is standard practice that relatives extol the virtues of the deceased, rather than criticise or publicly humiliate them. '*By custom, it follows a tripartite structure: first, you celebrate the dead person's virtues; second, you lament their loss; third, you affirm your hope in their eternal life.*'[135] In addition, family historians may assume that the information given in obituaries is correct, and utilise the information given to add to their research.

Conscientious Objectors

Many people are proud of their ancestor who served their country during a war. People can search for many types of war records. FamilySearch states that, '*Millions of brave men and women around the world left their homes to fight for their countries in the Great War. Discover if your ancestor is listed in the millions of free World War I records on FamilySearch.org.*'[136] However, those who objected to serving during the war, on the grounds of their conscience were arrested, imprisoned, struggled to find work after, and many of their families and communities felt that 'not helping the war effort' was shameful. This shame can be felt by descendants many years later. People will add many war records to their ancestors, but may not point out their ancestor's conscientious objection.

Brooks succinctly reported that, *'Before the First World War there had never been compulsory military service in Britain. The first Military Service Bill was passed into law in January 1916 following the failure of recruitment schemes to gain sufficient volunteers in 1914 and 1915. From March 1916, military service was compulsory for all single men in England, Scotland and Wales aged 18 to 41, except those who were in jobs essential to the war effort, the sole support of dependents, medically unfit, or 'those who could show a conscientious objection'. This later clause was a significant British response that defused opposition to conscription.'*[137] This explains the background context very well.

Bristol Museum ran an exhibition during 2018, entitled 'Refusing to kill: Bristol's World War I conscientious objectors,' which was the story of Bristol men who refused to fight in World War I, and the people who supported them. The exhibition described that it, *'explores the varied motivations of conscientious objectors and their experiences during the war and afterwards, using documents, photographs, artefacts and material from surviving relatives and archive collections.'*[138] The Bristol Radical History Group (BRHG)[139] explained that, *'Based on documents in the Central Library, we published details of 47 men from Bristol who were imprisoned as conscientious objectors during World War 1. For moral, religious or political reasons they refused to take part in the war... Cyril Pearce... has collated information about over 17,000 men... Many were subjected to harsh conditions in prison. After the war many found it difficult to return to their jobs. Others agreed to serve in non-combatant roles like the Friends' Ambulance Service. All paid a great price for having the courage to stand up for their principles... The list of names that we have found so far can be found in 'Do You Have A Conchie In The Family?'*[140']

This photograph shows three brothers, one of whom refused to take any part in the war, the second worked as an ambulance driver, and the third was conscripted. The text displayed with the photo in the exhibition read, *'The three Whiteford brothers lived with their parents in St. George. During the war Graham served in the army; Wilfred refused to fight but agreed to join the Non-Combatant Corps; Hubert refused to take any part in the war. Like other 'abolutists' he was repeatedly court-martialled and sentenced to hard labour. From August 1918, he served sentences in Wormwood Scrubs and Bristol. He was not released until May 1919. After his release, their father took all three brothers to a local photographer where this picture was taken. He was proud of each of his sons for the decisions they took in relation to the war.'* The brothers are (from left to right) Graham, Hubert and Wilfred. Mr Whiteford must have been a gracious man to have this photograph taken of his three sons, each in their respective uniform.

Reproduced with permission of Bristol Radical History Group
Thanks to Jeremy Clarke, one of the curators of the exhibition, for getting permission to
use the photo from Paul Shotton, the grand-son of Eric Crompton.

A dilemma here is that some people feel ashamed or awkward about having a conscientious objector ancestor, but why do conscientious objectors have to explain their decision? Why does not wanting to fight in an army in a war bring shame onto a family? I have never seen anybody referred to as a conscientious objector on any trees that I've viewed.

Find A Grave

The Find A Grave website states that you can, '*Find the graves of ancestors, create virtual memorials or add photos, virtual flowers and a note to a loved one's memorial. Search or browse cemeteries and grave records for every-day and famous people from around the world.*'[141] People have kindly taken the time to photograph and record memorials, and it's nice to read the inscriptions, especially if you don't live near enough to physically visit. *'The site provides tools that let people from all over the world work together, share information and build an online, virtual cemetery experience... Memorials generally include birth, death and burial information and may include pictures, biographies, family information and more. Members can contribute what they know and can leave remembrances via 'virtual flowers' on the memorials they visit, completing the virtual cemetery experience.'*[142] Jim Tipton, Find A Grave's founder, created the Find A Grave website in 1995, because he could not find an existing site that catered to his hobby of visiting the graves of famous people. Some dilemmas here include that, because it could be assumed that because this service is altruistic, that the information given is correct. However, it is not always known who the individual contributors are, and therefore there may be unsubstantiated information on the memorial. Close family can't 'own' the online memorial, and it could be argued that some memorials appear very quickly, maybe before the family have time to fully grieve.

Was your ancestor a Gypsy?

The Romany and Traveller Family History Society is the first and only, British family history society for people with Romany Gypsy, Traveller and Fairground roots. Their website asks, *'Is there a story in your family that one of your ancestors was a Romany Gypsy? Or have you come across people in your own research that look as though they may have led a travelling lifestyle?... Not everyone described as a traveller, vagrant or hawker in historic records was a Gypsy, but many were. By gathering other types of information about a person or a family, it may be possible to confirm that you have Gypsy blood.'*[143] People may not realise that some of the work named in censuses was traveller work. The website describes typical Romany occupations, such as hawker, pedlar, basket maker, mat maker, beehive maker, brush maker, tinker, tinman, knife grinder, general dealer, peg maker, umbrella mender, chimney sweep, horse dealer, or called 'Egyptian'. Family historians can also look for evidence of mobility, for example, *'a description in a document such as tent dweller, van dweller, stroller, itinerant or of no fixed abode. Or, in a census return, a different place of birth for each child.'* A dilemma here is that society tends to either romanticise or demonise Gypsies. *'The cultural dissonance that occurs between Gypsy travellers and the dominant culture in England and Wales has been well documented.'*[144] Matras reported that, sadly, *'Roma are one of Europe's most marginalised and deprived communities. Addressing their problems is made more difficult by lack of transparency in the methods used to collect data on them.'*[145]

Bristol Museum, UK, has a beautiful authentic gypsy caravan on display. It has a notice that thoughtfully states, *'Traditional Romany life is about close family and community bonds and the freedom to travel for work.'* The history of their Romany caravan is that, *'Horse-drawn caravans have been used as homes by the Romany community for about 160 years. Before that they were used by travelling show-people... Bristol Museum bought the caravan in 1953 and it was displayed outside Blaise Castle House Museum. After the wagon was burgled in 1957, it came to Bristol Museum and Art Gallery as part of a transportation display.'*[146]

People want to preserve areas

The Federation of Family History Societies (FFHS) website reported that, *'The former Longford Meeting House,*[147] *just north of Heathrow airport, is one of the many historical properties that will be destroyed if plans for a third runway go ahead. The building dates back to 1676, when it was opened by the Longford Monthly Meeting of the Religious Society of Friends (Quakers).'*[148] It was pointed out that many people are 'at rest' in the grounds which include a picturesque timber-framed property. On a positive note, the FFHS reported that, *'With strong backing from Suffolk Family History Society and FFHS, Suffolk Record Office*[149] *has been awarded £10.3 million to create a flagship heritage centre at Ipswich Waterfront and transform access to its archives, which is hoped to be completed by the end of 2019.'*

Meitzler reported that, in Nottinghamshire, UK, *'Families thought vandals had run amok in a cemetery when around fifty headstones were knocked over. Some were in tears when they saw the state of graves at Nuthall Cemetery... But the 'culprit' was Nuthall Parish Council,* (who left) *messages attached to each headstone explaining that the council had moved the headstones for health and safety reasons.'*[150] A dilemma here is how long can people's remains lay undisturbed? Renovation can be costly, but, once completed, can attract visitors and tourists. A positive angle of redevelopment is that it can lead to informing the next generation with archive-related events, learning activities and digital programmes.

Unclaimed bodies

Some people die without the local authorities being able to find living relatives to claim the body and organise and pay for burial or cremation. Smolenyak explained that, *'It's essentially 'lost and found,' but for human beings, rather than gloves and umbrellas... Because we've become such a mobile, churning society, people are going to their graves with no one to claim them. They aren't John or Jane Does. Their identities are known, but finding their family members is another matter...'*[151] Smolenyak altruistically set up a Facebook group for volunteers. In the USA, medical examiners and coroners' offices are required by law to make a 'best faith' effort to locate the next of kin for the each individual, but may be over stretched for time and money. The disposition of the unclaimed varies throughout the USA, and people whose family can't be found will receive an anonymous dispersal. Five hundred and fifty eight cases from thirty six counties in eighteen states had been attempted, with three hundred and forty solved, and one hundred and five were closed.

Rape

Family historians may investigate records and add men to their tree, not knowing the full information about the circumstances of a child's conception. This could later be revealed through newspaper accounts, for example, and cause great distress to family or descendants. Woodhouse stated that, *'I'm calling for a change in the law, a simple amendment to the Children's Act 1989 that would ban any male with a child conceived by rape from applying for access/ rights.'*[152] Labour MP Louise Haigh said, *'Convicted rapists should have no parental rights. We're campaigning for a change to the Children Act to stop the courts being used to re-traumatise victims and remove the rights of men who've fathered children through rape.'* However, a family law barrister and head of the Transparency Project[153] said current legislation was clear, explaining that, *'It is derived from our obligation under human rights legislation that a child, rather than a parent, has the right to family life.'*

Hitler's babies

Loveland described that, *'Lebensborn, meaning 'fount of life,' was a secret program carried out by the SS, which encouraged genetically 'pure' women (blonde-haired, blue-eyed women with the right measurements) to breed with SS officers... Between 1936 and the end of World War II in 1945, between 6,000 and 8,000 babies were born in Lebensborn clinics (though some sources estimated the number was a much higher 20,000).'*[154] Schmitz- Köster[155] who wrote a book about Lebensborn,[156] stated that she felt that, *'The children were conceived in all the usual ways: love affairs, one-night stands, and so forth... Abortion was not legal in Germany then, and in many cases, the women did not want to keep the babies.'* However, the women were given incentives to have a baby, and for some, it was a matter of survival in a poor, warn-torn country where families starved. Some mothers told their children that their father had been killed in the war. Those babies, who may well be alive today, may want to compile their tree. If they found that they were conceived in those circumstances, would they include their biological father on their tree? Can the past be eradicated?

Some case studies of a professional genealogist's ethical dilemmas

Here are some examples of ethical dilemmas produced while working on client's research, kindly provided by John Boeren,[157] a professional genealogist from The Netherlands.

Example 1

One of my clients told me she had already done quite a lot of her family history research, back to the beginning of the 19th century. She wanted me to check her results and to add - if possible - a few extra generations. When I took a look at her father's grandfather, I immediately saw that his birth certificate said he was acknowledged by the new husband of his mother, five years after his birth. In those cases, it is very unlikely that this man was the biological father. I told my client that a DNA test could bring some answers. My client stopped the project because her father was so upset.

Example 2

A client learned through my research that her x-times great-grandfather was already married in the Netherlands when he married abroad. He had left his wife and daughters behind and never returned to them again. The marriage abroad made him a bigamist. My client could handle the situation, but told me her (religious) family members would never hear this, as they would not be able to deal with bigamy.

Example 3

A client asked me to investigate her grandfather's history. She had the feeling he did something 'wrong' during World War II but never heard the true story. I found many records about him. Some testimonies said he did the right things. Other testimonies said he did bad things. In times of war, it is really difficult to say what one should do. What seems right at the time, may seem wrong years after the liberation.

Example 4

When I was working in the archives, I helped a woman who was in her 70s with finding records of her father and grandfather. After a while, I saw her sitting behind the microfiche reader, with tears in her eyes. She had learned that her grandfather was married twice. She never heard about the first marriage, nor about the children from this marriage. Her (deceased) father had had half-siblings.

Boeren concluded that, *'In all these cases the main question is: how to deal with right and wrong, how to deal with your own emotions and with those of others involved. As a genealogy professional, I signed some ethical codes that tell me (more or less) how I should behave. What is okay and what is not. Nevertheless, I have to ask myself every time again: what do I want to know, what do I tell my client, my friends or my family and how do I tell what I have found? The best thing to do, is to inform the other party – whether a client, or a friend or a family member – that genealogy is a wonderful pastime and a great job but that it also comes with risks. You never know what you will find... and in many cases, you always find the unexpected. Once you have finished your research:*

stick to the facts as much as possible, without judgement. But how difficult that is, when, for example, your own family is involved!'

Many thanks to John for these case studies, and his overall impression of working through ethical dilemmas as a professional genealogist.

The next chapters look at genealogical ethical dilemmas involved in DNA testing, adoption, and ethnicity.

Chapter 3: DNA testing

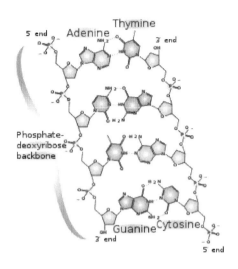

DNA chemical structure[158]

What is DNA?

DNA (deoxyribonucleic acid) is a chemical made up of two long molecules arranged in a spiral, a double-helix structure. DNA carries genetic information which has all the instructions that a living organism needs to grow, reproduce and function. Genes are short sections of DNA, and carry information for particular characteristics. In a cell nucleus, DNA is organised into coiled strands called chromosomes. There are many genes in a chromosome. Humans have forty six chromosomes in each cell, half of the chromosomes (twenty three) are inherited from one parent and half (twenty three) from the other.[159]

DNA discoveries timeline

1866   Gregor Mendel[160] published results of his research on the inheritance of factors in pea plants

1869   Friedrich Miescher[161] discovered 'nuclein' in the pus of discarded surgical bandages

1919   Phoebus Levene[162] identified the base, sugar and phosphate nucleotide unit

1928   Frederick Griffith discovered the transfer of traits in two forms of Pneumococcus[163]

1937   William Astbury produced the first X-ray diffraction patterns showing regular structure of DNA[164]

1943   Avery-MacLeod-McCarty experiment identified DNA as the transforming principle[165]

1952	Hershey-Chase experiment[166] showed that DNA is the genetic material of the T2 phage
1952	Rosalind Franklin and Raymond Gosling produced single X-ray diffraction image[167]
1953	James Watson and Francis Crick suggested the first correct double-helix model of DNA structure[168]
1958	Meselson-Stahl experiment confirmed replication mechanism as implied by the double-helical structure[169]
1962	Watson, Crick, and Wilkins jointly received the Nobel Prize in Physiology or Medicine[170]

Timeline adapted from DNA Research: A Timeline of Discovery & Developments.[171]

c2000	DNA testing for genealogical applications became available to the commercial market

DNA testing for genealogical purposes

DNA testing for genealogical purposes is a very new discipline. A fascinating background context was given by The International Society of Genetic Genealogy (ISOGG) wiki, which explained that, *'In the late 1990's, there were several highly publicized cases, i.e. the 'Cheddar Man', Thomas Jefferson and Sally Hemmings, and the last Czar of Russia's family, to name a few, in which DNA was utilized to prove or disprove relationships to people that have long since been deceased. The media coverage of these, and other cases, helped to bring DNA testing for genealogical applications to the commercial market in the year 2000.'*[172]

By 2019, 'DNA testing' has become a household phrase, and many people have undertaken DNA tests. A massive increase in advertising has led to many people undertaking a test and encouraging others to do so, *'The boom in testing may be a direct result of how much companies spend on advertising. Ancestry.com spent $109 million on TV and other ads in the US during 2016. It was on track to spend even more in 2017. The next-largest amount of ad spending, $21 million, was from 23andMe.'*[173] Regalado, 2017, reported that, the number of people who have had their DNA analysed with direct-to-consumer genetic genealogy tests, *'...now exceeds 12 million, according to industry estimates... around 1 in 25 American adults now have access to personal genetic data... Ancestry.com announced that it has tested more than 7 million people... The second-largest player, 23andMe, has tested more than 3 million, followed by MyHeritage and FamilyTreeDNA.'*[174] Hunt, 2018, reported that, *'AncestryDNA says it has tested more than 10 million people in 30 countries. 23andMe says it has more than 5 million subscribers; FamilyTreeDNA claims 2 million.'*[175] Lardinois, 2018, reported that, for MyHeritage, *'While the DNA sales account for much of the company's recent growth spurt, it's worth noting that the company's subscription business is also growing between 30% and 40% year over year, with a retention rate of more than 75%.'*[176] Larkin reported that, across the four DNA databases she looked at (Ancestry, MyHeritage, 23AndMe, and FTDNA), nearly 43,000 new people are testing every day.[177]

Bettinger and Woodbury explained that DNA testing is now a 'normal and vital' part of undertaking family history, stating that, *'Genetic genealogy will play an increasingly important role in the future of family history. In fact, it has become so prevalent that we can no longer ignore DNA testing as a valuable resource for family history research. The Genealogical Proof Standard, a set of standards for crafting proof arguments, suggests that a conclusion can only be proven if reasonably exhaustive research has been performed. DNA testing is now considered to be a common element of reasonably exhaustive research.'*[178]

Which DNA test to take?

MacEntee[179] has compiled a useful and succinct DNA Buying Guide[180] which, *'If you are planning on purchasing a DNA test kit for yourself, as a gift, several tests for family members, or have a specific testing need, 'DNA Buying Guide' provides you with the best strategy as you navigate all the different sales offers on DNA test kits and related genetic genealogy products.'* Larkin, 2018, succinctly summarised the pros and cons of the main autosomal DNA testing companies, *'Usually, the first questions someone new to genetic genealogy asks are, "Which test should I do? And which company should I use?" In almost all cases, the answer to the first question is an autosomal test, which looks at DNA inherited from all sides of your family... which (test) is best for you depends on your goals and family history.'*[181] Brown, 2018, reported on seven DNA companies and summarised his findings as, *'Ancestry.com's DNA test was the best because it is affordable, contains personalized results and has the largest database of any company on the market... MyHeritage is the least expensive of all the kits we tested. This company's website is easy to navigate, and in our testing it was easy to connect and chat with matches... 23andMe offers the best features in addition to straightforward geographical ancestry percentages ... (for) paternity testing, Paternity Depot is our top choice because it's the most affordable and offers great accuracy. DNAFit is the best health and fitness test because you get your results in 10 days. If you're testing your dog, Wisdom Panel 4.0 is the most affordable and tests the most dog breeds.'*[182]

Many of the DNA testing companies give discounted offers before Mother's Day, Father's Day, Christmas, 'Black Friday,' and 'Cyber Monday.' Cara warned about unthinkingly buying DNA tests for Christmas, *'They're pegged as a novel, exciting experience, one that might even bring a family closer together by revealing their shared genetic past.'*[183] Cara explained that, in his opinion, DNA tests are imprecise, barely regulated, and could expose your identity to people you'd rather not know anything about you. A marketing email entitled 'Celebrate Mom genes'[184] was based on an incentive to *'save on Family Finder and mtFullSequence during our Mother's Day Sale'* (offer ended 14 May 2018). The six women all look really happy in the three pictures of different ethnicity mothers and daughters cuddling, but what if you don't have a mother, or that it's your biological mother that you're looking for. Testing various members of the family can be really enjoyable, but can alternatively create major problems from revealed secrets.

Krueger asked whether genetic testing sites are, *'the new social networks, like Facebook, but for fifth cousins, adoptive mothers and sperm-donor dads.'*[185] She described how doing a DNA test *'...started me down this genealogical rabbit hole.'* She connected with a number of relatives, including via Facebook, and met and developed relationships with some, and went to visit her ancestor's village abroad. Because of the 'more affordable' testing fees, Krueger noted that, *'in many cases, long-lost relatives are reuniting, becoming best friends, travel partners, genealogical resources or confidantes'* and wanted to visit their family's places of origin, often finding *'an in-elecutable connection.'* But for others, connections and relationships made via DNA matches and conducted through social media may be different to 'face to face' ones.

Gill[186] reported that an unexpected outcome of the interest in DNA testing for genealogical purposes, is the increase in numbers of paternity tests being sold, as Alphabiolabs reported that up to 30,000 paternity tests are being performed every year, with 20% of men learning that they are not the father of the child they are testing. Gill explained that a huge ethical dilemma here is that that, *'the shock of learning a child is not biologically theirs can lead to severe emotional distress for some men, for which they may not be prepared.'*

There are a number of testing sites available, each with their own advantages and disadvantages.

Ancestry[187]

Ancestry Publishing was founded in 1983, publishing more than forty family history magazine titles and genealogy reference books. Ancestry was launched in 1996. In 2000, Ancestry published census images. In 2002, Ancestry partnered with Relative Genetics to offer Y and Mitochondrial testing. In 2007, Ancestry offered to combine DNA with online family trees. In 2010, 'Who Do You Think You Are?' television programme was launched in the USA. AncestryDNA was launched in May 2012, and during 2019 has more than 10 million people in its consumer DNA network, making it the largest in the world. AncestryDNA is available in more than thirty international markets. Ancestry has one thousand six hundred employees located around the world, with one thousand employees in Utah, four hundred employees in San Francisco, and approximately one hundred employees in Dublin, Ireland. Ancestry's company overview explains that, *'Ancestry, the global leader in family history and consumer genomics, harnesses the information found in family trees, historical records, and DNA to help people gain a new level of understanding about their lives.'*[188] MacEntee alerted people that AncestryDNA has posted a warning on Amazon listings for AncestryDNA test kits, *'AncestryDNA highly discourages the purchase of our DNA kit from unauthorized resellers. To ensure the best experience and service, please purchase directly from AncestryDNA Official. DNA kits that are fraudulently purchased and then resold through Amazon may be deactivated by AncestryDNA, and may not be eligible for a refund.'*[189] Orwig concluded that Ancestry is the best DNA test for cousin matching and for having the most geographic regions for ethnicity.[190]

FamilyTreeDNA (FTDNA)[191]

In 2000, FamilyTreeDNA was the first company to deliver direct-to-consumer DNA testing for ancestry, pioneering the field of genetic genealogy, the use of DNA testing to establish relationships between individuals and determine ancestry. '*Bennett Greenspan, President and CEO, is an entrepreneur and life-long genealogy enthusiast. Mr. Greenspan founded Family Tree DNA in 1999, turning - dare we say - a hobby into a full-time vocation.*'[192] Greenspan was born and raised in Omaha, Nebraska, and has been interested in genealogy from a very young age; he drew his first family tree at age eleven; he explained that, '*With DNA testing we are able to unravel that history book that is contained within the cells of all of us.*'[193] The strapline is, '*You are a brushstroke drawn from history.*' FamilyTreeDNA is a division of Gene by Gene, a commercial genetic testing company based in Houston, Texas. FamilyTreeDNA offers analysis of autosomal DNA, Y-DNA, and mitochondrial DNA to individuals for genealogical purpose.[194] Orwig concluded that FTDNA tests are the best for, '*serious genealogy, YDNA and mtDNA tests.*'[195]

MyHeritage[196]

Gilad Japhet started his MyHeritage company from his living room in Bnei Atarot, in Israel, in 2003. Japhet became interested in family history at the age of thirteen, after interviewing his mother for a school project.[197] Gilad attributes his fascination with family trees and family history to his inspiration from his grandfather, Chaim Japhet[198] who was a member of the pre-state Jewish National Council, the deputy to American Jewish scholar and Zionist leader Henrietta Szold,[199] and one of the pioneers of social work in Israel.

As of 2015, MyHeritage supports forty two languages and has around eighty million users worldwide. In January 2017 it was reported that MyHeritage has thirty five million family trees on its website.'[200] MyHeritage sends email alerts when there is a new shared match, which is really useful, as it gives a summary of the person who manages the tree, an estimate of the DNA percentage overlap, and the number of shared centiMorgans. The flag in the alert is an interesting visual point, but is an indicator of where the person lives now, not their heritage, and, as it's a DNA matching service, the flag could be a bit misleading. In addition, there are some objections to the use of flags as symbols, '*How can a country's history, geography, culture, politics and religion be squeezed into one design? Wars, revolutions, political unions and public competitions have shaped the colours and content of these most evocative of symbols.*'[201] People can add photographs of themselves to their profile and add photographs of their relatives to their tree, and it could be argued that it looks like a friendly platform, and then people may assume that people they message will reply, and feel surprised and disappointed when they don't.

A hugely altruistic side to MyHeritage is that they are involved in three main pro bono projects:[202] the 'restitution of looted assets,' which involves returning heirlooms from WWII to their rightful owners; 'Tribal Quest' which involves documenting family histories and cultures of remote tribes; and 'DNA Quest,' which involves potentially reuniting adoptees with their biological families, through offers of free DNA tests to adoptees during specific time periods.

23andMe

23andMe was founded in 2006 and the website explains that this was, *'to help people access, understand and benefit from the human genome. We have more than five million genotyped customers around the world... 23andMe offers two Personal Genetic Services: Health + Ancestry and Ancestry. The 23andMe PGS test includes health predisposition and carrier status reports.'*[203] Customers can choose between an ancestry-only test or a more expensive combined health and ancestry test. In 2015, 23andMe was granted authorization by the US Food and Drug Administration (FDA) to market the first direct-to-consumer genetic test.[204] Orwig concluded that 23AndMe was the best test for genetic health screening.[205]

Gedmatch

A very useful resource for collaboration is GEDmatch. You can download your DNA from the testing site you had your DNA analysed by, save the file, then upload the file to GEDmatch, which potentially has about four times the amount of matches from the site you tested with, because you can upload from a variety of testing sites. The website states that, *'GEDmatch provides DNA and genealogical analysis tools for amateur and professional researchers and genealogists.'*[206]

GEDmatch includes many free sophisticated tools to utilise, including:

- 'one-to-many' matches
- 'one-to-one' compare
- X 'one-to-one'
- admixture (heritage)
- people who match one or both of two kits
- are your parents related?
- archaic DNA matches
- multiple kit analysis

People seem to have uploaded their data to this site with different intentions from just seeing their ethnicity estimates, and therefore seem to collaborate more. However, a key to columns would be useful, as the site includes abbreviations which may not be standard for many people. People may not understand some jargon used in the explanations, for example, *'To qualify as a 'match' in the genealogical time frame, results must have a largest Autosomal segment that has at least 700 SNPs and be at least 7cM. It must have both. In general, the results shown below use thresholds less than 7cM / 700 SNPs.'*

A useful section to use is 'one-to-many matches.' Matches are listed in descending order of DNA closeness, an immediately visible ranking. People may draw what could be considered 'incorrect' conclusions from their observations, and may not understand how to use these tools, nor understand the implications of the findings given, despite there being some useful video links from experienced, and often expert, advisors.[207] If the first few people you overlap with don't have anything in the 'GED/ WikiTree' column, people may not scroll down too far and may miss an important tool, that is, that some people have also uploaded a tree. Some may not notice the explanation that the, *'intensity of green background indicates how recent (within last 30 days) a match is'* which indicates a 'new' match that you can potentially collaborate with.

It is very useful that email addresses for any match are given in the right hand column, so you can collaborate directly, and don't have to message through a DNA testing company's messaging system. Although it clearly states in red and capitals, *'do not create mass mailing lists from these results,'* people may well do so; there is a potential for people to cut and paste the emails and produce a group email list, whether it be for genealogical or other purposes. The quirky tool 'are your parents related'[208] may cause problems, because, although it may be useful to think that, in the past, many people married someone from their village, and it may be inevitable that your parents' DNA would overlap through previous generations; it could also 'open a can of worms' if people found that their parents matched more closely, such as half siblings, cousins, or as a result of incest.

The most useful aspect of using GEDmatch is that you can see matches with people who have uploaded their DNA from a variety of different testing sites, which gives a much greater potential for collaborating. GEDmatch allows uploads from Ancestry, 23AndMe, FTDNA, with more companies potentially being added,[209] including Chinese companies 23Mofang[210] and GESEDNA.[211]

Matching

A useful DNA Relationship Chart has been produced by Tierney, who explained that, *'To give me the visual my brain needs to absorb the info, I created this chart. If you'd like a copy for your very own, feel free to click and download a full size copy.'*[212] This makes for a great handout, as it is so easy to read and understand.

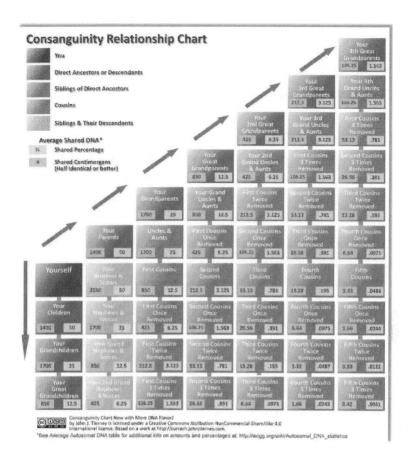

Consanguinity Relationship Chart

You can find out what potential relationship you have with a DNA match, and you can see what theoretical percentage overlap you have with known relatives. If you know the percentage DNA overlap, sometimes you can slot someone into your tree in a potential relationship. For example, I live in the UK, and have about 3% overlaps with people the same age as me in the USA, so I can start investigating where we 'fit in', by consulting this chart, which tells me we may be second cousins, or first cousins twice removed. If the match has a thorough tree, then you can make an educated guess where you match, by studying charts such as Tierney's. You can also eliminate or potentially include lines by triangulating with two or more matches, by investigating whether two people that you match with, also match with each other.

There are a numbers of dilemmas with 'matching,' for example, when the testing company gives a predicted relationship from the amount of overlap. Many people could feel that the predicted relationship given by the testing company was an exact reflection of the relationship, and not pursue other possibilities. However, a second cousin relationship (when you share great grandparents), could also be other specific relationships; for example, great-great uncle or aunt (shares your great-great-great grandparents); first cousin once removed (shares your great-great grandparents); first cousin twice removed (shares your grandparents); but this could be confusing for some people, such as those starting their tree or those with gaps in their tree. If your closest match is only a second or third cousin, some people don't know what to do next with that information, or where to potentially slot that match into their tree. Estes quoted Corbeil, who warned that, *'it is extremely difficult to assess any predicted relationship at the 4th cousin level. Even 1st, 2nd and 3rd cousin predictions had wide variances. The only conclusion we can draw from this is to use Ancestry predictions with extreme caution.'*[213]

DNA matches can contact, or maybe even contact you too much through email or social media. On the other hand, and disappointingly, many matches don't reply to messages and that feels unhelpful or rude. Even though some matches won't reply to any messages, you can still glean some information from a public tree. Some matches collaborate fully and broaden your information, along with potentially providing a whole branch of relatives. A dilemma is whether to pursue relationships with these new relatives that we don't have a history with, other than a sometimes obscure common ancestor. Subsequently meeting DNA matches can be along a continuum of great joy to immense pain, whether online or in person.

Misattributed paternity (MAP)

One of the main features of DNA testing is that when people's results come back, they can see immediately where they overlap or match with other people. The testing companies give a statistical overlap, and a predicted relationship between testees. This is great news for filling in blanks on a tree. However, some people are not able to understand their statistical overlap (or lack of) with, for example, a parent or a sibling. After disbelieving the implications, the reality can be that people just aren't related biologically. This can be a huge, life-changing blow for all concerned, create enormous rifts in the family, have implications for inheritance, legal implications, and maybe even trigger some mental health issues. One or both parents can be seen in a new harsh light.

Larmuseau warned that paternity issues resulting from DNA tests purchased for genealogical purposes are not receiving enough attention because any criticism of DNA testing, *'deals mainly with general issues, that is, the accuracy of the ethnicity analyses, the privacy and ownership of the supplied DNA profiles, and their secondary use for police investigations in cold cases. Also, attention is mostly given to adopted children or children conceived through anonymous sperm or egg cell donation and their search for biological relatives... paternity issues receive too little attention in this debate, despite their substantial potential impact on customers' lives.'*[214] Some families give or receive DNA kits for Christmas, for example because family tree enthusiasts want to expand the DNA evidence on their tree, or to test for ethnicity. Larmuseau lamented that there is a noticeable absence of any help with coming to terms with the implications of the DNA test findings, and recommended that the companies should make the possibility of finding a MAP (misattributed paternity) event clearer to the consumer, and that professional help should be more readily available. An ethical dilemma here is that who has the overall responsibility for these findings?

Discovering errors in your tree because of mis-attributed paternity

DNA testing is revealing a variety of previously unexpected relationships, and people's construction of their tree may have to be re-addressed. For example, what if you discover through DNA testing that your dad wasn't actually your biological father, but he did bring you up all of your life or for many years, and you had relationships with his family? Do you delete your dad from your tree, and add your biological father? Lents argued that, '...*the important feature of genealogy is the family history and the connection with our past, not the precise genetic relationships.*'[215] Some people didn't know that their relative was adopted, and that this person's parents weren't their biological relatives. If you found out at a later stage that a relative had been adopted, what would you do with the information about the inclusion (or not) of that person's family? A dilemma here would be whether to add the person's adopted or biological family to the adoptee on their tree? A solution could be that people who know the adoptee and their (adopted) family would add that family to their tree, whereas those who don't know the adoptee, but match on a DNA testing site, would add biological relatives.

Using DNA for non-genealogical purposes

Familial searching was reportedly first used in the UK when a brick was thrown through the windscreen of a lorry on the M3 motorway in March 2003, causing the driver to have a fatal heart attack. Harman was traced through DNA he left on the brick he threw and was jailed for six years for manslaughter. But the investigation into an elderly British widow, Gladys Godfrey, was the first time familial searching had ever been used to trace and convict a murderer. The pioneering technique used to identify her killer has led to many crimes being solved around the world. The senior intelligence officer stated that, '*The result is actually quite a long list of potential relatives of an offender and it's down to the local police to use knowledge that they have access to.*'[216]

Using familial DNA to solve a crime gained notoriety through the much-publicised case of 72-year-old former marine and former police officer, Joseph DeAngelo, who was arrested on 25 April, 2018, on suspicion of being the so called 'Golden State Killer.' He was believed to have committed at least twelve murders, forty six rapes and numerous break-ins in California in the 1970s and 1980s. It was reported that the police had used genealogy DNA to apprehend him. Paul Holes told reporters that he had a breakthrough in the case after uploading a DNA sample from one of the crime scenes to GEDmatch. '*He was able to use the sample to trace DeAngelo's family tree back to his 4 x great grandfather, and identify distant living relatives. This allowed investigators to narrow* down their search using factors such as ethnicity, height and residence until they identified DeAngelo as the suspect.'[217]

On 28 April, 2018, presumably because of voiced concerns about the methods used in the DeAngelo case, GEDmatch stated that, *'While the database was created for genealogical research, it is important that GEDmatch participants understand the possible uses of their DNA, including identification of relatives that have committed crimes or were victims of crimes.'* GEDmatch subsequently warned that, *'... If you are concerned about non-genealogical uses of your DNA, you should not upload your DNA to the database and/or you should remove DNA that has already been uploaded. Users may delete their registration/ profile and associated DNA and GEDCOM resources. Instructions are available.'*[218] Many people then didn't know what to do about this situation, creating a dilemma about the usefulness of the information being on the site, compared to the privacy and confidentiality of all the people sharing your DNA. *'Individuals who contribute to genetic genealogy databases have an expectation of privacy in their genetic data that may be violated by familial genetic searches'*[219] However, many family tree enthusiasts haven't asked their children or close relatives' permission to upload their DNA. Even if your living relatives are labelled private, they are still visible relationships.

Then, on 20 May, 2018, GEDmatch produced a revised Terms of Service and Privacy Policy stating that, *'GEDmatch respects your privacy and recognizes the importance of your personal information. We are committed to protecting your information through our compliance with this Privacy Policy. This Privacy Policy describes our practices in connection with information we may collect through your use of our website (our 'Site'). By using our Site, you consent to our collection and use of the information described in this Privacy Policy.'*[220] Many people were worried that this use of genealogical data had been used in a different way to its' intended purpose of expanding on a family tree, but in a quandary because it was great news that unsolved crimes from many years ago were now solved.

GEDmatch's purpose is that it, *'...exists to provide DNA and genealogy tools for comparison and research purposes. It is supported entirely by users, volunteers, and researchers. DNA and Genealogical research, by its very nature, requires the sharing of information. Because of that, users participating in this Site agree that their information will be shared with other users.'*[221] Gedmatch[222] clearly states that, *'While the results presented on this Site are intended solely for genealogical research, we are unable to guarantee that users will not find other uses, including both current and new genealogical and non-genealogical uses. For example, some of these possible uses of Raw Data, personal information, and/ or Genealogy Data by any registered user of GEDmatch include but are not limited to:*

- *discovery of identity, even if there is an alias, unidentifiable email address, and other obscuring information*
- *finding genetic matches (individuals that share DNA)*

- *paternity and maternity testing*
- *discovery of unknown or unidentified children, parents, or siblings*
- *discovery of other genetic and genealogical relatives, including both known and unknown or unexpected genetic and genealogical relatives*
- *discovery of ethnic background*
- *discovery of a genetic relationship between parents*
- *discovery of biological sex*
- *discovery of medical information or physical traits*
- *obtaining an email address*
- *familial searching by third parties such as law enforcement agencies to identify the perpetrator of a crime, or to identify remains*

** each one of these represents an ethical dilemma **

A further Gedmatch alert on May 26, 2018, explained that, *'We are still working to hide GEDCOM entries for Living Individuals, as required by GDPR. Until we complete this effort, you will likely see many entries hidden.'*[223] GDPR (General Data Protection Regulation)[224] came into force in the UK on May 25, 2018, and was designed to modernise laws that protect the personal information of individuals. It also boosts the rights of individuals and gives them more control over their information.[225]

Other cases have been similarly solved, such as that reported by Crime Feed, *'...using DNA crime scene evidence obtained from chewing gum and a water bottle, Pennsylvania police arrested a wedding disc jockey DJ Freez, for the cold case 1992 rape and murder of a local teacher... authorities created a DNA profile of the suspect and put it into a database... After a relative of Raymond Rowe uploaded DNA to the genealogy website GEDmatch, investigators got a match... Technicians from Parabon Nanolabs then linked that DNA to the semen left at the crime scene.'*[226] Also recently, the so-called NorCal rapist, Waller, was arrested after police searched the genealogy site GEDmatch for leads. The Washington Post reported that, *'In DeAngelo's case, officials did what's called a familial DNA search of GEDmatch... which has come into wider use around the country, but it raises complicated questions about whether it means that the privacy rights of people are forfeited, in effect, by the decisions made by their relatives.'*[227] Collins pertinently asked, *'What are the risks of using DNA websites in criminal investigations'* and *'what does this mean for the safety of our genetic data?'*[228]

Genealogists helping police may be worried about any reprisals from their involvement. Murphy, reporting for the New York Times, reported that Barbara Rae-Venter, a seventy-year-old former attorney, did not want to be named at the time of the DeAngelo case, because she was worried about her safety. Rae-Venter's involvement has, however, apparently subsequently inspired others to offer their services to law enforcement. Murphy said that, *'While this has resulted in at least eight arrests over the past four months, not everyone in the genealogical community is so comfortable with the alliance,'* and she went on to state that, *'Although she insists that she still considers genetic genealogy a hobby, she's now talking to various law enforcement agencies about fifty cases involving homicide and unidentified victims.'* [229]

Combining DNA information with known information about family members has recently appeared ground breaking, and has received huge media attention, but, mixing DNA results with known people in family trees to identify 'unknowns' is what many genealogists probably do routinely. Gleeson explained that, *'This use began shortly after the first DTC (direct to consumer) autosomal DNA tests were introduced in 2007. It is the same technique that has been used to help adoptees and foundlings identify and locate their birth families, to help donor-conceived children find their genetic father, and to solve illegitimacy mysteries in our family trees.'* [230] If a DNA match is predicted as cousin for example, you can look at their tree to identify their parents, and yours, work out who fits where in a merged tree, and can fill in gaps. A dilemma here is that law enforcement agencies can also circumvent the request process entirely, by creating fake profiles on sites using the DNA of a suspect. So, potentially, you could approach a DNA match to ask about collaborating, or a match could approach you, and it could be a fake profile. [231]

Should anybody be utilising genealogy websites, other than those looking at DNA for genealogical matches, and should police specifically be utilising genealogy websites? Guerrini reported that, *'DeAngelo's arrest was widely celebrated as a clever investigative coup that may have finally brought to justice a man who had terrorized California residents for years. Yet as details of his arrest emerged, privacy concerns were quickly raised about police searches of personal genetic data of the kind used to capture DeAngelo.'* [232] District Attorney Stedman expressed gratitude to the DNA analysis firm, stating, *'We were not close to making an arrest; we didn't even have a direction to go until Parabon pointed us in the right path,'* implying that, 'the end justifies the means.'

Ethical issues concerning using DNA for non-genealogical purposes include the fact that many family historians probably hadn't understood that their DNA information could be utilised for other purposes. DNA information could theoretically be used for many not-intended purposes. Molteni advised that, *'although many genetic service providers warn users about the potential for third parties, including law enforcement, to access personal genetic data, these warnings are usually buried in privacy policies and terms of service that users may never read.'* [233]

Some people may now be reluctant to load their DNA onto GEDmatch, but Guerrini reported that, *'in relation to violent crime, missing persons, and crimes involving children, most responders (89-91%) felt that law enforcement should be allowed to search genealogical websites that match DNA to relatives.'* [234] GEDmatch has had to edit and re-word their policies. Collins explained that, *'Commercial DNA testing companies have privacy policies designed to protect data from being used for other purposes, but these do not apply to GEDmatch, a free public database where users upload the results of DNA tests.'* [235]

An interesting blog by Dick Eastman succinctly explained the ethical dilemmas and legal implications of the police using DNA results, stating that, *'Privacy advocates and many others have since questioned the legality of using the information for law enforcement purposes. Admittedly, the information is publicly available for all to see. The genealogists who contributed the information did so willingly and presumably gave permission for the family DNA to be available to all. However, the relatives of the uploading genealogists may or may not have given permission for their personal DNA information to be made available to the public. After all, it isn't the DNA of any one individual; it is indeed the family's DNA information. Not all family members have agreed to having that information made available to genealogists, law enforcement personnel, insurance companies, and worldwide hackers alike.'*[236] This is an excellent overview of the many issues and dilemmas raised by utilising DNA for solving crimes.

Uploaded DNA results aren't just the DNA of that person, because the DNA includes the family's DNA information too, and through processes of deduction, relationships can be deduced. Erlich *et al* warned that about 60% of the searches for individuals of European descent will result in a third-cousin or closer match, which theoretically allows their identification using demographic identifiers.[237] Wee reported that, *'Chinese officials, who are building a broad nationwide database of DNA samples, have cited the crime-fighting benefits of China's own genetic studies. In Xinjiang, in northwestern China, the program was known as "Physicals for All." From 2016 to 2017, nearly 36 million people took part in it, according to Xinhua, China's official news agency.'*[238] The article suggested that the check-ups were mandatory, and that there was a strong coercive element to the procedures. Is this the way forward for crime detection?

DNA and bone marrow transplants and stem cell transplants

People who have had a bone marrow transplant or a stem cell transplants may not know whether a DNA test would reveal their DNA, or whether it be merged with their donor's. *'Depending on the type of donation, the DNA stays for a short time, a long while or maybe even forever.'*[239] Ancestry explained in their Frequently Asked Questions page that, *'We recommend that recipients of bone marrow transplants do not take Ancestry's DNA test. Instead, we recommend that a close relative, such as a parent or sibling, be tested... If you received a bone marrow transplant, your saliva will probably include your own DNA and the DNA of your bone marrow donor... However, there is no impact to your results if you are a bone marrow donor.'*[240] People may have tested and not realised that the combination of DNA can cause their results to be inconclusive, or even include the results of their donor. It is useful to have the suggestion that a close relative, such as a parent or sibling, be tested, although some relatives may not actually be as biologically related as was thought (if, for example, siblings are half siblings). Also, it is more enjoyable to have your own DNA tested, especially when siblings from the same two parents can have different ethnicity results, for example.

Genetic health information

During 2017, the U.S. Food and Drug Administration (FDA)[241] allowed marketing of 23andMe Personal Genome Service Genetic Health Risk (GHR) tests for ten diseases or conditions.[242] These are the first direct-to-consumer (DTC) tests authorised by The Food and Drug Administration that provide information on an individual's genetic predisposition to certain medical diseases or conditions, which may help to make decisions about lifestyle choices, or to inform discussions with a health care professional.

The ten diseases or conditions include:

- Parkinson's disease, a nervous system disorder impacting movement
- Late-onset Alzheimer's disease, a progressive brain disorder that destroys memory and thinking skills
- Celiac disease, a disorder resulting in the inability to digest gluten
- Alpha-1 antitrypsin deficiency, a disorder that raises the risk of lung and liver disease
- Early-onset primary dystonia, a movement disorder involving involuntary muscle contractions and other uncontrolled movements
- Factor XI deficiency, a blood clotting disorder
- Gaucher disease type 1, an organ and tissue disorder
- Glucose-6-Phosphate Dehydrogenase deficiency, also known as G6PD, a red blood cell condition
- Hereditary hemochromatosis, an iron overload disorder
- Hereditary thrombophilia, a blood clot disorder

Hattenstone explained that DNAFit, a nutrigenetics company, *'is an emerging, and as yet largely unproven, science that studies the interaction between genes and nutrition, with the hope of preventing disease... Last April, DNAFit was bought by a Hong Kong-based genetics company, Prenetics, for $10m (£7.8m). Many scientists believe we simply don't know enough about nutrigenetics for companies such as DNAFit to deliver on its promises.'*[243] Brown warned that, *'23andMe definitely is selling your data to third party companies, research institutions and nonprofits. But it is not selling your genetic data to those entities in order for them to sell you things. It is selling de-identified, aggregate data for research, if you give them consent... Without genetic privacy protections, the information stored in our genes might be used to discriminate against us or send us targeted ads... 23andMe is not using your genetic information in an Orwellian ploy to help companies sell you drugs or shoes your DNA suggests you might want. At least, not yet.'*[244] However, Gymrek et al[245] argued that sharing sequencing data sets without identifiers has become a common practice in genomics. They reported that, *'Surnames can be recovered from personal genomes by profiling short tandem repeats on the Y chromosome (Y-STRs) and querying recreational genetic genealogy databases. We show that a combination of a surname with other types of metadata, such as age and state,* *can be used to triangulate the identity of the target. A key feature of this technique is that it entirely relies on free, publicly accessible Internet resources.'*

Farr[246] reported that Veritas is studying the DNA of people who live to 110, looking for clues to longevity. Veritas Genetics says it has the largest collection of DNA for people who have lived to the age of 110. The company is *'focused on people at the edges of the human experience, whether it's the really old, really young or super performers.'* Are these companies going nearer towards 'designing' humans?

Collecting DNA samples at death

Many people have 'what-ifs' and regrets about not asking relatives more about their lives. Some people regret not asking elderly relatives for a DNA sample. If this regret is instant, when a relative passes away, it may be that people want to retrieve a DNA sample from a deceased person. This could be seen as the last chance for one line of genealogical enquiry. Russell described an interesting scenario in her online blog[247] in which she debated the genealogical and legal implications about whether or not relatives could obtain DNA samples from a deceased relative, explaining that, *'There is no law anywhere in the United States that I could find that bars the next-of-kin from authorizing the taking of a DNA sample from their loved one except, perhaps, in the extraordinary situation where the loved one had expressly stated in writing beforehand that he or she did not want DNA testing to be done.'* The article gave nine useful references, including the consent form which Cuyahoga County Regional Forensic Science Laboratory Office of the Cuyahoga County Medical Examiner Parentage and Identification Department have issued, *'Deceased Patient Custodian/ Next-of-Kin Consent for DNA Testing.'*[248]

Collecting DNA samples at death is not just a legal issue, it is a potentially very upsetting scenario for many people involved. It may even sound 'creepy' for some people. Potentially, someone who wanted to do the DNA test on their recently deceased relative may find opposition from other close relatives. Attending nursing staff may disagree with the procedure, and may not know the legal points about undertaking DNA sampling. If someone felt strongly that they didn't want their DNA tested after death, they could fill in a form clearly explaining that they don't want DNA extracted and utilised.

Overview of ethical dilemmas with DNA testing

DNA testing has come a long way since Gregor Mendell[249] published the results of his research into the inheritance of factors in pea plants in 1866, and James Watson and Francis Crick put forward their double-helix model of DNA structure[250] in 1953. DNA tests are now successfully marketed to the eager family historian. The overall tone of DNA test advertising is very positive, for example, *'With more than 10 million people now in our database and the unique ability to connect with Ancestry's billions of historical records and millions of family trees, AncestryDNA can help deliver the richest family stories - and solve the toughest family mysteries.'*[251] This can lead to false raised expectations. DNA testing has become hugely popular, *'It's a billion-dollar industry that has spawned profitable websites, television shows, scores of books and, with the advent of over-the-counter genetic test kits, a cottage industry in DNA ancestry testing.'*[252] The kit prices are now reasonably priced, which means that less affluent people can be involved, but because the kits are relatively cheap, maybe many are buying DNA tests without fully considering all the implications. Many people don't know what to do after they receive their DNA results, and don't include a public tree or any information about themselves on their DNA testing site. The statistics and jargon words can be overwhelming at first, for example, what are 'centimorgans' (CMs) and 'DNA segments'? Does it help, knowing that a centiMorgan (cM) or map unit (m.u.) is, *'a unit of recombinant frequency which is used to measure genetic distance. The genetic genealogy testing companies 23andMe, AncestryDNA, Family Tree DNA and MyHeritage DNA use centiMorgans to denote the size of matching DNA segments in autosomal DNA tests.'*[253] People generally just want to see what their DNA overlap is with someone else, and knowing how DNA works isn't vital to them.

The DNA testing companies don't necessarily explain that a lot of work goes into compiling a family tree; for example, one company's strapline is *'Give us 5 minutes, and we'll give you your past.'*[254] Customer service at the major companies seems to vary hugely, and some complain that the company has taken their money for the DNA test or membership, but that they can't seem to get practical help afterwards.

DNA testing can reveal that some family members may not be related, including key figures such as a parent[255] or sibling. This information can make or break a family. DNA results can be the key solution for adoptees because potential parents can be deduced from other people's DNA and trees. But whilst many people are overjoyed to be contacted, equal numbers are not happy with the renewed contact. Some people get quickly drawn into relationship with DNA matches, either online or in person, and there are numerous potential benefits and drawbacks with this method of meeting a relative.

Where is all the DNA information going to? Some companies have added incentives of receiving health information. On the face of it, this sounds useful, but, where is this information going? *'The sheer number of people who have the data could spur growth in websites that offer to reanalyse it. Companies including Habit and Promethease take the files and provide a breakdown of people's diet or health risks, frequently with little oversight from regulators.'*[256] Some are concerned about potential cloning. Others are concerned that Governments will have access to their DNA. There is a concern that 'future hackers could amend stolen DNA.'[257] It could be argued that, *'In a world riven by race, ethnicity, religion, nationality and other factors, such focus on DNA for any other than scientific knowledge and advancement seems divisive.'*[258] ('Riven'[259] - *'a tall order, particularly in a field characterised by diverse and conflicting interests'*).

The major positive of DNA testing is the potential great joy to be had from family historians adding relatives to their tree. *'DNA testing gets all the attention these days, from shining light on your ethnic background to identifying serial killers, but for real genealogy buffs, searching for the paper trail in old censuses, wills, and marriage records to build a family tree is a hobby that they will happily spend money on for years.'*[260] Many people get caught up with the fascination of DNA testing and hadn't thought through all the ethical dilemmas DNA testing raises. Boyle warned that, whilst DNA holds the keys to your identity, your true parentage, your inborn talents, and your chances of falling prey to a wide range of diseases, you should consider where all that information is going to, asking, *'How do you feel about handing those keys to someone else? The answer could determine how you proceed with the search for your family roots.'*[261]

The next chapter will look at the genealogical ethical dilemmas involved for people who have been fragmented from their biological families through adoption.

Chapter 4: Adoption

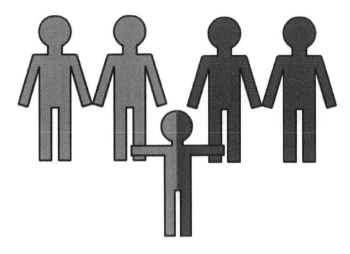

Adoption[262]

Children born outside marriage

Children whose parents weren't married when they were born have been labelled a variety of terms, for example, 'baseborn,' 'illegitimate,' 'bastard,' or people said that the baby was 'born on the wrong side of the blanket.' A politer description is 'natural child,' although this still distinguishes from a child born within a marriage. Baseborn can be defined as, *'of humble parentage; born out of wedlock; illegitimate,'* but also *'having a base character or nature; mean.'*[263] Illegitimate can be defined as, *'born of parents who are not married to each other; born out of wedlock; not legitimate; not sanctioned by law or custom'* but also *'unlawful; illegal'*[264] (implying an illegal child). Because of inheritance laws, people born outside marriage would have been given these labels, but, as less people have a child within a marriage, these old terms can feel more offensive now. In the UK, from 1839, all bastardy cases were heard at Petty Sessions, and initiated by the mother, who had to produce corroborative evidence to convict the putative father. What would corroborative evidence have been in those times? Bastardy Bonds/ Agreements, *'determined which adult male was to support a child... Bastardy Cases were often reported in local newspapers, and gave the names of both the mother and father.'*[265]

The Stack Exchange website reveals that many people are interested in 'which bastards became kings.'[266] Some suggestions put forward by respondees included: William the Conqueror; Bernard of Italy, illegitimate son of Pepin of Italy (himself a legitimate son of Charlemagne); Edward the Martyr, briefly king of England from 975 to 978, who was probably illegitimate as his father Edgar I acknowledged his younger son Æthelred as his only rightful heir; Vladimir the Great, who became 'Knyaz' of Kiev in 978; João I of Portugal was an illegitimate son of King Peter I; Atahualpa, who became Sapa Inca, was the illegitimate son of Huayna Capac; Paul I of Russia could have been the son of Sergei Saltykov, and not of Peter III, husband of his mother Catherine (who became Catherine II). There is a book devoted to bastardy[267] which is a guide to sources for illegitimacy; and a half day course organised by the Society of Genealogists, in which the speaker Professor Probert, *explains the concepts of legitimacy and legitimation and the legal and social implications for children born outside marriage.*[268]

Adoption

Why do people from so many cultures make young girls give up their babies? ...

Lents explained that, *'Secret adoptions have been commonplace in the western world since the Middle Ages. A pregnancy in an unmarried young woman was often 'handled' by attributing the baby to a different family member or even through adoption to an unrelated family. This was almost always concealed from official registries and kept as a tightly guarded secret taken to the graves.'*[269] Herman, of The Adoption History Project[270] contextualised that, *'Adoption is a significant public and private issue... history is an indispensable resource for understanding the personal, political, legal, social, scientific, and human dimensions of this particular form of kinship.'*[271] The American Adoptions website succinctly explained that, *'adoption taking place during the 19th century and before was conducted in a very secretive manner. Many of the children who were adopted were placed with other families to avoid them being labelled as illegitimate. In other words, the stigma against unmarried mothers and their children was enough of a social threat that birth mothers chose to place their children for adoption rather than raise them. Other reasons a birth mother placed her child for adoption could include poverty, illness and family crisis.'*[272]

People know that some women and girls put their baby up for adoption, but many perhaps don't realise that there are so many background issues to the decision. Gordon summed it up that, *'A percentage of these mothers, possibly most, were able to ... go on to create purposeful, productive lives for themselves. Others... never recovered from the loss of the child they bonded with in pregnancy and childbirth and desperately wanted to keep. Strict social convention stood in her way at every possible turn. Women and girls simply did not enjoy the agency to make reproductive decisions for themselves.'*[273]

The Irish Times, 2008, reported three very different reflections on adoption, to explain how people can experience vastly different feelings about adoption. One lady painfully explained that, *'In the late 1970s I had a child who was adopted - at a time when 30% of Irish children born outside marriage were adopted... I always wondered about how my child was progressing and what was happening to him, and knew very little until I contacted the relevant adoption society after my child had reached the age of 21...Giving up a child for adoption has a lifetime impact. One of the things which I've found helpful to remember is that what we did was the most generous act anyone could undertake.'*[274] Whereas a lady who also gave her baby up for adoption gave a different viewpoint, explaining that, *'I'm afraid that birth mothers speaking about their pain would put off young girls today from seeing adoption as a viable choice. There are so many couples who can't have children, and I would love to see adoption coming back in again. Abortion can be hard to live with and women should have the choice to continue their pregnancies and have their babies adopted if that is what's right for them.'*[275]

The third adoptee featured, heart wrenchingly explained his numerous dilemmas, *'I am an adopted person who has successfully made contact with his birth mother...From our meeting in 2005, I got enough information to trace back into the ancestry of both my parents, and I am very glad to have had that opportunity... I have collected a folder of documents recording the facts of my ancestors' lives, but I have no real access to my living relatives...because I continue to be my mother's secret, my sense of identity remains muted. Some part of me - the essence or core that non-adopted people may take for granted - is always suppressed...the charade of secrecy continues... I am not just the object of secrecy, but a participant in the process. Not only must I carry with me someone's secret, I am that secret incarnate. What am I to do if my mother dies? Am I to appear after a decent interval of mourning and reveal myself to her family?'*[276]

Many societies don't 'like' a girl to have a baby out of wedlock, with a presumption that she won't be able to care for the child, and this can be revealed through a number of other (sinister) 'lenses'. Some girls/ women report that they felt, or they were, coerced into giving up their baby. *'Dozens of mothers have said they were forced by social workers, medical staff and churches into surrendering their child because they were young and unmarried. But some of these women say they never surrendered their child at all: they say they were told their child was stillborn or died shortly after birth, when in reality they allege their baby was adopted or essentially handed to a married couple.'*[277]

In Saskatchewan, (western Canada) Lombard, an associate with Maurice Law, the first indigenous-owned national law firm in Canada is representing a proposed class action detailing sixty indigenous women's accounts of being sterilised without proper and informed consent.[278] The women were told that they could not leave the hospital with their new baby, until their fallopian tubes were tied, cut or cauterised. Some of the women's complaints about this enforced sterilisation were as recent as 2017. A dark warning from Senator Yvonne Boyer pointed out that, *'If it's happened in Saskatoon, it has happened in Regina, it's happened in Winnipeg...'* A number of American women were told their newborn had died[279] but, in fact, he or she was adopted. This has recently been termed 'baby scooping', which was, *'a period in United States history starting after the end of World War II and ending in approximately 1972, characterized by an increased rate of premarital pregnancies over the preceding period, along with a higher rate of new-born adoption.'*[280]

Disturbingly, many baby skeletons that were found in Tuam, County Galway, had reportedly[281] all died between 1920 and 1960. The Mother and Baby Homes Commission of Investigation[282] began excavations, as a result of Catherine Corless' persistent allegations about the deaths of what may be as high as eight hundred babies.[283]

The 'altruistic' world of adoption

Verrier wrote extensively about the 'primal wound'[284] of a baby being separated from his/ her mother. When a baby/ child is given to strangers, this forms what could be termed an 'adoption triangle,' the baby, the birth parents, and the new family. However, it seems to be assumed that adoption has little/ no effect on children (people are replaceable and children 'bounce back') and that it is possible to substitute mothers (like a replaced teddy bear or pet). Verrier explained that whilst adoption can be a good solution for the child to have a family, and that long term or permanent foster care is not the answer in the long term, that irreparable damage can be felt by all three parties (the baby, biological parents and adopted parents). It is assumed that because there are professionals involved, everything must have been done correctly, and that it is a wonderful solution for everyone: parents receive a new baby, the baby gets a loving family, and the birth mother feels the baby has gone to a 'good' family. The bottom line is that 'love will conquer all.'

This Rod Stewart song *'The first cut is the deepest'*[285] isn't about being adopted, but sums up the feelings for some adoptees.

> *I would have given you all of my heart*
> *But there's someone who's torn it apart*
> *And she's taken just all that I have*
> *But if you want I'll try to love again*
> *Baby, I'll try to love again, but I know...*
> *The first cut is the deepest...*
> *When it comes to loving me she's cursed*
> *When it comes to loving me, she's worst.'*

Adoption language

The language people use to describe their adoption can indicate their attitude to it. People can say:
- *'I'm adopted...'* (current)
- *'I was adopted...'* (past)
- *'I'm an adoptee...'* (status)

(similar to *'I'm a non-smoker'* or *'I'm an ex-smoker,'* or *'I am disabled'* versus *'I have a disability,'* or I *'suffer from'* a disability).

There are a variety of terms used for 'mother', and these can indicate feelings towards the lady:
- 'birth' mother ('BM') birth 'mom'

- 'natural' mother
- 'blood' mother
- 'biological' mother
- 'real' mother

When and why do people want to 'find' their birth family?

- some people become inquisitive as soon as they have been told
- even just deciding to search can be empowering
- some had a general 'uneasiness'/ felt 'different' through childhood
- *'the decision to search for a birth relative is a slowly accumulating process rather than a one-off trigger'*[286]
- wanting to know why they were 'given away'
- Feast and Philpot's (2003) study revealed that 82% of adoptees had a long-standing curiosity about their origins[287]
- *'uncertainty is a complex phenomenon'*[288]
- many adoptees have never met a blood relative
- there is a 'trigger' event, for example, birth of their own child, death of someone close
- many say they never had anyone who looks like them
- after having their own child, an adoptee may feel that the baby looks like herself or the baby's father, and this can make adoptees wonder who they look like[289]
- some adoptees are unhappy (even abused) within the adopted family
- death of adopted mother/ father, people then feel 'allowed' to search
- there has been a huge surge in televised successful searching for ancestors/ relatives
- seeing something in the media or meeting others who have searched[290]
- nationality/ ethnicity not known
- some people are approaching older age and may feel a realisation of their own mortality, and feel urgent in their search
- health reasons
- infertility issues of self or others
- unhappy image of a woman who had her baby taken away from her (leads to a sense of injustice)
- impact of 'big occasions' or family events[291]
- wanting to search for siblings[292] rather than birth parents
- genealogy is an interesting hobby, and can be undertaken for interest to look for ancestors, not necessarily to search for alive relatives
- *'when you know nothing about the biological background of one of your parents, it's easy to see how that search could become addictively all-consuming'*[293]

The question that always seems to be asked when you mention that you were adopted is *'Have you ever found your **real** family? ....'* This can be a hurtful question. Because there are so many reasons for searching, each person's incentive can involve many different emotions and many different solutions, all of which are ethical dilemmas. Someone who is desperately searching for a birth mother will potentially have different feelings, attitudes and solutions to someone who would like to know their medical history, or someone who had an unhappy adoption. At the other end of the continuum of people wanting to search, are people who have had a happy upbringing and feel no need to search for birth family. An ethical dilemma is that those adoptees who don't feel the need to search for their blood relatives often results in them having to justify not searching.

Bureaucracy

The Massachusetts Adoption of Children Act, enacted in 1851, is widely considered the first 'modern' adoption law.[294] It was made legal to adopt, in 1926 in the UK[295] and the Adopted Children's Register[296] was established in England and Wales on 1, January 1927, in Scotland in 1930, in Northern Ireland in 1931, and in the Republic of Ireland in 1953. If you choose to investigate your birth parents, then there can be a lot of bureaucratic paperwork. There are a number of records held in the UK, by the General Record Office, GRO[297] including:

- Adopted Children Register
- Adoption Contact Register
- Abandoned Children Register
- Thomas Coram Register

In the UK, you fill in the form[298] on the Government website[299] but you need to be eighteen or over to do this. Everyone adopted before 12 November, 1975 has to attend a counselling session with an approved adoption advisor before obtaining their birth certificate. There is also The Adoption Contact Register, which you can add yourself to, at the General Register Office to find a birth relative or an adopted person. The Adoption Contact Register is not a tracing service though; for a connection to be made between people, you must both be on the Adoption Contact Register. I'd assumed this was a 'tokenistic' service, with an elderly man in a basement looking for papers, and matching the contactees, *'I know it's in here somewhere...'* but it is computerised and if both parties want contact, then it can work. Adopted people and birth relatives can also use the Adoption Contact Register to say that they don't want to be contacted. Adoptees should tell their agency and register an 'absolute veto' or a 'qualified veto' if they don't want to be approached by an intermediary agency. Some people don't want to be approached in any circumstance, and some would only accept contact by specific people.

Sealed records

In the USA, an adoptee can face a bureaucratic nightmare to obtain their birth certificate or birth family information as, *'in nearly all states, adoption records are sealed and withheld from public inspection after an adoption is finalized. Most States have instituted procedures by which parties to an adoption may obtain both non identifying and identifying information from an adoption record while still protecting the interests of all parties.'*[300]

An adoptee, BH, summed up his feelings, and raised a number of ethical dilemmas in a post on a Mental Health website, in his eloquent commentary entitled, 'I am not property.' He explained that, *'we are not the property of the state and our records should not be treated like a state secret, or any secret... as an adoptee how can I be bound by an agreement that not only did I not sign but I am not allowed to see and the other people who signed it never received a copy of... how can any of this information be kept from me once the age of majority is reached. I am no child any longer and any protection by the state is not needed nor wanted... Society sucks sometimes and pregnant girls were forced to give up children as a consequence, we can either accept that this happened and fix it by allowing access to information that is my human right or keep the atmosphere of secrecy and act like we never happened... The adoption industry needs to be regulated so much more than it is when talking about the methods that are used to convince these young women to choose adoption.'*[301]

UK help and advice sources

- Adopted Children Register[302]
- NORCAP[303]
- The Adoption Authority of Ireland[304]
- Scottish Adoption[305]

There was a useful service, The Natural Parents Network (NPN), which explained that, *'Whether you are a birth parent, birth relative, adopted adult or have been affected in some way by the difficulties that arise as a result of adoption, including forced or coerced adoption, NPN is here to help. NPN is a self-help organisation run by those who have lost children to adoption. We offer non-judgmental, confidential and independent support to those who have suffered such a loss.'* After thirty one years, the NPN will close during 2019, but their Facebook page[306] will still be active.

Example of a scenario

This was adapted from a post on a Facebook Adoption help page:

> *'I'm trying to search for my birth father. I'm adopted. I traced my birth mother about twenty five years ago (I'm in my 50's now), however the relationship with*

her was short lived because she had a husband and my two half siblings didn't want to know. This felt like being rejected all over again. I'm older now, and better equipped to deal with that but it still hurt me all over again. When I asked about my birth father, she wouldn't tell me anything other than she had to choose between two men at the time. She put her husband as my BF on the birth certificate, rather than my BF. If I ever asked about him, my BM would clam up and refuse to answer, and our relationship became very difficult, and quickly ended. I've slowly recovered from that, but have now resuscitated my interest in my BF, especially as he'd probably be in his seventies now. I have no name and I don't know where to start. Should I try a DNA test? It's going to be like looking for a needle in a haystack isn't it? Can anyone can suggest my next step please? Thank you so much.'

There were many varied replies (paraphrased here):

- *children would like to know who their biological parents are, regardless of who they are, and to not let those children know the truth by the time they are approaching adulthood is cruel*
- *I don't know why parents put husbands before their own child, my birth mum won't tell me either*
- *as you have the info on your BM you can use the time you have whilst you wait for your results to build her family tree (if you haven't already) which should help you work out which matches are from her side of the family, then you have more ideas about the matches that will help you find your BF*
- *one advantage to Ancestry is that the test results can be downloaded and transferred to several other testing sites as well to see if you have matches there - which saves having to pay for multiple tests*
- *when results come back, the real work begins, assume that your father's family is not related to your mother's family, try to identify anyone related to your maternal line (name, geography, research) and mark their file in some way*
- *YouTube is a great way to learn about genetics and centiMorgans*
- *there is a Facebook group that helps adoptees, DNA Detectives*
- *some women had valid reasons for not naming a father but most don't seem to*
- *my friend was adopted, and using DNA matches and mirror trees I found the identities of both her mother and father (now deceased) and she is in touch with 2 half-brothers, it takes hours of work but it's worth it*
- *if you get any matches that come up as a second or third cousin, or an aunt might be all you need, my advice is to be careful not to get too personal too soon, and start a tree as soon as you get your results, if not before then*
- *no cranky, estranged, unloving, unhelpful BM to deal with*
- *as you've had a bad experience with the BM, and the BF may well have passed away by now, focus in on doing your ancestral tree rather than looking for alive relatives*

Mental health issues[307]

Verrier warned that the separation of a baby and mother is a trauma that can have lifelong consequences, which she felt is, *'a physical, emotional, psychological and spiritual wound which causes pain so profound as to have been described as cellular.'*[308] She explained that people feel grief over the loss of a relationship with their birthparents and the loss of the cultural and family connections, and this feeling of loss can be very intense when little or no information is available and grief feelings may be triggered randomly. It can be felt that the birthmother 'rejected' the child; revealed through explanations such as, 'she gave me away' or 'she didn't want me enough.' The person can 'feel abandoned' and comes to feel 'abandonable' or 'not good enough' to have been kept. Even if the adult adoptee understands the birth mother's feelings of guilt and shame, he/ she may carry these as a burden. All these negative feelings can be compounded if the child learns that the birth mother had other children that she kept. The adoptive mother can come to be viewed in a 'wicked step mother' stereotype, who took the baby away. The adoptee can develop feelings of being a 'victim.' Darongkamas asked, *'Do searches often spring from dysfunction, and should mental health professionals be alive to this potential marker, and prepared for the possibility of psychological distress as a result of the search?'*[309] Some adoption issues can develop into mental health issues, both short and long term, including self-esteem issues, relationship problems, drink or drug over-use or abuse.

Compiling a biological family tree

Some searches can result positively in further information about an ancestral tree, rather than living relatives, and this can be very rewarding, and add to an ancestral narrative which had previously been missing. A huge dilemma for adoptees is whether to compile one or two trees. A useful solution is to have your adopted family tree and also compile a separate biological one. DNA matches can be added to a biological tree.

Some people also utilise a bow tie tree,[310] which is a great way to graphically represent the two families, but this could be seen as the adoptee in the middle, with two very separate families pulling in opposite directions.

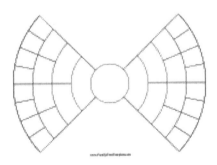

When I added people onto my online biological tree, people were immediately labelled 'mother', 'father', 'grandparents' and so on, which felt uncomfortable, as I'd never used that label for any of those people before. This can make an adoptee wonder why they are spending a great deal of time compiling a tree for people that they have no 'real' connection with. Lents observed that, '...the emphasis on genealogy as a source of identity seems acutely harmful to at least some adopted people.'[311] Are these additions 'relatives' as such, or just names on a tree? I have compiled a narrative for each person, but mainly based on their names, dates of birth, marriages, deaths, address, names of siblings, and their occupations given on the censuses, because there can't be much 'meat on the bones' for people you've never met. Argyle commented that, 'Family links entail long-lasting bonds of concern and mutual obligation, and do not depend on common interests or values in the way that friendships do.'[312] Maybe this is why some adoptees can't work out how to 'slot' into a new-found family, because they were a unit and the adoptee has to take a new 'role', the adoptee probably isn't a 'child' any more, but they aren't a new 'friend' or 'colleague'. Sadly, most of the people I was adding were already dead, but doing an ancestral search can become a really positive and spiritual task.

Ancestry has a drop down box, under the Edit Relationships section, where people can add relationships, such as 'adopted' to a tree. The relationships include: 'biological', 'adopted', 'step', 'foster', 'related', 'guardian', 'private', 'unknown'. There is a support page[313] describing the procedure. It may feel ok to add these labels for some people, but for others it may feel awkward to label your child 'adopted child' when you've looked after and loved that child all his or her life, and he/ she is your child. Professional genealogists who help adoptees with their tree are often filling in what was literally a blank canvas. Professionals need to acknowledge that there may be many emotions behind compiling an adoptee's biological tree.

Further dilemmas here include where should DNA results be added to, the adopted tree or biological tree? Should you state someone was adopted on the birth information section on a tree. If an adoptee does not want this information to be known, do you document it anyway because it's true? An adoptee's birth parent(s) may want to add the birth of the child who they gave up for adoption. Future generations may not understand their DNA test results if they find they were (or weren't) biologically related to someone.

DNA testing

If adoptees have a DNA test done, then they can potentially match with other people, and can then work out what the percentage overlaps mean when interpreted as relationship predictors. If birth family aren't known, then collaborating with matches can help fill in assumed relationships, and potentially identify biological parents from other people's trees. When I joined Ancestry and only had a few DNA matches, I had a match with a man from the USA, who shared 32cM across 3 segments, and Ancestry predicted that he was my fourth to sixth cousin. I could have ignored that quite low match, as this relationship seemed very difficult to work out, but I initiated that collaboration because he had a friendly picture on Ancestry and, at the time, was my top match (apart from my children). This match was waiting for his mother's DNA test results, and, shortly afterwards, she was predicted as my third to fourth cousin, with a match of 121cM across 7 segments. Consulting our trees, looking for common ancestral names and filling in potential positions, revealed that I was a second cousin once removed from his mother, and a third cousin to the man I was collaborating with. When he had his brother tested, our DNA match was 108cM across 6 segments, and was similarly predicted to be a third to fourth cousin, when our actual relationship is third cousin. The brother doesn't engage with Ancestry, so I could have become discouraged by any potential lack of replies to messages by him.

So, a tip here would be for an adoptee to look at the variety of relationships that a DNA match could potentially be, hopefully collaborate with the DNA match, and then work out the real relationship, based on the starting point of the potential relationship based on DNA evidence. Ancestry predicted a DNA relationship with a match of fourth to sixth cousin, but collaborating based on this starting point was a useful start to finding our actual relationship of third cousin. This is gold dust for an adoptee. This collaboration with a low DNA match added a whole branch to my biological tree, and taught me many lessons about mixing DNA results with a paper trail, which have been turned into lectures and articles.[314] By filling in our trees in more detail, as he added my information and I added his information, we then matched with another DNA match and triangulated with our trees. Our relationship on GEDmatch was predicted as an 'MRCA' (most recent common ancestor) 3.9 generations ago, which is borne out by looking at our trees, where we overlap four generations ago with our great-great grandparents. This collaboration with a low DNA match took us back to ancestors who had twelve children during the Irish Famine, and it appears that the daughters went to the USA as domestic servants and the boys went to coalmines in South Wales. These information from these matches added to my micro-history narrative.

Uploading DNA results from the testing company to other websites, or to GEDmatch[315] can increase matches that an adoptee can potentially collaborate with. There seems to be slightly incorrect information on the Ancestry help page 'Ancestry DNA testing can help you find members of your biological family. To find a relative using DNA, you both need to have taken a DNA test with the same company.'[316] GEDmatch allows uploads from Ancestry, 23AndMe, FTDNA, with more companies potentially being added.[317]

After adoptees have done a DNA test and received their results, some comments adapted from various Facebook forums included:

- *there must be a lot of us adopted people out there; I wish things were easier to find out; we wait all our life to find out who we are*

- *if your close matches have trees, screenshot everything before attempting contact because some matches close down communication or block you when you say you're adopted*
- *I did a DNA test to find my biological father; I am very confused about the results which only said one 1st cousin being managed by someone (what does that even mean?) and two 2nd cousins and a lot of 3rd - 8th cousins; I just don't know what this information means and don't know what to do next*
- *all of my top DNA matches are strangers and I have no idea how to insert them into my tree to find my biological family, or if they belong there*
- *I started by contacting my top ten DNA matches with just a generic message about me and what I was trying to find*
- *I sent several messages to DNA matches but only had one reply from someone, who feels that I am mistaken in the relationship I have suggested, because obviously the pregnancy and adoption was a secret*
- *I find it sad when you finally find your birth family and your half siblings or first cousins won't talk to you*
- *help is available to sort through the clues you get from your DNA results; what seems impossible becomes possible with DNA; not all the stories have positive endings but at least you will have answers and a sense of achievement whatever the outcome; there is strength in numbers as we search for the truth*

MyHeritage launched an altruistic (time limited) pro bono initiative[318] to help adoptees and their birth families reunite through genetic testing, by providing 15,000 MyHeritage DNA kits, worth more than one million dollars, for free, to eligible participants.

Some useful DNA aides for adoptees or people helping adoptees

- DNA Detectives[319] on Facebook, which is a discussion forum, and people can ask for help from 'search angels'
- Mirroring a Tree on Ancestry (for Adoptees)[320] which explains how to utilise information from DNA and combine that with a tree

Adoptees contacting birth families

There are a variety of ways of contacting birth families. Some people approach them as soon as they get contact details, others utilise an intermediary, and some people can spend many weeks, months, even years trying to decide the best way to approach them, others never feel emotionally equipped to initiate contact. Reunions are obviously on a continuum, ranging from perfect to disastrous. Verrier discusses the reunion process in depth and with sensitivity. '*The relationship may be quite different from that which was envisioned by the birth mother, the adoptee, or the adoptive parents... It may be that in neither the case of the 'perfect reunion' nor the 'difficult' reunion is the adoptee acting from his true feelings, but from a protective stance.'[321]* And she concludes that *'Even with mutual support, the reunion process is often misunderstood and can be difficult.'[322]*

Pat, my newly found second cousin, Australian 'mine of information' when asked why he stays in touch with me and sends lots of photographs, since we matched on our trees, and subsequently verified our relationship through DNA testing, said that, *'While as an adoptee you can dig into the birth family tree, but sadly miss the family 'culture', anecdotes and at least the near contemporary personalities. That's why I try to fill in as much as I can from my perspective for you.'[323]*

Inter-racial adoption[324]

Slingerland, in his 1919 manual for social workers, stated that, *'It is desirable in fitting children to applications, to select such as resemble one or both of the foster parents, or at least not specially different from them in appearance. A strong contrast between parents and children causes endless remarks and calls for continued explanations, which are often irritating and sometimes embarrassing to the foster parents, and frequently a source of trouble to the children.'[325]*

The Adoption History Project website includes an interesting debate from Herman about transracial adoption and also the problems with 'matching'[326] potential adoptees and new parents. *'During much of the twentieth century, matching was the philosophy that governed non-relative adoption. Its goal was to make families socially that would "match" families made naturally. Matching required that adoptive parents be married heterosexual couples who looked, felt, and behaved as if they had, by themselves, conceived other people's children. What this meant in practice was that physical resemblance, intellectual similarity, and racial and religious continuity between parents and children were preferred goals in adoptive families.'[327]* This may also have meant that children would remain in state care until they matched a family that they resembled. This can, unfortunately, mean that many mixed race children are left in temporary care or institutionalised, as adoptive literal matches can't be found.

Chung explained that she was often made to feel guilty about looking for her biological parents because she had been raised by 'good people', and was told she was ungrateful.[328] *'That word, 'good', and all that it implies, is fascinating to me. As an adoptee, I've been asked to make this distinction over and over: only one family can be 'good'. Only one family can be 'real'. So I must choose between the white adoptive parents that have been regularly portrayed (by others) as selfless saviors, and the Korean immigrant family that, by default, has been relegated to illegitimacy, selfishness, otherness.'[329]* But J.J. described how 'nice people' had adopted her as a 'poor' child from another country, but felt a different outcome, *'I was adopted at about 15 months old by white people (I am an Asian female). I was put into boarding school at age seven ... People think adoptive parents are doing you a favour. They gave me all the basic living requirements. In return I lost my country, my culture, language, my identity, name and self-worth. I grew up feeling*

76

inferior, lost and unwanted... They should have left me at the orphanage, I would have had continuity and some identity through culture.'[330]

Compton stated that, *'most adoptive parents in the U.S. are white, many adoptions are transracial, as minority children are placed in white families. Are these children at risk for problems as they make sense of themselves as minorities in white families and communities?'*[331] However, Compton felt that, *'concerns about transracial placement have been overblown and that, in fact, children are capable of developing a solid sense of identity and family regardless of the racial composition of their families.'* The study by Hamilton *et al* found that, *'No mean differences were found in adoptees' ratings of affect about adoption or of curiosity about birth parents. Some differences were found in general identity development and adjustment. There were notable differences in communication about race/ ethnicity across groups and between parent and child reports.'*[332] DNA testing has pinpointed some ethnicities, but, alongside identity issues, another dilemma is that when people want to undertake research into their ancestry, many people who have been adopted from abroad or from another race, perhaps wouldn't know where to start.

Transgender adult reuniting with birth mother

The ITV programme, Long Lost Family, recently, during Series 8, featured an episode which included a transgender woman who was searching for the birth mother who gave her up as a baby boy. *'Francesca Barnes is in the early stages of transitioning from male to female. She was born with the name Paul and given up for adoption as a baby... Francesca wants to tell her birth mother that she understands that decision and has no resentment towards her. But Francesca is also aware that she is taking a big risk in searching for Norma. She dreams of her birth mother accepting and supporting her on her journey. However, she fears that her transition may be too challenging for Norma, and that she runs the risk of rejection.'*[333] It was reported that there was a positive outcome, *'The transgender care assistant who was put up for adoption as a baby boy 43 years ago is reunited as a woman with her birth mother, who says it's truly wonderful to have gained a daughter.'*[334] People can often assume that the child they gave up, or the mother they are searching for, will be the same as they were many years ago. It can be painful that people 'move on.'

Further genealogical adoption issues

Adopted children can get called names, be teased, or subjected to awkward or hurtful questions when others are told they were adopted. A strange scenario is that some people threaten a child who has been naughty, with being adopted out. This implies that being adopted was a child's fault. At home, many adoptees have to live up to expectations after being told they were special because they were 'chosen,' but often also, at the same time, have an inherent sense of loss and/ or grief over 'lost' relatives and relationships. Therefore, many adoptees don't know whether to search for their birth parent/s or not, and a big worry is about hurting their adopted family if they decide to search for biological relatives. Those who don't want to search for biological families often feel pressured into doing so, and are asked to justify why they don't want to search. Searching for, and then finding, biological relatives will, at the least, change relationships with the adopted family parents and relatives, and could even cause irreparable rifts. Because of this worry, many adoptees wait for their parents to pass away before starting a search for biological family, and this may often be too late to connect with biological parents. Finding that birth parent/s have died can be a huge blow.

People have to fill in forms and be interviewed by a Government clerk to be 'entitled' to get their original birth certificate, and it can take a long time to get a reply to your request, whilst dealing with all those mixed emotions on their own. Many adoptees don't realise that they would have a different name, nor that their birth mother's name and address (at the time) would be on the certificate. The father section can often be a disappointing 'father unknown.' There are many dilemmas about what to do next. The biological mother and father may not want to be found. There can be potential rejection for a second time by the biological family. Finding biological family many years after the adoption inevitably means that time has passed, the biological parents may well not be together, so there are two families to look for, and this can rake up many old memories and feelings, and needs to be handled sensitively and carefully. People can be found quickly, through social media, and there has been little time to absorb the implications. The excitement of finding biological family probably means that people can rush into contact too quickly, before they have thought through the variety of scenarios. The biological parents may well have had relationships or married other people, and therefore there are other partners and probably half siblings. So adoptees looking for biological parents are not just looking for two people, there are many more involved. Some people searching for relatives will have a fantastic 'reunion' with relatives, but some will have a less than positive reunion.[335]

Explanations around conception can be very upsetting or even traumatising, if the conception wasn't as a result of consensual sex. However, some adoptees have complained that when they reunited with their biological mother, and she said that the baby was given up for adoption because she was raped, however, when the biological father was traced, these claims were denied. If the biological mother didn't have any more children, it can imply that she chose not to have any more children, or couldn't have any more children after adopting the baby. There can be many 'what if's' especially if it is found that the biological family lived very near. There is the possibility of knowing biological relatives, without knowing that they were, and even the disturbing scenario of having had sexual relations with someone who subsequently turns out to be a relative.

People enjoy undertaking a study into their surname, and could join The Guild of One name Studies which has 8,284 surnames,[336] but adoptees don't definitively know which surname they belong to. Are you a product of your lifelong surname, your surname on your original birth certificate (usually your biological mother's) or your biological father's? Adoptees have at least two distinct surnames. *'The sense of personal identity and uniqueness that a name gives us is at the heart of why names interest us and why they are important to us as individuals and to our society as a whole. In spite of their importance, though, most people know very little about names and about the effects they have on us an on our children in everyday life. In a very real sense, we are consumers of names, and we have a need and right to know about the psychological, magical, legal, religious, and ethnic aspects of our names.'*

Never lose hope

An elderly Irish woman, Eileen Macken, aged eighty one, has finally tracked down her birth mother after a genealogist who heard the radio broadcast asking for help contacted her and helped to identify Eileen's birth mother through DNA testing. Everyone concerned was astonished to find out that her mother is alive and well at the age of one hundred and three, plus two half-brothers who are in their seventies. Because both mother and daughter have hearing problems, and live a great distance from each other, they haven't met yet, but Eileen was overjoyed during her radio interview.[337]

Interesting books

These books are interesting and helpful, and contextualise the need that some adoptees have for researching their biological family.

The Primal Wound, Nancy Verrier[338,339]

The blurb states that it, *'...is a must read for adopted people, adoptive families, birth parents and adoption professionals. Nancy Verrier, a psychotherapist and adoptive mother, coined the term 'primal wound,' which results when a child is separated from his or her mother and the trauma that it causes. She examines the life-long consequences this can have for adopted people, as they are growing up, underpinning this with information about pre- and perinatal psychology, attachment, bonding and the effects of loss. .. Adoptees have often felt misunderstood; it can bring solace to birth mothers, who have long been denied the truth of their loss; and it can be a source of information for adoptive parents, so that they can better understand and respond to their children.'*

Blue-Eyed Son, Nicky Campbell[340]

'Raised in a comfortable middle-class home, Nicky Campbell's Scottish Protestant family cared for and nurtured him as their own, while remaining open about the fact that he'd been adopted. His father, an ex-army man, and his mother helped him to a good school and a good university. Nicky rarely thought of his birth parents, until a combination of an imploding marriage and a chance meeting with a private detective led him to track down his birth mother. Nicky Campbell brilliantly recalls their reunion and tentative steps

towards a relationship, evoking all the complex and deep-seated emotions that being reunited elicited in each of them. In this emotionally gripping and refreshingly honest memoir, Nicky Campbell describes the many sides of a family's dark history, and how it feels to find out where you come from.'

Reunions: True Stories of Adoptees Meeting with Their Natural Parents[341]

'This work brings together the experiences of fifteen people who have two things in common: first, they have shared the experience of being adopted, and second, they have all chosen the path to meeting one or both of their birth parents. Their experiences are specific and highly individual, as are their personal histories and the circumstances surrounding their adopted families. The book covers a wide range of people that have decided to face up to their past and who have risked a great deal in tracing their natural parents. The accounts show that the actual reunion meeting itself is not the end of the process, but only the beginning.'

Adopting an animal

Are the 'Adopt an animal' campaigns,[342] for example, those championed by the World Wildlife Foundation, an adoption or a sponsorship? What is the similarity between purchasing a pack, which includes a rather sweet soft toy that 'you can love forever,' and adopting a child? Their website strapline states, *'Adopt an animal now. Help our work to protect some of the world's most vulnerable animals by becoming a WWF adopter from just £3 a month today. A WWF adoption also makes a fantastic gift. Choose from our range of adoption animals below.'*

'Three Identical Strangers,' the impact of an unethical adoption study

Triplet brothers were part of an elaborate psychological experiment designed in the 1960s, to study the effects of nature versus nurture. Psychiatrists partnered with the Louise Wise Services adoption agency on a 'Twin Study,' which involved splitting up identical twins and triplets, placing them in different home environments, and studying their development. Kellman, Shafran, and Galland were three of their test subjects. *'In 1980, two 19-year-old identical men who had been adopted separately as infants found each other when they were both students at Sullivan County Community College near New York City. A third triplet, a student at Queens College in New York, found the other two when he saw press reports of their meeting. Neither they nor their adoptive parents knew that they each had two identical brothers. The reunion of the triplets became a media circus.'[343]* During an interview, Kellman explained that, *'I feel like sometimes you don't know how you're injured until you see the results of the injury.'[344]*

Adoptee changing her name back to her original one

An Australian columnist explained that she was changing her name back to her original birth name, because, as she explained, *'Collier was a fiction, a fraud, an identity created by the Victorian government in the forced adoption era. I have occupied this identity for almost fifty years, but on October 31 it was put to rest. When a child is adopted, their birth certificate is declared invalid, eliminated. It is sealed in the records of the state. This process officially divorces the adoptee from their parents and everyone else in their family tree. They lose all of the natural rights that people who are not adopted take for granted. At the same time, a new, second birth certificate is created. The second birth certificate shows the adoptee as born unto people that a government agency has chosen and the child is issued a new name to suit. This trick, this lie, this erasure of identity and creation of a new one means an adoptee has two identities and is unable to retain important connections to their families of origin.'*[345] Grace stated that her second identity was expunged because she went to her County Court to have her adoption annulled, or 'discharged', and her request was granted. The article made for a very interesting read. Grace truly felt that her original identity had been removed from her in a variety of ways when she was adopted. She was given to a new couple to look after her, she was disconnected from her biological family, she was disconnected from other biological relatives, and was given a new name and identity by law. The article didn't explain how her adoptive parents felt about this matter.

A number of responses were raised in response to her online article, including:

- *'I'm so pleased for you. It seems to have been an exceptional process and journey that you've set out on, a quest to rediscover your identity.'*
- *'I am really sorry that adoption caused you loss, grief and pain. In my case, the adoption process was a loving one and enabled me to build a strong and resilient base on which to build my life.'*
- *'My wife and I adopted 10 years ago under the extant open adoption system. Our child was issued a new birth certificate appropriately in my view as it recognized how 100% welcomed and fully incorporated into our nuclear and wider family they are. Our adopted child bears my surname and will inherit what comes to a full member of my family.'*
- *'Closed adoption is child abuse. It is as simple as that.'*
- *'Another example of bureaucracy purging facts (the truth of one's birth) to ensure compliance with some weird political agenda.'*
- *'I applaud your strength in bringing this to the public eye, in the public interest.'*
- *'One cannot help but ask how the adoptive parents feel in this story? Assuming they are good people and it certainly appears they offered Grace every opportunity then it must be quite hurtful.'*
- *'Please don't generalise about what adoptees are "denied" - I was never denied anything, including details of the circumstances of my adoption, and I'm quite sure*

I'm not the only one. I hope you find what you're looking for, but please don't generalise - you are in no position to do that.'

- *'You cannot have got thus far without the love, support, nurturing and concern for your welfare that have been given to you by your adoptive parents. The declaration of the 'answer' to the question concerning your origin is, I hope, not a kick in the guts for them.'*
- *'You have chosen to take the name and identity of those who were prepared for whatever reason to abandon you and not seek you out while (well you did tell us) you had a wonderful childhood, and loving caring parents... I am wondering if your adoptive 'parents' if they still live are hurt or upset you took this route.'*
- *'So parents who wanted you are discarded for a family that did not care?'*
- *'While I mostly disagree with you, I enjoyed this beautiful brave story and wish you all the best under your correct name.'*

The next chapter with look at genealogical ethical dilemmas involved with ethnicity and identity.

Chapter 5: Ethnicity and identity

Globe[346]

Is there a difference between the terms 'ethnicity,' 'race,' 'heritage' and 'ancestry', when explaining where you are 'from'? Eilers succinctly explained that, *'**Ethnicity** is based on a group that normally has similar traits, such as a common language, heritage, and cultural similarities. Other variables that play a role in ethnicity include a geographical connection to a particular place, common foods and diets, and perhaps a common faith... **Race** is similar to ethnicity, but relates more to the appearance of a person, especially the colour of their skin... **Nationality** refers to the place where the person was born and/ or holds citizenship... **Heritage** generally refers to the ancestors of a person, and what they identified with... **Culture** may involve one trait or characteristic... **Identity** is whatever a person identifies with more, whether it be a particular country, ethnicity, religion...'*[347] (bold added). Official forms ask for you to give your address; and birth certificates and passports record for posterity where you were born. Therefore, where you were born and where you now live are vital for one's self concept of identity.

So, are my children English, British, mixed race, black, white, Jamaican heritage, black British, Gahanaian? All, or none? During their childhood my children were called 'half caste', and if they had been born during enslavement, three of them would have been labelled 'quadroon'[348] and the other three 'mulatto'[349] (from Spanish 'mulato' - a small mule, a word referring to a person who is born to one black parent and one white parent). Black friends might call them 'light-skinned.' Do these words matter? It is sometimes difficult to know 'which box to tick' on forms, and some terms can be seen as acceptable, or very offensive, in different circumstances.

Being Black British

South London (Streatham) rapper Dave (David Orobosa Omoregie)[350] sings about the many ways of being black in his recent song 'Black.'[351] In a recent interview, Dave remarks, *'Black is confusing. Where does the line start and stop?'*[352] Here are some (family history) excerpts from the lyrics.

> *'Black is so much deeper than just African-American*
> *Our heritage been severed, you never got to experiment*
> *With family trees, 'cause they teach you 'bout famine and greed*
> *And show you pictures of our fam on their knees...*
> *Your mummy watchin' tellin' stories 'bout your dad and your niece...*
> *It's representin' countries that never even existed while your grandmother was livin'*
> *Black is my Ghanaian brother readin' into scriptures*
> *Doin' research on his lineage, findin' out that he's Egyptian*
> *Black is people namin' your countries on what they trade most*
> *Coast of Ivory, Gold Coast, and the Grain Coast...*
> *But black is all I know, there ain't a thing that I would change in it.'*

A perhaps typical black British family history story

We didn't have much information to go on when researching my children's ancestors. I know that three of my children's grandfather came from Kingston, Jamaica to London, UK in the 1960s. The word 'Jamaica' appears to have derived from the Arawak word 'Xaymaca'[353] meaning *'land of wood and water'*. Many people went to the UK, in response to a call from the British Government for skilled workers to help the re-building work, following the bombings and devastation of many towns and cities, during World War II.[354] The National Archives state that, *'West Indians came to Britain for many different reasons. Some were seeking better opportunities for themselves and their children. Some came to work for a while, save money and return home. Some had been recruited because Britain was short of workers to run the transport system, postal service and hospitals. Other West Indians were returning soldiers who had fought for Britain during the Second World War (1939-1945)'.*[355] The International Organisation for Migration reported that, *'Responding to the British post-war labour shortage, the first large-scale migration of Caribbeans, four hundred and ninety two of whom were Jamaicans, arrived in the UK on the SS Empire Windrush*[356] *on 23 June 1948, at the invitation of the British government of the day.'*[357] Between 1955 and 1968, a total of 191,330 Jamaicans arrived and settled in the UK.[358]

When my children's Jamaican great grandmother, Beatrice, passed away, I was given her commemorative 'Thanksgiving' paper, which had a lovely photograph of her on the front page, and her birth and death dates. We sadly never had the opportunity to visit her ourselves, and so all her stories and those of her (our) ancestors are now potentially lost, unless we investigate and resuscitate their stories. Not much 'meat on the bones' so, as family historians, we try to find out more. Many years later, her address on letters gave information about where she lived, so we could see what kind of area it was on Google maps, and potentially see what kind of work was available there. More careful reading of letters can give more information, even such as the writer simply saying, for example, 'I'm going shopping later with my sister Maude...' and then Maude can be added as her sibling on the tree.

Beatrice's birth record was accessed on FamilySearch,[359] which added to the information on her Thanksgiving paper, that she was born in Galloway, Sutcliffe Mount, Westmoreland, Jamaica. (By a lovely coincidence, my grand-daughter was born on Beatrice's birth date, exactly one hundred years later). Beatrice's mother was Adella, and no father was listed. I then accessed Beatrice's death Registration form, which revealed that she had died from a 'cerebro vascular accident' (medical term for a stroke). Searching for Beatrice's mother, I found Adella Allen, in FamilySearch, baptised 28 November, 1875, in Roaring River, Westmoreland, Jamaica.

Adella Allen's baptism record[360]

Close-up of the baptism record

Information gleaned from this record is that Adella was black, her middle name was Maude; and that her parents were Charles Allen and Augusta, nee Quarry, who were married. Closer inspection of this record reveals that Adella was baby number 31 in the 'legitimate' column. On the same page are 'black', 'white', 'coloured' babies, and many in the 'illegitimate' column. There is also a 'rank/ profession' column, and on Adella's page, amongst the named fathers, there is a white book-keeper, a white clerk; a coloured carpenter; and the rest are black labourers. Charles George McGregor was the Church of England Minister.

Adella's baptism place was reported as Roaring River, Westmoreland, Jamaica, which now looks like a really pretty heritage and nature park, and I could view some lovely images of the area on Google or Trip Advisor. However, I then read that it was a former slave plantation, and that its' history is rooted in the sugar industry of the colonial era, beginning in the late 17th century. The estate of the Beckfords,[361] one of whom, William Beckford,[362] wrote a book[363] about 'the situation' of his slaves. Beckford employed an artist (George Robertson) to paint the landscapes,[364] all beautiful paintings, but none featured any enslaved people in them.[365]

The slave trade 'triangle'[366]

By 1662, there were about four hundred enslaved black people in Jamaica.[367] The English captured Jamaica from the Spanish in 1655. As the cultivation of sugar cane was introduced, the number of enslaved people grew to 9,504 by 1673; by 1734, there were 86,546 enslaved people; and, by 1775, there were 192,787. There are records of total numbers of enslaved people,[368] including figures gleaned from 'Long's Manuscripts' entitled 'Slaves Imported and Exported 1702-1787,' which were presented by C. E. Long, Esq. to the British Museum, in March, 1842.

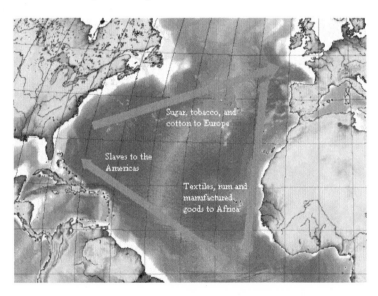

More than ten thousand vastly overcrowded[369] British ships[370] left Africa with more than four million enslaved people, travelled back via Britain[371] and onto America. By the abolition of the Slave Trade[372] in the UK[373] in 1807, it reportedly took more than twenty five years to affect the emancipation of the enslaved, circa August 1834.[374] After emancipation, many Jamaicans moved from island to island looking for seasonal work, usually returning home after the work was finished. They risked dangerous voyages traveling on tiny fishing boats over hundreds of miles of treacherous sea.[375] Thousands went to work in Panama, where they helped build the Panama Canal. Others moved to New York City, and had different or maybe 'better' opportunities. However, strict laws were also passed, designed to limit the mobility and civil liberties of free black people. The planters took control of the most fertile land, and left little room for emancipated black people to grow food. Many free Jamaicans moved from the coastal plantations to the interior hill country because they were unwilling to work under their former masters in still slave-like conditions. Many villages developed on the north coast of Jamaica.

Between the 17th and 19th centuries, Britain conducted censuses in Jamaica, but the records do not contain any names of individuals, just total numbers of people in various categories[376] which included such labels as 'black', 'white', 'free coloured', plus countries of origin, and occupation. Because of this history, individual people would be potentially difficult, if not impossible to find. However, some parental relationships could be implied from the colour naming on documents. Historically, in the context of enslaved societies of the Americas, a quadroon or 'quarteroon' was a person with one African and three European grandparents (or in the context of Australia, one quarter aboriginal ancestry). Similar classifications were 'octoroon' for one-eighth black (Latin root 'octo' which means 'eight') and 'hexadecaroon' which means one-sixteenth black.[377] Governments of the time sometimes incorporated the terms in law-defining rights and restrictions. The use of such terminology is a characteristic of hypodescent,[378] which is the practice within a society of assigning children of mixed unions to the ethnic group which the dominant group perceives as being subordinate. This labelling of people would be considered offensive now, but does give some insights about relationships, so, if a descendent now found reference to their ancestor being mulatto, it could be assumed that they had one black and one white parent, or if their ancestor was labelled quadroon[379] they would have had one black and three white grandparents, which could aid the genealogical investigation.

Civil Registration of births, marriages and deaths officially started between 1878 and 1880 in Jamaica, the start date differing slightly from parish to parish.[380] Some baptisms from 1752 can be found[381] and have been digitised by the Digital Library of the Caribbean (dLOC).[382] FamilySearch website reveals that that some earlier records[383] can be utilised, via Church records, wills and land records. These are potential sources for today's family historian. In place of slavery, the negotiated settlement established a system of 'apprenticeship', which tied the newly 'freed' people into another form of unfree labour for fixed terms. In the UK, slave owners were granted c£20 million in compensation[384] paid by British taxpayers, for the owners' loss of their 'workforce.' Many of these records are available for researchers to view. Guy Grannam usefully explained that until emancipation, most African-Caribbeans were considered to be the property of their owners, *'families could be split up, people could be sold, gifted and inherited as property. The enslaved people migrated with their owners to other countries, and were often denied an education and not allowed to attend church. Therefore, enslaved African-Caribbeans are not listed in the usual records used by family historians.'*[385] Many family historians would not envisage seeing ancestors as part of a list of property in a will, but, in these instances, people's names were given in wills, and descendants may find their ancestors' names included.

In addition, because enslaved people were, by law, the 'property' of a master, their naming traditions had to change. Many babies born to enslaved women were given their master's surname, women didn't always have the opportunity to 'be allowed' to get married, many families were broken up, people had to form new relationships and continuity of family ties was broken. If the child was given his father's surname, that may well have been that man's slave owner's surname, not the child's 'inherited' name. Generations later, people still carry those surnames. After emancipation, some people changed their name to add a religious or hopeful connotation, such as Wisdom, or Sojourner, and some made up a name to dis-associate themselves from their previous terrible situation.

People can now visit some historic buildings to get historical context, for example, The Georgian House[386] in Bristol, UK, to see how slave traders invested their money, and many buildings have searchable archives, which could be useful. The Georgian House Museum website explains that you can, *'Discover what a Bristol sugar plantation and slave owner's home might have looked like around 1790. Eleven rooms spread over four floors reveal what life was like above and below stairs, from the kitchen in the basement where servants prepared meals to the elegant formal rooms above. Free entry.'*[387] The house was built in 1790 for John Pinney,[388] who was a slave plantation owner and sugar merchant. The website states that you can walk round the house including the bedroom, and it sounds as though it is a positive statement that, *'from the window, John Pinney could have seen ships on the river bringing his plantation goods into Bristol.'* However, it was also where his valet, an enslaved man of African descent, Pero Jones lived, and he would have looked out of the same window, presumably with very different feelings on seeing the ships. The website notes that, *'a small display explores John Pinney's involvement in the sugar trade and the life of his enslaved valet, Pero Jones.'*

The Georgian House, Bristol[389] has a huge painting of Nevis, in the West Indies, which the Pinneys' enslaved valet, Pero must have had to look at every day. Pero Jones was born enslaved on Nevis, was bought when he was twelve years old by John Pinney and brought to Bristol in the UK in 1784, when the Pinneys left Nevis. Pero was Pinney's valet, and worked for him for over thirty years, though he was never freed. A footbridge[390] opened in Bristol in 1999 was named after Pero, in tribute to the many unknown African men, women and children who were enslaved by Bristol's merchants.

On the top floor of the house is a small display about enslavement, and this iconic and moving picture of soldier Private Gordon[391] is included in the display:

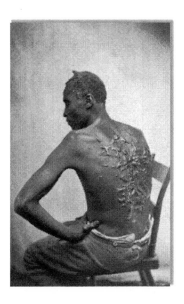

Private Gordon c1863[392]

In 1863, it was reported that, *'There has lately come to us, from Baton Rouge, the photograph of a former slave - now, thanks to the Union army, a freeman. It represents him in a sitting posture, his stalwart body bared to the waist, his fine head and intelligent face in profile, his left arm bent, resting upon his hip, and his naked back exposed to full view. Upon that back, horrible to contemplate, is a testimony against slavery more eloquent than any words.'*[393]

Slave traders

Family historians may be able to find out more about those involved in slavery, than about their enslaved ancestor. Many people have called for any commemorations to slave traders to be addressed. One such example, is that of Edward Colston (1636 - 1721), *'a Bristol-born English philanthropist, merchant, slave trader, and Member of Parliament,'* who *'built up a lucrative business, trading with Spain, Portugal, Italy and Africa... his name is commemorated in several Bristol landmarks, streets, four schools, and the Colston regional bread bun. He is also remembered, particularly by some schools, charities and the Society of Merchant Venturers, on Colston's Day on 13 November, his birthday, at a church service now at St Stephen's Church...'*[394] The first description is philanthropist, and the third is slave trader. A large commemorative statue, designed by John Cassidy[395] was erected in Bristol city centre, in 1895.

Photographs taken by Penny Walters, during a Slave Trail walk[396]
October, 2017, facilitated by Edson Burton[397]

In 1998, someone wrote the words 'slave trader' on its base, and then a small plaque was put on the bottom of the statue, reminding people that he was a slave trader, but I noticed that it has since been removed (September, 2018). Some people, especially in the Bristol area, will find the name Colston as an ancestor's middle name, because he was famous at that time. Colston as a name for boys is an old English name, and Colston means *'swarthy (dark) person; coal town or settlement. Colston is an alternate form of Colton (Old English).'*[398]

Two petitions, gathered in Manchester in 1806, both in favour of and against the Abolition of the Slave Trade Bill, may enable some readers to search for their ancestors.[399] Some comments included, *'I was pleased to find the signature of my ancestor Richard Bindloss on the anti-slavery petition. Richard (1765-1842) was a partner of Bindloss and Gardner, fustian manufacturers, in Manchester.'*[400]

How would people feel if they discovered that their ancestor was involved in the slave trade? If we can feel pride about our ancestors' accomplishments and good virtues, should we also feel any shame for their actions, or, indeed, make reparations?

Names and surnames which became offensive

Colston Hall was built on the site of Sir John Young's house, the first Bristol merchant to trade with Africa in the 1550s. Reportedly[401] Bristol's first known black resident worked there in the 1570s, and it was later converted into the city's first sugar house, to process

Caribbean sugar. Colston Hall as a building, therefore has historical importance. It is now a prestigious music venue, and it was recently reported that, *'The Colston Hall in Bristol is to change its name to escape its 'toxic' associations.'*[402] There are a diverse range of opinions[403] about changing the name. Many bands and customers actively boycott attending the music venue; and artistic Bristolians explain that they feel excluded. Ros Martin[404] (a Bristol-based poet and playwright) and Madge Dresser[405] (associate professor of history, University of the West of England) debated the issue at length.[406] The decision to change the name of was apparently a, *'moral and not a financial one.'*[407] The Colston Hall official website laments that, *'We have been at the heart of Bristol's entertainment and cultural life for over 150 years, but for a long time the Hall has been the lightning rod for a debate on the legacy of the slave-trader and philanthropist Edward Colston, which has distracted from our core purpose: to share the brilliance and joy of live music with everyone.'*[408]

Names linked to the slave trade can be disconcerting for people living in an area named after people who were prestigious at the time. Many roads and buildings in Bristol are named after Colston, should their names be changed too? There are many roads with what could be considered 'disturbing' connotations for the names, such as, for example, Black Boy's Hill[409] which leads onto White Ladies Road, in Bristol. Elton Road is named after the Elton family,[410] who were investors in the brass industry, and owned slave ships; Farr Lane is named after the Farrs, who were rope makers and slave traders, Thomas Farr built Blaise castle;[411] Tyndalls Avenue is named after the Tyndalls,[412] who invested in slaving ventures; Winterstoke Road is named after Lord Winterstoke, who was head of the Wills family, associated with the slave-grown commodity of tobacco. The Theatre Royal was funded by fifty merchants, of whom at least twelve were slave merchants or slave ship owners, and at least another six were suppliers to the slave ships, plantation owners or sugar traders. The street where the Theatre Royal is based, King Street, was also home to Henry Webb, captain of the slave ship Nevis Planter, and Robert Walls, surgeon on the slave ship Guinea. A step towards an atoning solution could be to erect a commemorative statue honouring the contribution which enslaved Africans made to Bristol's prosperity.

Whilst street names serve as a reminder of slavery, some surnames can be a constant reminder. Some would consider, for example, the surnames Lynch, Brown, Black, and White offensive. Lynch relates to 'lynching' which is defined as, *'to punish (a person) without legal process or authority, especially by hanging, for a perceived offense or as an act of bigotry.'*[413] Grenham points out that Lynch is today one of the most common surnames in Ireland, and is unusual in that it has two completely distinct origins. *'The first is Norman, from de Lench... The family settled initially in Co. Meath, and a branch then established itself in Galway, where they rapidly became one of the strongest of the famous 'Tribes of Galway'... One of their number, James Lynch, mayor in 1493, is reputed to have hanged his own son for murder when no one else could be found to carry out the sentence... The second origin for the name is Gaelic, from the Irish O Loingsigh, grandson of Loingseach, meaning 'seaman''*[414] or mariner.[415] Three schools in Portland (USA)

(Lynch Meadows, Lynch Wood and Lynch View elementary schools), named after the Lynch family who donated the school's land will be renamed because decision makers felt that 'Lynch' has racial connotations. 'While there is no connection between the Lynch family and the often racially motivated, murderous practice associated with the word, it's still been a disruption for some students.'[416] It's not known whether the word 'lynch' therefore originates from Irish roots, or is connected to the word 'lynching.'

An ethical dilemma is that if someone finds their surname offensive, should they change it or not? The surname can be a constant reminder of something abhorrent. Surnames can be carried on for many generations and maybe indefinitely. Do these words carry the same or more offense now? You can't delete the past, so is there any point in changing your surname? 'If we're going to eliminate some words because they're homonyms or contain sounds or allusions that resemble, but have nothing to do with, ethnic slurs or terms like 'lynch', then we'll never stop renaming stuff. Anything named 'White,' for instance, could be and probably is disruptive to some.'[417] Enslaved people often changed their names changed to Biblical or Graeco-Roman, or place names, for example, Solomon, Caesar, or Bristol. After emancipation these names often became surnames, though, more often, the surnames are those of their former masters.[418]

Archives

Family historians and genealogists can investigate records through many avenues, including searching through birth certifications; private narratives, for example the fascinating accounts of Sojourner Truth[419] and Edward and Eliza;[420] some census records; cemetery records; manumissions;[421] letters, private testimonies; and compiled lists of, for example Black Bristolians.[422] In addition, researchers can utilise trader orientated archives, such as slave trade transactions; port customs archives; maritime insurance records; ship inventories; and plantation records. Other archives include: newspaper accounts; legal documents; Index of Slaves and Their Owners in New York state;[423] records of the trial of those charged in the Rebellion of 1741; records of abandoned babies born to enslaved women who were placed in foster care; runaway slave notices and ads; and Naturalisation Records[424] for example in Find My Past's Naturalizations in Travel and Migration.

The arrival records of thousands of immigrants from the Windrush Generation have recently re-emerged in the National Archives.[425] 'It could be the vital evidence the immigrants need to prove citizenship after it emerged the Home Office destroyed its archive of landing slips in 2010. Filed in nearly 1,500 boxes at the National Archives, the records include names, birth dates, and journey details, all taken down on ledgers that date back until the late 19th century... Recent restrictions in immigration law require people to have paperwork proof of near-continuous residence in the UK...'[426]

By-product businesses

Whilst the slave trade triangle essentially involved enslaving people; transporting and selling people; and returning home with goods, many other perhaps 'unseen' or not immediately obvious businesses would benefit. These records are also useful for a family historian, and include those ancestors involved in a variety of businesses such as ship builders, sailors, local pubs, brothels, churches, providers of accommodation, oil producers. Businesses were also involved with producing, then selling, for example, sugar, rum, cocoa and chocolate.

University College London (UCL) has succinctly summarised the 'Legacies of British Slave-ownership'[427] to include six main categories, including: commercial (evolution of firms receiving slave compensation and their redeployment of slave wealth into other investments); cultural (the role of British slave-owners as connoisseurs and collectors, as philanthropists and as founders or participants in new cultural and social institutions for example, *'Pinney's study, furnished simply but to impress, this is where Pinney could discuss business or talk with his friends after dinner. The bookcases contain a collection of his books that reveal his interest in the study of plants and geography'*;[428] historical (the role of slave-owners and their descendants as writers and historians constructing memories of the slave-trade and slavery); imperial (the wider circuits of Empire, as investors, administrators and settlers in colonies beyond the slave-colonies); physical (physical legacies include country houses, domestic residences and public monuments); and political (involvement in national or local politics of any kind). Many artefacts in beautiful houses may have been taken from countries with land worked by enslaved people. A family historian may feel proud of their ancestor's beautiful painting, or interesting novel, but then realise that it was based on observing land worked on by enslaved people.

Individual accounts

Sojourner Truth, born Isabella (Belle) Baumfree when she was born (c.1797 - 26 November, 1883), *'was an African American abolitionist and women's rights activist. Truth was born into slavery in Swartekill, Ulster County, New York, but escaped with her infant daughter to freedom in 1826. After going to court to recover her son, in 1828 she became the first black woman to win such a case against a white man.'*[429]

I was going to reduce this quote from her autobiography... but where would you begin?

> *'You have common sense and a conscience....That slaves in the United States are treated with barbarous inhumanity; that they are over-worked, under-fed, wretchedly clad and lodged, and have insufficient sleep; that they are often made to wear round their necks iron collars armed with prongs, to drag heavy chains and weights at their feet while working in the field, and to wear yokes and bells and iron horns; that they are often kept confined in the stocks day and night for*

weeks together, made to wear gags in their mouths for hours or days, have some of their front teeth torn out or broken off, that they may be easily detected when they run away; that they are frequently flogged with terrible severity, have red pepper rubbed into their lacerated flesh, and hot brine, spirits of turpentine, &c., poured over the gashes to increase the torture; that they are often stripped naked, their backs and limbs cut with knives, bruised and mangled by scores and hundreds of blows with the paddle, and terribly torn by the claws of cats, drawn over them by their tormentors; that they are often hunted with bloodhounds and shot down like beasts, or torn in pieces by dogs; that they are often suspended by the arms and whipped and beaten till they faint, and when revived by restoratives, beaten again till they faint, and sometimes till they die; that their ears are often cut off, their eyes knocked out, their bones broken, their flesh branded with red hot irons; that they are maimed, mutilated, and burned to death over slow fires; are undeniable facts.[430]

People are now researching for ancestors who endured this.

Sojourner Truth c1870[431]

Alex Haley's 'Roots'

Alex Haley's 1976 seminal book 'Roots', subtitled 'The saga of an American family' inspired many people to do their family tree. Rodriguez summed it up that, *'Haley's best seller, and the blockbuster television miniseries that aired a year later, were the beginnings of a genealogy craze that would sweep the nation... (and became) part and parcel of a newfound need to locate oneself in uncertain cultural terrain.'*[432] Roots originally aired on the USA's ABC channel for eight consecutive nights from January 23 to 30, 1977. In the United Kingdom, BBC One aired the series in six parts, starting with parts 1 to 3 over the weekend of April 8 to 11, 1977. The concluding three parts were broadcast on Sunday nights, from April 15 to May 1, 1977. I remember as a young teenager, watching Roots on a Sunday evening, after my parents watched Jess Yates' religious chat show with various celebrities, 'Stars on Sunday'[433] (1969-1979).

I was really so very disturbed by this television programme. I had never heard of anything so terrible and, as a child, had no idea where to find out any more about it.

Hareven stated that, *'Roots' most compelling aspect was not the book's rendition of the story of slavery in a humane and moving way, but rather, the successful trace of the connection between a contemporary man and the origins of slavery through an individual line of descent... Its key message is the resilience and survival of African traditions, demonstrated in the effort of Chicken George and his descendants to transmit their family history from generation to generation. Its uniqueness lies in the process of search and trace of the history of one family, whose odyssey fits closely the contours of the collective experience.'*[434]

Obama's 2007 book, 'Dreams from My Father' was written with his belief that, *'...the story of my family, and my efforts to understand that story, might speak in some way to the fissures of race that have characterised the American experience, as well as the fluid state of identity...'*[435] A summary of the context to the book is that, *'Obama was born in 1961 in Honolulu, Hawaii, to Barack Obama, Sr., of Kenya, and Ann Dunham of Wichita, Kansas, who had met as students at the University of Hawaii. Obama's parents divorced in 1964, when he was two years old... (Obama Sr.) returned to Kenya to fulfil his promise to his nation... (but) died in a car accident in Kenya in 1982. After her divorce, Ann Dunham married... a Javanese surveyor from Indonesia... The family moved to Jakarta. When Obama was ten, he returned to Hawaii under the care of his maternal grandparents (and later his mother) for the better educational opportunities available there...'*[436] The book was described as, *'the tale of a young man desperately trying to find his own identity by exploring his unknown family past.'*[437]

The preface to the book begins with an excerpt from a Bible passage, *'For we are strangers before them, and sojourners, as were all our fathers.'* (1 Chronicles 29:15)[438] Sojourner can be defined as *'a person who resides temporarily in a place.'*[439] This name was chosen by Isabella (Belle) Baumfree who changed her name to Sojourner Truth after emancipation from enslavement.[440] Obama noted that during the writing of his book, his mother would read drafts, correcting stories that he'd misunderstood,[441] as his narrative was about her story too.

Staying positive when researching heritage

Everyone who wants to investigate their family tree and finds an enslaved ancestor would be devastated to think what a horrendous life some of their ancestors had, and may feel disillusioned about continuing with researching their family tree. Killingray and Hanley raised important issues about how people write 'black history' and who people study in black history, suggesting that people need to, *'dig deep in the archives, and find more and different black people in order to develop a broader perspective. For example, not all black people in Britain in the late eighteenth century were formerly enslaved Africans and nor were they all focused on slavery and abolition.'*[442] Undertaking family history from another country to the one being researched is difficult, and descendent diaspora can feel ashamed about illegitimacy and colour.[443]

It could be easy to get discouraged, after realising that Caribbean ancestors may well have been enslaved from Africa. However, in Ghanaian Akan mythology, a bird flies with its head turned backwards, to symbolize the exigency of reconciling one's past with the future, termed Sankofa[444] or 'Go Back and Fetch It', meaning *'It is not wrong to go back for that which you have forgotten.'*[445] African Diaspora have used this symbol to represent the need to reflect on the past, to build a successful future.

UK/ USA   ⟶   Caribbean   ⇢   Africa

Many people don't realise that a variety of records are available. Stone[446] for example, explained that he was unaware of any Caribbean records available in the UK, as he had heard that Jamaican records were destroyed, and that births were rarely registered, which is why he initially only collected oral accounts from family, but with diligence, he has traced his family back nine generations to 1788, when his African ancestor was captured and sold into slavery. Stone found his ancestor, Peggy Ann Smith, in the Slave Register of Former British Colonial Dependencies,[447] which is held at The National Archives, but is also on Ancestry.[448] Poignantly, Stone explains, *'... over hundreds of years I'd made a connection to my ancestor. She was the first person who came to Jamaica from Africa... Growing up in Bristol in the 1970s and 80s I only knew the Jamaican community... it took a while for me to embrace my African heritage. Through doing the research I started to feel much prouder about my heritage...The journey has not finished... our history does not start with slavery and I want to go to Africa to experience my ancestral homeland and carry on building our family tree.'*[449]

Celebrity search programmes

In the spirit of going back for that which you have forgotten, a number of celebrities have been featured in episodes of the UK's Who Do You Think You Are? (WDYTYA) series.

These can be watched just for interest, or you can take notes throughout and add some pointers to your searching repertoire.

Actor and producer, Noel Clarke,[450] born in 1975 in London, England, known for roles in films Brotherhood (2016), Star Trek: Into Darkness (2013) and Mute (2018), grew up with his single-parent mother, reportedly[451] 'leaving one side of his family tree a mystery to him.' His search started in Trinidad, where both of his parents grew up. He said at the start of the programme, '*I want my kids to know about their bloodline...*'[452] As a black British actor/ celebrity, his family history story is both interesting and informative. The Who Do you Think You are? team of researchers reportedly used three key sources: Slavery records; Naturalisation records; and Birth, Marriage and Death records to investigate Noel's ancestors.

The team firstly took Noel to Trinidad to find out more about his family. During WWI, Trinidad had a boom, partly because of the demand for cocoa and sugar needed to provide chocolate for the troops fighting. Research revealed that his great grandparents Elizabeth (a seamstress) and William (a mason) emigrated to Trinidad together from St. Vincent in 1917, which was a shock to Noel. Sadly, he hadn't realised exactly which exact island his Caribbean ancestors came from, *"There's me shouting Trini, Trini for all my life and actually I'm waving the wrong flag."* This exact ancestral location had been 'lost' over the years.

Noel then went to Carriacou to learn more, as the team of researchers had found information which revealed that Noel's four times great-grandparents were Mary and Glasgow Bedeau. The 'Annual Return of the Increase and Decrease of Slaves' on an estate revealed that Glasgow was born into slavery in 1821. He commented that, '*You know the thing is...being black, I thought this might end up here at some point. But it's still crazy to see it, you know?'* The history of Carriacou (now belonging to Grenada), part of the British Empire from 1763, involved plantations worked by transported enslaved Africans. Glasgow's mother was listed as '2nd Genevieve', because there was already another enslaved woman called Genevieve there. Noel commented, '*So they just called her Genevieve 2. Wow...'* The estate on which his ancestors worked had been owned by absentee planters who lived in London, and he quirkily commented, '*Brunswick Square in London. Just north of Soho...I'm around that area all the time... I might go look for them...'* (This begs the question of whether descendants of slave traders and those involved in the slave trade triangle should feel the shame of their ancestors, and should they make reparations or atone for crimes against humanity from a number of generations previously?)

The team facilitated Noel to attend 'the Big Drum', which is the traditional musical and dance ritual of Carriacou. The performance honours ancestors and, performed on his ancestor Glasgow's land,[453] welcomed Noel to the large Bedeau family. It was pointed out that with this music, Noel can directly trace his African origins. It was reportedly sung by the first enslaved Africans on the island and passed down through the generations, and was free from outside influence for generations. Evidence was pointed out that, through his Bedeau family, Noel is a descendant of the Akan people of present-day Ghana. Noel stated, *'This song, through a family line goes all the way back to Ghana, before they were enslaved. Glasgow Bedeau... Genevieve... they would have sung that song... and then two hundred years later these guys are singing it for me.'*

The programme also featured an episode with 'Strictly Come Dancing' televison judge Shirley Ballas[454] who wanted to pursue a rumour that she had black ancestors on her father's side. This ancestral trail led her to colonial Cape Town and the era of slave trafficking to South Africa, via the Indian Ocean. During the programme, Shirley discovered her four times great grandmother was sold as a child slave in South Africa after being snatched from Madagascar.[455] Madagascar[456] is an island country in the Indian Ocean, off the coast of East Africa, and not where she'd envisaged her ancestors as having come from. These revelations resulted in a variety of mixed feelings for her.

Another dilemma arose for Marvin Humes, a black British singer (JLS, 2006-2013), who featured in the 6 August, 2018 WDYTYA? episode[457] and found that some of his ancestors were enslaved, but then was devastated to find that they had gone on to subsequently own enslaved people. It wasn't clearly pointed out that some people who gained freedom bought relatives as a way of freeing them too. WDYTYA? Magazine[458] usefully listed the five places he visited to look at archives, namely Mico University College in Kingston; St John's Church; Royal Sea Bathing Hospital in Margate; The Historic Dockyard, Chatham; and Dunkirk; and explained the usefulness of each place for a family historian, which would be helpful tips for viewers. They also listed six useful websites for tracing Caribbean ancestors.[459]

Whilst it's nice to see a celebrity in a real-life story, rather than their television 'persona,' viewers may feel that the outcomes on the screened TV programme may occur for them too. A team of professionals researched the celebrities' stories, and the celebrity often visits other countries, whereas many people wouldn't be able to afford to travel for their genealogical investigation. People might not have that help or budget available and the programme usually only reports positive outcomes; it wouldn't make 'good television', to have a disappointing outcome from a fruitless search. Whilst a team of people are at hand to help discuss or diffuse any problems or upsetting findings, viewers wouldn't have that emotional support, but the tips given during these programmes may help someone with a similar trail. WDYTYA? magazine usefully lists the places they took their celebrities, explained the usefulness of each place for a family historian, and the websites that could be used, which would be helpful tips that people could investigate for themselves, or get an idea of somewhere to search for information about their own ancestor

One Name Studies

One Name Studies may be glad to hear from people with different ethnicities. The 'Allen' (Allan/ Alleyne/ Allin) One Name Study[460] gave a free FTDNA test[461] to my eldest male son, as they were really pleased to have a new line of investigation. *'FREE yDNA 12 marker tests will be made available to any males carrying the Allen surname and residing outside the United States who are willing to join the project and participate in the testing. The only requirement for a free yDNA test in a known Allen/ Allan (any spelling) lineage to at least the participant's Great Grand-father Allen/ Allan (any spelling) in any non-USA country. Additionally, The Allen DNA Project is setting aside a specific Sub-group within the Project with a full commitment of assistance from Allen Project Co-Administrator Dr. Eric Allen who will be overseeing this specific International Sub-group.'* The surname Allen has mostly a Scottish history, so to have a Jamaican heritage male was of great interest to them.

Joining a local group

This can be useful, for example, Jamaica Family Roots,[462] a Birmingham, UK, based community group, which hosts monthly meetings, invites guest speakers, and organises trips and events for members. Also Sparkbrook Caribbean and African Women's Development Initiative (SCAWDI)[463] are a Birmingham, UK based community group who specialise in working with local volunteers to research the early presence of Black people in the West Midlands. Their family history research led to the publication of the book, *'History Detectives: Black People in the West Midlands, 1650-1918'*[464] which identified many black individuals who came to the West Midlands before 1918, and constructing short biographies and including photographs of a number of them.

DNA testing

The increase in DNA testing has now led people to want to investigate the missing links to their ancestors. AncestryDNA uses two different processes, *'to determine the regions provided in your DNA Story: a reference panel and Genetic Communities™. One way we create estimates of your genetic ethnicity is by comparing your DNA to the DNA of other people who are native to a region...'*[465] There is a short video which explains that, *'Before you take a look at your new ethnicity results, our lead scientists would like to personally give you some insight into how we determine your unique ethnic mix.'*[466]

After I did a DNA test, and it revealed an estimated 71% Irish heritage, my six children wanted to do a DNA test too. The specificity of my Irish heritage helped me to pinpoint further searches. Three of my children with a Jamaican grandfather had thought that 'Jamaican' would be one of their named ethnicities, but were surprised to see no mention of Jamaica in their results, which is a similar scenario with other black British people.[467] Ancestry succinctly explained that, *'Most African Caribbeans in this Genetic Community can trace their ancestry back to West Africa, from areas in present-day Ivory Coast, Ghana, Benin, Togo, Nigeria, the Republic of Cameroon, Republic of the Congo, and Mali.'*[468]

This map shows a screen shot of my children's main African DNA from their Ancestry DNA tests, but sadly we had to look for some specific countries on a detailed map. Their ancestors' context has already gone.

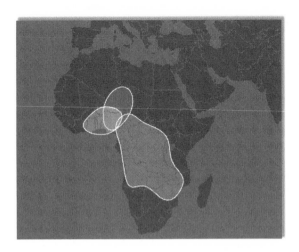

However, this huge interest in obtaining ethnicity estimates may mean that many people haven't added a tree or have a private tree, or don't respond to messages regarding collaborating. Estes stated that, '... *about 50% of the people taking autosomal DNA tests purchase them for the ethnicity results... I think a lot of people who aren't necessarily interested in genealogy per se are interested in discovering their ethnic mix - and maybe for some it will be a doorway to more traditional genealogy because it will fan the flame of curiosity.*'[469] Sometimes this can be really exciting and spur on researching the family history further. However, for some, seeing African regions as the ethnicity of known Caribbean ancestors can be truly upsetting, as it is a stark reminder of the enslavement of ancestors. Disappointingly, the likelihood of matching with some ethnicities is lower, as some countries haven't had many people who have tested, so these areas wouldn't show up in ethnicity estimates.

Kearns[470] suggested three useful ways to utilise DNA testing when exploring African ancestry:

- examining DNA Admixture results
- identifying African-born DNA matches
- exploring DNA haplogroups

'*Advances in DNA testing offer African Americans the intoxicating possibility of leapfrogging research brick walls created by slavery to connect to African roots by analyzing the family history etched within our DNA.*'[471]

Differences in ethnicity estimates in siblings

Some people have different members of their family tested, and a point of great confusion and debate is that different, but closely related, family members have different ethnicities in their test results, and that children's ethnicity estimates don't appear to be exactly half of each parent. Swayne explained that, *'My sibling's DNA results are all different - because we are all different... Genetic inheritance is random and my sibling's ethnicity results are a great example of that. But because our ethnicity results are different doesn't mean we aren't siblings. We all show up as 'immediate' family in the matching section which is expected... Each of us carry unique pieces of DNA that can unlock our family's story...'*[472] Starr explained that, *'...because of how DNA is passed on, it is possible for two siblings to have some big differences in their ancestry at the DNA level... DNA isn't passed down from generation to generation in a single block. Not every child gets the same 50% of mom's DNA and 50% of dad's DNA. (Unless of course they are identical twins)... DNA ancestry can be very different from cultural ancestry.'*[473]

Ethnicity results can therefore be difficult to understand, and the results could cause problems between parents over paternity. In addition, some hidden ethnicities could reveal themselves more in different siblings. My first three children's ethnicity estimates varied slightly from each other, with Ireland varying between 42% and 52%; Great Britain varying between 29% and 33%; Benin and Togo varying between 1% and 10%; Ivory coast and Ghana 0% and 8%; whilst Cameroon and Congo, and Nigeria all appear the same.

	Child 1	Child 2
Ireland	52%	42%
Great Britain	29%	33%
Ivory Coast/ Ghana	-	8%
Cameroon/ Congo	7%	7%
Senegal	-	2%
Nigeria	2%	2%
Benin/ Togo	10%	1%
Others	-	5%

Two of my children's ethnicity results on Ancestry, September, 2018

Can the ethnicity estimate change over time?

Ancestry explained that, *'Your ethnicity estimate is based on the data we have and the methods we use to compare your results to that data. Because we're always collecting more data and our methods are constantly improving, your estimate may change over time... You could see new regions* (because) *when AncestryDNA launched in 2012, we compared your DNA against 22 possible regions. We now have more than 380.'*[474] Ancestry provided a full explanation in their thirty five page 'Ethnicity Estimate White

Paper'[475] of the two primary pieces of information provided to customers to aid genealogical discovery. The first is identity-by-descent (IBD) analysis, which identifies pairs of customers with long shared genetic segments suggestive of recent common ancestry. The second piece of information, which is the subject of Ball *et al*'s White Paper, is genetic ethnicity or genetic ancestry.

Cooper concluded that, '*From a scientific perspective, the new estimates are a huge improvement over the previous version.*'[476] Replies on her blog reveal a variety of people's happiness, dismay and even disbelief at their updated ethnicity estimates, and, reflecting on her own updates, a typical response included, '*The decreases in Irish, English, and Scandinavian are all much more in line with my known ancestry, as is the loss of Italian/ Greek. I was disappointed to see the Iberian estimate disappear. I'm proud of my Spanish ancestry... The Sardinian is a complete head-scratcher.*'

A number of dilemmas occur here. People are interested in their ethnicity results and, for many people, this was the main reason for purchasing a DNA test, so they may be disappointed to receive different results, especially if the change is big. Some feel that the new DNA ethnicity updates have fine-tuned their previous more vague results, and feel happier, but others may feel that their previous estimate was somehow 'wrong,' and may have spent a lot of time pursuing evidence about an ethnicity, which has disappeared, and it may feel like time has been wasted. The change in ethnicity estimates can add to the argument that the DNA estimates are (somehow) made up. An advantage on Ancestry, is that you can view previous and updated ethnicity estimates, to compare. GEDmatch[477] can still provide an insight into ethnicity with their tools, such as 'Admixture/ Oracle with Population Search,' and 'Archaic DNA' matches. Cousin matches remain the same, so collaboration can still take place.

Music in your DNA

When you access your DNA ethnicity estimates, there is a new link on Ancestry, '*We've partnered with Spotify to create a custom playlist - tailored especially for you - from your AncestryDNA results.*'[478] Ancestry then invites customers to, '*Discover your World of Music ... Tell us which regions you're from based on your AncestryDNA kit results, and we'll make a playlist out of your heritage. What does your DNA sound like?*' Is this new option quirky, interesting, useful, silly, or valid? Wylde's interesting blog explained that '*...If you found out that you have a DNA connection to a place in the world that you're not familiar with, or have a limited knowledge about, listening to various musicians from that region will help introduce you to its culture and its history and its people.* [479]

Spotify lets you pick a region and find music from musicians who came from there, which sounds very interesting, but who were the playlists chosen by? Ancestry stated that you can use this feature 'to broaden your musical taste, region by region, and learn about what types of music each region influences.' People may want to visit a homeland, and listen to music beforehand, so this could feature be useful. It was interesting to note that, '...once you get your results, you can see if the music that you were drawn to was actually in your DNA the whole time.' People who want to hold onto practices from their ancestors refuse to allow the disappearance of their ethnic group into the host society. But is this 'cultural appropriation' (the 'use or mimicry of artefacts or manners from another culture without permission from any members of that culture'[480]) or 'cultural appreciation'?[481]

The Ireland and Scotland playlist included:[482]

Songs	Artist	Time
All Apologies	Sinéad O'Connor	2:38
Guiding Light	Foy Vance	5:52
Causing Trouble	Saint Sister	3:19
Your Love Is An Island	Talos	3:56
Feel It Again	Hudson Taylor	3:46
Guiding Light	Foy Vance	5:52
Causing Trouble	Saint Sister	3:19
Your Love Is An Island	Talos	3:56
Feel It Again	Hudson Taylor	3:46
Take Me Out	Franz Ferdinand	3:57
Eloise (Lean Into the Wave)	Brian Deady	3:31
Echo	Talisk	4:55
No Pressure	Odd Mob	3:27

Benin and Togo playlist included:

Songs	Artist	Time
A Min We Vo Nou We	Les Sympathics de Porto Novo	6:17
La Musica en Verite	Ghonnas Pedro And His Dadjes Band	4:15
Togol'aise	Flash Marley	2:02
Agoo	X N'djao	2:12
Feeling You Got	El Rego	3:45
Wait for Me	Roger Damawuzan	3:20
Papaoutai	Richard Flash	3:40
Ago Kae Medze	Wini and Fefe	5:24
Mighty dread - Reggae	Susu Bilibi	4:21
Au coeur de l'océan	The Magician King	3:00
It's a Vanity	Gabo Brown	4:23
African Fiesta	Singuila	3:24
Can't Imagine	Kezita	3:53
Ne Noya	Cos-Ber-Zam	4:12
Love Song to the Earth	Paul McCartney ** (That famous artist from Benin and Togo?) **	3:52

Some further investigation showed the origins of some of the artists:

- Sinéad O'Connor[483] (born 1966, Glenageary, Republic of Ireland)
- Foy Vance[484] (born 1974, Bangor, County Down, Northern Ireland)
- Saint Sister[485] (formed in 2014, music draws from early Celtic harp traditions)
- Les Sympathics de Porto Novo[486] (a band created in 1972 in Porto-Novo, Benin, by Herman F. Laleye, the former leader of the Black Dragons Orchestra)

Some countries are grouped together in the playlist, but separate in ethnicity estimates, for example Ireland and Scotland playlists are merged, but indigenous people may argue these two music genres are quite separate. The aim of the Ancestry and Spotify partnership is stated as, *'making learning about music history really fun and creative'* (but also encourages people to buy a DNA test if they haven't already done so). It is stated that *'you're bound to learn something new and most importantly, listen to something new'* (but this is an assumption).

Diaspora, 'So, where are you from?'[487]

People have dispersed from many places. *'Where are you from?'* is usually an easy enough question to answer, but what happens when you don't feel like you 'come from' where you live at present? And, when does where you live, feel like 'home'? Knowing where you are from usually means a specific place. Official forms will ask for your address, and birth certificates and passports record where you were born, *'Where someone was born has a special importance for identity.'[488]*

Many people move from one area to another, for a huge variety of reasons, for example, to change jobs, leave or get involved in new relationships, or retire. However, some groups of people are forced to leave their home, which is termed 'diaspora,' which probably originated from the Greek word *'diaspeirein'* which means *'disperse,'* (from *'dia'* which means *'across,'* and *'speirein'* which means *'scatter')* and which can be defined as *'the dispersion of any people from their original homeland.'[489]* The term can be found in the Septuagint (Deuteronomy 28:25) in the phrase, *'esē diaspora en pasais basileias tēs gēs,'* which means, *'thou shalt be a dispersion in all kingdoms of the earth.'[490]* The mitigating factors for dispersion can include, for example, famine, war, religion, and people having to flee from different forms of persecution.

Having looked at African dispersal, we can now turn to other countries, for example, Ireland. Estimating the size of the Irish community abroad is difficult. Does stating that you are 'Irish' mean that you were born in Ireland, your parents were born there, your grandparents, your great grandparents? You lived there? When does one's connectivity with a place end? Some people 'feel Irish' because their parents were from Ireland, and they had direct contact with living in a family and 'being Irish.' Other people may say they are Irish because their grandparents came from there, and they were given lots of contact with Irish traditions, food, and music. Others that say they have Irish heritage, but their Irish connection was from many years ago, for example their ancestors had to leave because of the Famine, and the Irish-ness is felt through heritage rather than anything current. Are you Irish if your DNA tests says so?

In the past two hundred and fifty years, more than six million Irish people reportedly left Ireland 'in search of a better life'.[491] The total number of Irish heritage diaspora has been put as high as seventy million, because each generation has had children. In the United States, nearly thirty five million people reported Irish ancestry, and six million reported Scottish-Irish ancestry, according to the USA 2000 Census. However, reportedly, more Americans claim German ancestry than any other ethnicity.[492]

In the UK, the figure varies between five million people stating they had an Irish parent or grandparent (10% of the British population at the time) in the 1991 census, to a total of fourteen million (24%).[493] In Canada,[494] people said their ethnicity was from over one hundred countries, firstly Canada, then England, France, Scotland, Ireland. In Australia,[495] people reported that they were English (32%), Irish (9.1%) and Scottish (7.6%). Bowden suggested that there are one million Irish-born people living currently abroad today.[496] County Cork seems to be the main producer of Irish diaspora; and Murphy, Kelly and Sullivan are the most common diaspora surnames.[497] When asked by a Census enumerator, 'where are you from?' people may have said Cork, as that was where the ship had left from (Cobh), rather than stating their actual village or homeland.

Nash, 2003, argued that people nostalgically yearn for that point in time when, '... *where you lived was where your ancestors had lived and there was no dissonance between cultural identity and location.'*[498] Bettinger and Woodbury hypothesised that, *'genealogical interest is most often born of a displacement and disconnect from an individual's cultural roots.'*[499] They explained that immigrants and their children often maintain connections to their native land. *'However, by the third and fourth generations, descendants of an immigrant may not know the immigrant themselves, may not have connections with their distant family, and in their absence may have increased interest in discovering their cultural roots and heritage. Accordingly, interest in genealogy often increases about one hundred years after migration.'*

Grenham stated that, *'...in medieval and early modern Irish society the real concern was kinship, not ancestry......when tribes shrink and scatter like this, the question of origins becomes more insistent and the answer more problematic. Why prosperity should have this effect is open to debate, but prosperity also provides the time and the education to explore the question.'*[500] An interesting dilemma for people who have researched ancestors and homelands is whether to move 'back' there, but descendent diaspora may not speak the ancestral home's language; people living somewhere in a specific time period had their own context, which can't be re-created today; and the land now doesn't consist of the families and communities that lived there.

Visiting where your ancestors came from[501]

Family historians often love to visit where their ancestors came from. A problem for descendants of diaspora is that, when visiting an ancestral homeland, they are 'tourists', but they feel like 'long lost relatives' who are eager to re-establish their heritage. Before they visit, descendants often have to research the country, its history, religious struggles, economy, politics and geography. People often have to consult a map to even find the name of the place their ancestors were from. The main issues which can be faced may include: being sure you have the right names and places for ancestors, whether any relatives still live there, understanding how to travel around that country, language barriers, not knowing or understanding local music, not knowing about traditional food, not knowing how to access civil records, for example, birth, death, and marriage records.

Many people want to return home with things with 'their' surname on (for example, key rings, mugs, fridge magnets) which do reflect being a tourist rather than diaspora. People often also mistakenly purchase heraldry items such as items with coats of arms on, which are for an individual not that surname.

Diaspora souvenirs
Photographs taken by Penny Walters, 2017

My paper trail and collaboration with DNA cousin matches revealed that 'my' Irish ancestors separately left counties Cork and Kerry during the Famine, to work in South Wales' coalmines, and their sisters went to New York, USA, to work as 'domestics.' I have found myself adding this new angle to my narrative, that I'm Irish heritage. I began reading all about Ireland, and became a 'mine of information.' My DNA test revealed 71% Irish ethnicity, so, because I'd never even been to Ireland, I had to research it. 71% sounded like a lot of my ancestors had Irish heritage. Over the years, and with more reference samples being included, my Irish heritage has increased to 94%. I embarked on a couple of 'touristy' weekends in Cork and Dublin, which mostly consisted of going on really informative Open Top bus tours, and wandering round famous places I'd Googled.

However, I thought *'I'm not a tourist'*, my ancestors had to leave here; my bloodline was dispersed, they didn't just emigrate.

'I'm home!'

I located my O'Reilly great grandparents' derelict cottage in Drimoleague,[502] south west Cork. With the aid of Google, it turned out to be one straight bus trip (236) from Cork city centre. Drimoleague appears to now be a small village, just a few houses up and down, and some cottages in fields. It's a very pretty place, *'Here at the heart is to be found rich folklore, warm friendliness, down-to-earth faith, lively cultural expressions and a varied and interesting history going back to St Finbarr of the 6th century and beyond. Here also is a landscape of remarkable beauty, comprising mountains, undulating farmland, pristine riverbank, woodland and a largely unspoiled flora and fauna.'*[503]

I felt sick with excitement looking round my ancestors' cottage, but equally dismayed by the small size and dereliction of it. The O'Reillys had tried to bring up twelve children in a two bedroom cottage, during the Famine. The view of fields and hills was spectacular, but you can't feed children on a pretty view. My O'Reillys must have never seen ten of their children again. But I felt grounded.

Having got my bearings from a couple of Cork and Dublin weekends, and, despite my newfound Irish-ness, I was, in reality, a tourist. I decided to get the ferry to Ireland, and do a one week road trip[504] with my youngest daughter, around the south of Ireland, and incorporate Kerry as well, to look where 'my' O'Neills came from.

We got the four hour ferry from Fishguard, south west Wales, to Rosslare, south east Ireland, and then drove south to Waterford (visiting the Museum, Castle, and a luxurious crystal glass showroom); Midleton (we saw the 1696 College; and Jameson Whiskey distillery); Skibbereen (we visited the heart-wrenching Famine Heritage Centre, and met the managers Terri Kearney and Philp O'Regan, authors of the book, *'Skibbereen, The Famine Story'*[505]). We then drove down as far as Mizen Head[506] (Ireland's most south westerly point, home to the Marconi signal station), and then back up the coast to Glengarriff; Kenmare; onto Sneem[507] (where my O'Neill ancestors were supposed to have come from; with the nearby Staigue Iron Age Fort, c400AD); Valentia Island (where another cousin match from Ancestry assured me our O'Neills were from; we saw a bleak 1816 slate quarry,[508] with its religious shrine towering over the quarry); Killarney (we went round the Cathedral, a mansion, and the National Park); Maynooth (we stayed with a friend, and saw traditional Irish dancing); up to Dublin city; and then back to Rosslare.

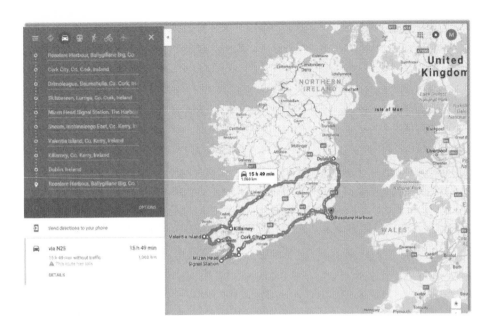

Diaspora trail down through county Cork, through county Kerry, and back
Google maps screenshot of the route, by Penny Walters, 2017

My O'Neill line has been harder to trace, as it is such a common surname. I have matched with two helpful DNA second cousin Americans who have separately assured me, through their own very thorough research that our County Kerry O'Neills came from Sneem, or Valentia Island. This became a dilemma. The two places aren't too far apart, but how infuriating not to know for sure. They're my ancestors, so I'd really like to know. It was interesting, however, that when I was driving towards Sneem, I got an overwhelming desire to stop my car, get out, and wander through some trees, and I emerged at a tiny waterfall, near the river, and I felt overwhelming déjà vu. I took some pictures, and researched where I was (Drimnamore), and it appears that it had previously been an oyster bed inlet. Fascinating! Is there such a thing as 'race memory' defined as memory, present at birth, and that exists in the absence of sensory experience, that arises from the common experience of one's ancestors?[509] Psychologists are now suggesting that, *'The idea of inherited, or genetic, memory of a different kind has some degree of plausibility.'*[510] Or am I getting too excitable thinking that spirits are sending me messages about my ancestors?

We spent a few hours in each place and then drove an hour or so to the next one, spent a few hours there, then stayed in an AirBnB room, which is cheaper than hotels or B&B (because hotel costs can mean that visiting where ancestors came from can end sadly up being a once-in-a-lifetime trip); and that filled up a whole week. Actually visiting where your ancestors came from is so much more informative than collecting their birth, marriage and death records, especially when you're adopted, and have no anecdotal stories, and it can help you 'feel' how they lived. It must have been so bleak during the Famine; the rain, the poverty, lack of food, the distances. I got to witness how far apart all the villages were, and how many hopeful and beautiful religious shrines there were. We had local food, gossiped and chatted to local people, who loved my reason for visiting, and we brought back home-made marmalade, rye and soda breads, and new memories.

My daughter enjoyed her holiday, but she wasn't as moved as I was. It's funny how these ancestral ties can be cut after so few generations: I saw it as visiting my ancestral home, whereas she just didn't. It could be argued that, *'The culture in which we are raised shapes us as much as our parents do. The cultural influence of our ancestors fades with each generation anyway. The cultural imprints that were left on your great-great-grandparents have long since given way to the more recent cultural milieu.'*[511]

Genealogy tourism

Many diaspora want to visit where their ancestors came from, and this has developed the term, 'genealogy tourism.' The lecture *'Genealogy Tourism: a new niche market'* was presented at the 2018 Irish Famine Summer School, which had the theme of *'Irish Journeys: Famine Legacies and Reconnecting Communities'* held at Strokestown Park,[512] Co. Roscommon in the west of Ireland. This venue was where the landlord at the time, Major Denis Mahon was assassinated in November 1847, at the height of the Great Famine. The National Famine Museum[513] was established at Strokestown Park in 1994, using the archive of original documents, which were found during the restoration of the house.

Abstract: *'Genealogy Tourism: a new niche market'*[514]

'The recent huge interest in DNA testing, and paper trails within family history has developed into an increase in the number of people loyally (maybe over-romantically) viewing Ireland as their 'homeland', and this can develop into a huge desire to visit. The total number of Irish diaspora has been put as high as 70 million, including c35 million in the USA, and c14 million people in the UK. County Cork is the main producer of Irish Diaspora; and Murphy, Kelly and Sullivan are the most common diaspora surnames. There are, therefore, potentially thousands, if not millions of descendent diaspora who want to visit their ancestors' homes, 'feel' how they lived, and seek out records with the help of experts. There are a number of new tourist initiatives, such as The Cork Foundation; journals such as 'British Connections' and 'Irish Lives Remembered;' 1916 Easter Rising commemorative exhibitions, and the 2018 20th anniversary of the Good Friday/ Belfast Agreement (10 April, 1998). People can visit fascinating heritage centres such as that at Skibbereen, workhouses such as Portumna, as well as more traditional museums, Universities, and archives. Instead of being a costly once-in-a-lifetime visit for overseas visitors, businesses should make access to visiting

Ireland easier and cheaper, for example, people could stay at AirBnBs instead of hotels, and utilise buses and trains instead of taxis. Genealogy tourism is a new niche market, but this huge untapped source of income could be vastly expanded upon and be profitable for those running a business in Ireland, and a great source of pleasure for the diaspora who visit.'

Helping diaspora 'connect' with ancestors' countries

In Bristol, UK, people were encouraged to, *'celebrate African textiles and culture with an exciting evening of catwalk fashion, Afrobeats music and special guest speakers. Hosted by Vanessa Kisuule, the highlight of the evening is the fashion show curated by Christelle Pellecuer featuring designers of African heritage. Dee J Neyo will be providing a live DJ set and you can catch the exhibition. Free entry.'*[515]

Photographs taken by Penny Walters, September 2018, while attending the Bristol exhibition

The display shows beautiful clothes, but people may feel these are standard clothes to wear, not realising they are traditional dress. *'Multiculturalism and its accompanying value of diversity have become institutionalised such that individuals regard ethnic difference as something to be recognized and celebrated.'*[516] Looking at clothes from other countries doesn't necessarily inspire empathy for people.

A different approach is that of Ireland's Cork Foundation, whose mission is *'to connect with the Cork network globally to support Cork people locally'*[517] which involves connecting diaspora with businesses currently in Cork. Their method is to:

- match donors - connect local and international donors to social enterprise projects in the community
- create jobs - contributions go towards creating sustainable jobs
- improve lives - the jobs help improve the lives and families that make cork great

- give back - provide a meaningful way to give back to your people, place and heritage

Joining Your Family's Native American Tribe

Native Americans were greatly affected by the European colonization of the Americas, which began in 1492, and their population declined precipitously due to warfare, diseases, and enslavement.[518] Gates and Arnold stated that, *'Many Americans believe they have at least one Native American ancestor.'*[519] Could it be argued that people have a rather 'romantic' notion of having a Native American ancestor? As many as nine hundred or more nations, peoples, tribes, and bands once lived on the North American continent, and people now want to know about how to become a member of a tribe.

One dilemma is that uniform membership requirements do not exist, so each tribe may have different requirements. Membership rests on your 'blood quantum,' (the exact number of Native American ancestors, stated as a percentage), and your ability to prove your paper trail Native American lineage. Gates and Arnold gave useful hints for researching American Indian research, including that Ancestry has more than two dozen record collections[520] that may reveal your ancestor's tribe, plus photographs, marriage records, allotment records, and an index card file. Tennant's blog[521] gives useful advice about searching for potential Native American ancestors, with a clear list of instructions.

The main five Native American nations: Cherokee, Choctaw, Chickasaw, Muskogee (Creek), and Seminole are termed by the Federal Government as, *'The Five Civilized Tribes.'* Frank explained that the phrase 'Civilized Tribes' came into use during the mid-nineteenth century and was most widely used in Indian Territory and Oklahoma.[522] Although the Indian tribes had various cultural, political, and economic connections before removal in the 1820s and 1830s, they were termed 'civilized,' *'because they appeared to be assimilating to Anglo-American norms. The term indicated the adoption of horticulture and other European cultural patterns and institutions, including widespread Christianity, written constitutions, centralized governments, inter marriage with white Americans, market participation, literacy, animal husbandry, patrilineal descent, and even slaveholding.'*[523] Frank poignantly went on to explain that, *'Elements of 'civilization' within Southeastern Indian society predated removal. The Cherokee, for example, established a written language in 1821, a national supreme court in 1822, and a written constitution in 1827. The other four nations had similar, if less noted, developments.'*[524]

The Dawes Commission[525] was established to oversee land redistribution within the Five Civilized Tribes (Choctaw, Creek, Chickasaw, Seminole, and Cherokee Indian), and an official list of members of each nation was drawn up, whereby people had to fill out forms for acceptance, basically asking them to prove that they belonged to their tribe. Reportedly about two thirds of the applications were rejected, so people purporting to be descendants will have a difficult, if not impossible task, finding any paper trail, even though a DNA test can support the claim. According to the Dawes Commission rules, a person who had mixed heritage had to choose one nation and register, which meant that people lost a recorded part of his or her inheritance and heritage, which could affect descendants searching for evidence.

Some people proudly publically announce their Native American Indian ethnicity, but others can mock them for that. For example, Senator Elizabeth Warren (D-Mass.) made public the results of her DNA test,[526] which an expert, Carlos D. Bustamante, a Stanford University professor, who analysed the results said shows 'strong evidence' that she has a Native American ancestor. The 'vast majority' of Warren's ancestry is European, but the results[527] strongly support the existence of a Native American ancestor between six to ten generations ago. This means she could be between 1/32 to 1/512 Native American. How do indigenous people, for example, Nubians, Aborigines, Native American Indians, feel about people claiming descendent diaspora heritage? At what stage is claiming inheritance a tenuous link?

Royal Wedding

The recent wedding between Prince Harry (fifth in line to the UK throne) and American actress Meghan Markle perhaps reminds us that colour and heritage still feature prominently in people's minds. Meghan Markle is the daughter of Thomas Markle and Doria Ragland. Journalists[528] were quick to point out that Meghan's great-great-great-great grandfather was enslaved in the Deep South plantations, and was freed after the Abolition in 1865. When he was permitted to choose a new name to mark his emancipation, he called himself 'Wisdom.' Afua Hirsch reported, after the wedding, that, *'At this royal wedding, talented black people were more than adornment,'*[529] including the sermon, delivered by the Reverend Michael Curry[530] (who perhaps 'stole the show'),[531] actor Oprah Winfrey,[532] tennis star Serena Williams[533] and husband Alexis Ohanian,[534] actor Idris Elba[535] and Sabrina Dhowre, and Gina Torres,[536] Markle's fellow Suits actor. Hirsch felt that, *'Winfrey's attendance was a reminder that, between her and Meghan Markle, perhaps the two most famous women in the world today are of African heritage.'* It seems that people have discussed Meghan's ethnicity more than any of her other points, and that many people have been pleased that the British Royal family will have a black person within it, possibly forgetting the mixed European heritage of the Royal family.

Conclusions: dilemmas within DNA ethnicity testing

Some might argue that we are all of a mixed ethnicity. During a video of ethnicity 'reveals' by 23 And Me, some cynical comments included, *'So, some ethnically ambiguous people took a DNA test, and found that they were ethnically ambiguous.'*[537] A pertinent comment was that, *'I think these "oh my god, my ancestry is suddenly so important and shocking" kind of videos have a weird aftertaste. Why, after fighting so long for making "race" as unimportant as possible, we now make a big deal out of it again?'* Another wry comment was that, *'the lady doing the reveals must still be reading out the list of ethnicities.'*

Are the DNA tests measuring 'ethnicity,' or proof of where our ancestors used to live? Some countries haven't had many people who have tested, so the likelihood of matching with some ethnicities is lower. Some groups of people were isolated from neighbouring populations; isolation gives populations a chance to develop a unique genetic signature.[538] When individuals from different countries next to each other begin intermarrying, the previously distinct populations becomes more difficult to distinguish.[539] Enslavement would have changed the DNA makeup of African diaspora. *'Africa is massive. It also has the highest human genetic diversity in the world because our species originated in Africa and has had hundreds of thousands of years to form distinct populations. Not many Africans have tested yet, so that immense diversity is currently poorly sampled. The good news is that AncestryDNA is launching an African Diversity Project to improve their sampling.'*[540]

Testing with different companies can produce different ethnicity results; some vary somewhat but some people's ethnicities vary hugely, which can decrease confidence in them. *'GEDmatch results are for comparison only and will likely be somewhat different than those shown by your testing company.'*[541] Many people's sole interest in ethnicity estimates may mean that many people haven't added a tree or have a private tree, or don't respond to messages regarding collaborating.

Some people find unexpected ethnicities, including a black testee who found about one third European heritage, remarking that she, *'I Celebrated Black History Month ... By Finding Out I Was White,'* revealing her ethnicity was Sub-Saharan African, 67.2%, European, 31.5%, concluding that that, *'Of all the emotions which materialised from the results, the two strongest were disorient and shame.'*[542] However, my English friend has Indian, Middle Eastern and west European DNA heritage estimates, which reflect the Silk Route, which she was so excited to have revealed, as she had a rather 'romantic' image of people wandering from country to country, selling beautiful silks. People's DNA results may not resemble what they feel they know about their ancestors through their paper trail. Estes commented that, *'...Liv Tyler discovered something in the race column of the 1870 census that did not match the 1860 census - spawning questions that many of us have experienced as well...'*[543] A reply by RBM to the blog post said, *'They only gave out what they deemed eye catching. George W. Elliott was obviously only ¼ African American but they played up his 'passing as white' and trying to get ahead in society by joining the Masons.'*[544]

The next chapter includes a potted history of genealogy, and ponders on the potential future of genealogy.

Chapter 6: Potted history and potential future of genealogy

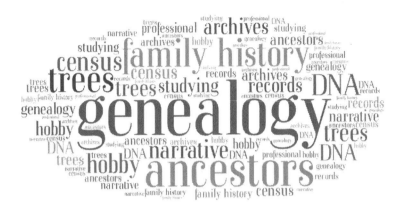

Background

What is the difference, if any, between the practices of 'genealogy' and 'family history'? Genealogy (from the Greek: γενεαλογία genealogia from γενεά genea, 'generation' and λόγος logos, 'knowledge') is the study of families and the tracing of their lineages and history.[545] It could be explained that genealogy involves the extracting of evidence, from reputable and valid sources, of how people and generations are linked, and this aids devising a 'family tree.' Family history could perhaps be described more as the narrative story of the family and of the community, era and country in which they lived. Family history incorporates genealogy. Researching family history traditionally used to be for the rich, elite and peers because, as Hareven noted, *'Genealogies originally functioned to provide pedigrees and legitimisation for status, claims for property, inheritance, or access to skills or political positions.'*[546] Rodriguez would have agreed, commenting that, in the USA, *'…elites often sought to maintain their social status by promoting a definition of whiteness that excluded newcomers. Genealogy became a way for them to prove their credentials.'*[547]

Genealogy is a popular hobby now, and is more accessible to many different people through online records, family history societies and libraries. *'A hobby once dominated by persnickety elites was now fully democratized and focused on identity rather than pedigree…'*[548] People are now recording events for a variety of people, and including records for lives that may have gone somewhat un-noticed in the past. For example, plenty of my ancestors worked as 'ag. labs.' (agricultural labourers), but these simple folk are now recorded, potentially for posterity in my tree, with a variety of birth, marriage and death records, census returns, and dog licences. None of these people would have appeared in historical accounts, apart from my tree, and their information can theoretically now be recorded forever, and in some context as an informative micro-history.

So, how has genealogy developed over time?

'Potted history' of some key dates in genealogy
(this is a compilation, not an exhaustive list)

1741- Collins - The English Baronetage book comprises six hundred and fifty nine pages of English baronets' descents, marriages and issues, memorable actions, religious and charitable donations, deaths, burials, monumental inscriptions, coats of arms; and it's provenance is that the author compiled it from, *'authentic manuscripts, records, old wills, our best historians, and other authorities.'*[549]

1786 - Her Majesty's Stationery Office (HMSO), UK.[550] The British government set out to establish an official stationer who would be singularly accountable to the Treasury. HMSO provides a variety of documentary support to the British government, including passports, parliamentary records, manuals, forms, computers, and office equipment.

1812 - The American Antiquarian Society (AAS),[551] both a learned society and national research library of pre-twentieth century American history and culture was founded, by Isaiah Thomas (1749 - 1831). It is the oldest historical society in the United States with a national focus. The mission of the AAS is to collect, preserve and make available for study all printed records of what is now known as the United States of America. This includes materials from the first European settlement through the year 1876.

1820s - John Farmer (June 12, 1789 – August 13, 1838)[552] is considered the founder of systematic genealogy in America.

1826 - Burke's Peerage[553] was compiled by Sir John Bernard Burke (1786–1848) and is useful for people to find established trees and pedigrees for the elite in society. The website includes information about elite families, royal genealogies from a variety of countries, arms and heraldry, book sales; but to view them requires a subscription.

1838 - Public Record Office Act was passed to, *'...keep safely the public records... The Public Record Office was organised in a number of branches with headquarters at Rolls House on the Rolls Estate in Chancery Lane, central London.'*[554]

1853 - microfiche invented[555] by English scientist John Benjamin Dancer. Microfiche[556] are flat and small sheets of microfilm on which newspapers, manuals, books, newspapers, and other documents can be photographed in reduced form. They came about when companies had a lot of documents or files but didn't really have the space or wanted to save a lot more space in and around their offices.

1866 - Gregor Mendel[557] published results of his research on the inheritance of factors in pea plants.

1880s - The 'Complete Peerage of England, Scotland, Ireland'[558] was compiled by George Edward Cokayne[559] (1825-1911) and is a detailed summary of elite families, with dates and facts intertwined with a narrative.

1880s - William Phillimore Watts Phillimore[560] (1853-1913) was an influential genealogy publisher in the UK.[561]

John Horace Round[562] (1854-1928) became famous for the translation and discussion of the Essex Domesday Book.

1894 – FamilySearch, USA was founded; historically known as the Genealogical Society of Utah, it is dedicated to preserving the records of the family of mankind. The Church of Jesus Christ of Latter-day Saints is the primary benefactor for FamilySearch services. *'We pioneered industry standards for gathering, imaging, indexing, and preserving records.'* Their home page states that you can, *'Find your family. Discover yourself. Bring to life your family's history by exploring the lives of those that came before you.'*[563]

1930s - Percival Boyd[564] (1868-1955) was responsible for compiling many UK civil registration indexes, including a Marriage Index which lists about an eighth of all marriages recorded in parish registers before 1837.

George Frederick Tudor Sherwood[565] (1890-1958) was one of the founding fellows of the UK Society of Genealogists.

1903 - National Genealogical Society[566] founded in Washington, D.C., USA is dedicated to genealogical education, exemplary standards of research, and the preservation of genealogical records. Wilcox has produced a fifty eight page, one hundred year history of NGS.[567] Hosts an annual family history conference.

1903 – G. W. Marshall, The Genealogist's Guide To Printed Pedigrees *'lists printed family history information to be found in local and county histories, biographical studies, national and local periodicals, transactions of county archaeological and record societies...'*[568]

1910 - American and English Genealogies in the Library of Congress preliminary catalogue.[569] This eight hundred and five page book contains titles of American and English genealogies before 1910; available through The Internet Archive[570] and can be purchased on Amazon.

1910 -The Complete Baronetage[571] was published by George Edward Cokayne.

1911 - The Society of Genealogists, London, UK was founded. *'The Society's collections are particularly valuable for research before the start of civil registration of births marriages and deaths in 1837.'* [572]

1926 - A Catalogue of British Family Histories was published, which consists of one hundred and eighty four pages, compiled by Theodore Radford Thomson.

1938 - Burke's Genealogical and Heraldic History [573] was published.

1953 - James Watson and **Francis Crick** suggested the first correct double-helix model of DNA structure [574]

1960 – Americans of Jewish Descent: 600 Genealogies (1654-1988) [575] by Rabbi Malcolm H. Stern was published.

1967 - The UK Public Records Act and the thirty year access rule [576] meant that the fifty year closure period was reduced to thirty years. This allowed records relating to the First World War and those created before 1923 to be available for public inspection.

1974 - The Federation of Family History Societies (FFHS) UK [577] is an educational charity formed in 1974 and granted charitable status in 1982. The organisation represents over one hundred and eighty societies throughout the world, including national, regional and one-name groups.

1975- Federation of Genealogical Societies (USA) was formed, *'Despite the patriotic fervor to save the nation's personal and collective past, historical records were being lost to floods, fires, neglect, and legislative acts. Vital records, critical to genealogical inquiry, were closed to researchers in some states, and the threat of more record closures was real. Concerned individuals and small organizations were having little influence on preservation and legislative efforts. A collective voice was needed.'* [578] The FGS mission statement explains that they, *'Represent the members of hundreds of genealogical societies across the United States and other nations, the Federation of Genealogical Societies (FGS) is here to link the genealogical community by helping genealogical societies strengthen and grow.'* [579]

1979 - The Guild of One-Name Studies [580] *'is the worldwide centre of excellence in one-name studies and promotes the interests of both the individuals and groups who are engaged in them. Established in 1979 and registered as a charity in 1989... The new organisation was set up as a guild. The founders were keen to liken members to skilled craftsmen...The Guild encourages all new members to enter into that same spirit of sharing.'* [581] As of 28 July, 2018, The Guild of One-Name Studies had 2,861 members, 2,444 studies, 8,712 surnames.

5 February 1979 – The Association of Professional Genealogists, USA was registered in Utah, USA. *'APG is an independent organization whose principal purpose is to support professional genealogists in all phases of their work: from the amateur genealogist wishing to turn knowledge and skill into a vocation, to the experienced professional seeking to exchange ideas with colleagues and to upgrade the profession as a whole. The association also seeks to protect the interest of those engaging in the services of the professional.'* [582] A history of the APG was published in the 20th Anniversary Issue of APG Quarterly, August 1999. [583]

1983 - Ancestry Publishing was founded, publishing more than forty family history magazine titles and genealogy reference books.

1987 - JewishGen is a non-profit organization, affiliated with the Museum of Jewish Heritage, A Living Memorial to the Holocaust, and was founded in 1987 as a bulletin board with one hundred and fifty users who were interested in Jewish genealogy. *'Primarily driven by volunteers, there are more than 1,000 active volunteers throughout the world who actively contribute to our ever growing collection of databases, resources and search tools. JewishGen hosts more than 25 million records, and provides a myriad of resources and search tools designed to assist those researching their Jewish ancestry.'* [584]

1989 - Family Tree Maker [585] was released by Banner Blue Software. This program ran on DOS (Disk Operating System), an operating system that runs from a hard disk drive, and came on 3.5 and 5.25 floppy disks.

17 August, 1991 - The Genealogical Speakers Guild [586] was founded in Fort Wayne, Indiana, USA, to facilitate better communication between speakers and societies.

1996 - Ancestry was launched.

2000 - The Peerage [587] is a comprehensive elite family history website, compiled by Darryl Lundy [588] which is *'A genealogical survey of the peerage of Britain as well as the royal families of Europe.'* The site is often updated, and by 13 September, 2018 had received 709,417 visitors. Lundy stated that he isn't an expert, and asks for help with updates/ errors.

2000 - FamilyTreeDNA became the first company to deliver direct-to-consumer DNA testing for ancestry.

2003 - MyHeritage was founded.

2003 - The National Archives [589] **was founded.** Based in Kew, UK, TNA *'are a non-ministerial department, and the official archive and publisher for the UK Government, and for England and Wales... the guardians of over 1,000 years of iconic national documents...*

expert advisers in information and records management and are a cultural, academic and heritage institution.'[590]

2005 - The International Society of Genetic Genealogy (ISOGG) *'was founded by DNA project administrators who shared a common vision: the promotion and education of genetic genealogy. Our mission is to advocate for and educate about the use of genetics as a tool for genealogical research, and to promote a supportive network for genetic genealogists.'*[591]

April 2006 - 23andMe was founded by Anne Wojcicki and Linda Avey. On 17 November, 2007 the 23andMe test was officially launched in the US.[592]

November 2008 - GenealogyInTime Magazine[593] was launched.

2010 - 'Who Do You Think You Are?' television programme was launched in the USA.

2012 - AncestryDNA was launched.

5 January 2014 - Burke's Peerage Foundation[594] was established on the 200th anniversary of the birth of Sir John Bernard Burke.

26 April, 2019 - The Federation of Family History Societies rebranded as the Family History Federation.[595]

Professionalising genealogy

When people start researching their tree in earnest, and then helping others with theirs, they may then start considering asking to be paid for undertaking the research, as it is very time consuming. People may not initially realise that there are genealogy courses that can be studied, professional bodies that can be joined, and conferences that can be attended. They may then want to engage with others, and expand on their knowledge and skills.

Family historians invariably become a 'mine of information' because they are researching their tree, but that also involves knowing about, for example, maps, trends, wars, history, politics, economics, laws, archives, and, more recently, DNA. But, when does someone feel that they have enough skills to undertake investigating trees for others, and 'qualified' to undertake genealogy work for a fee? Researching trees does take a lot of time, and it is reasonable to get paid for doing that. Some people would like to ask, or pay others, for some help with their family history. Maybe when people start paying you a fee, you would consider yourself a 'professional'? However, lawyers, doctors and nurses, for example, study strictly prescribed courses; and then join a published Register, with a Professional Code of Conduct. Do family historians/ genealogists need/ want/ should have to do the same?

Amateur or professional

Once people know you 'do' genealogy, they often ask for your help. But, when do you step over from being an amateur hobbyist to being a professional? There is a difference between 'being professional' in your methods, and being 'in a profession.' An 'occupation' is an activity undertaken by the person to earn his/ her livelihood. A 'profession' is an activity which requires specialised knowledge, training, qualification/s and skills. These two terms are often used interchangeably, but there is a thin line of demarcation between them. Joseph explained that, *'Being a professional in your chosen field means much more than wearing a coat and tie or possessing a college degree and a noted title. Professionalism also has to do with how you conduct yourself during your business affairs.'*[596] Grenham wryly observed that, *'this is a self-evident truth about expertise in general: it is perfectly possible to extract your own tooth, but the job is better left to an expert.'*[597]

How do you know when someone is a 'professional genealogist'? Is it when they've done a thorough tree for themselves, and their friends; when they've had paying clients; when they were listed on a professional body's website; when they are recommended by people; when they have a great website; because they've undertaken a course? Which course? 'Approved' by whom? What type of course: an evening class; a certificate; a Post Graduate certificate; a Diploma; a Masters, a PhD? Was the course specifically in genealogy, archiving, librarianship, history, or family history? What about those who haven't studied a course, but have successfully been doing genealogy for many years? Joining a professional body can involve a variety of criteria, and may involve paying a membership fee, proving that qualifications have been obtained, submitting a portfolio, and/ or the requirement that CPD (continuing professional development) is being undertaken, to keep up to date.

If people are paying you, other and different ethical dilemmas may arise. For example, for a hobbyist, finding information that someone hadn't previously known about, perhaps an affair, an illegitimacy, criminal activity, family secrets, or an unknown living relative, can be awkward; but for a professional genealogist this can involve more formal and serious ethical and professional dilemmas. How do you approach people with your findings if previously unknown information is potentially very upsetting for the recipient? With the addition of DNA interpretations being included in some people's family histories, some evidence is irrefutable, and DNA findings raises its own set of hopes, fears, expectations and ethical dilemmas, when presenting information to a client.

Professional genealogists may giving bad news or sensitive information a difficult task to undertake without training. We're all clever with hind-sight, but it can be unprofessional to just learn from your mistakes with clients, so fore-warned is fore-armed. People paying you can add responsibilities to the process; going from hobby to work includes all the processes involved in setting up a small business, and running a business also has financial and legal implications. Understanding research standards and knowing about business practices are very different. An initial dilemma is how much should you charge? What should you do if you find nothing 'new' for the client?

Wanting to become a 'professional' genealogist leads some people to want to obtain an academic qualification

There are a number of academic, mostly online, courses that can now be studied. They vary from a few weeks, to a few years.

* I am not specifically advocating them, these are just ones that I know about *

FutureLearn and the University of Strathclyde run a free MOOC ('taster' course) entitled Genealogy: Researching Your Family Tree. *'This free online course will help you develop an understanding of basic genealogy techniques and how to communicate your family history. We will consider how to effectively find and analyse sources and explore the potential of DNA testing as applied to genealogy. We'll help you add historical context to your family history and discuss how to record and communicate research findings in a clear fashion. The course is primarily designed for people at beginner to intermediate level.'*[598] The MOOC is six weeks in length, and it is suggested that it will involve four hours per week studying; and students can then optionally upgrade for a fee, which would give unlimited access to online materials and a certificate of completion.

The University of Strathclyde, Scotland, UK[599] offers online academic short and longer Postgraduate Certificate, Postgraduate Diploma, or Master's degree in Genealogical, Palaeographic and Heraldic Studies.[600] The short genealogy classes include: online beginner to intermediate level genealogy eight week classes, and on-campus beginner to intermediate level genealogy eight week classes. Alternatively, The Postgraduate Certificate, Diploma or MSc in Genealogical Studies *'is for anyone with an existing interest and some experience in genealogy and related subjects. It has been developed by academics and genealogy professionals to provide a thorough grounding in the theory and practice of genealogical research, family history, records, archives and heraldry. You may wish to study the field in more detail or use it in your career.'*

The University of Dundee Centre for Archive and Information Studies (CAIS), Scotland, offers an academic Postgraduate Certificate, Diploma or Masters in Family and Local History, also short accredited courses, and 'taster courses' (non-accredited short introductory courses). *'If your aim is to discover more about sources and archives that could assist your research, to find out about the historical context in which your ancestors lived, to put further names on your family tree or to do sustained research into a local area, CAIS' programmes are suitable for you.'*[601]

Pharos Teaching and Tutoring, UK offers a joint distance learning certificate programme, in partnership with the Society of Genealogists called, 'Family History Skills and Strategies.' *'Together we want to help you become a better genealogist. We can't* promise that you will find all those elusive ancestors. That's up to you. But we can promise that one of our courses will equip you with the know-how to expand your family tree accurately and quickly. Pharos are specialists in online genealogy education. Our teachers are professional genealogists and archives professionals with many decades of teaching experience.'[602]

Genealogy Diploma Level 3 / PI990, NCC Resources Ltd. (Conwy, UK) provides 'a dedicated Genealogy Diploma which is aimed at providing you with background knowledge in the area of Genealogy and also expanding into more detail in specific areas such as Census information and Immigration Records.'[603] There are ten modules, awarded by ABC Awards, consisting of an average duration of three hundred and sixty hours.

The Institute of Heraldic and Genealogical Studies (IHGS) Correspondence Course in Genealogy, UK was launched in 1961, and, 'provides an in-depth knowledge of UK genealogical sources and their application. The course prepares students for examination at the level of Higher Certificate in Genealogy... The course is suitable for both beginners and experienced genealogists and the academic standards followed and depth of learning are also suitable for those intending to operate a professional genealogical practice.'[604] There are twenty four modules, which are Open and Distance Learning Quality Council (ODLQC) accredited.

The Society of Genealogists, UK offers 'Courses and Talks' and 'Visits and Walks.' 'We offer an extensive programme of events: guided walks, visits to places with historical value, talks and workshops delivered by family history experts, and special events aimed at updating and enhancing your skills and knowledge.'[605]

Local Societies that are members of The UK Federation of Family History Societies also publish information about events. 'The courses and talks mentioned can help you discover more about what is available.'[606]

The National Archives, UK includes, 'A growing range of audio and video items are available to view free of charge. The family history section of the online catalogue takes you to a menu of over one hundred and twenty items.'[607] These include a variety of webinars and podcasts.

The Center for Family History and Genealogy, Brigham Young University, Provo, Utah, USA[608] provides a Family History (Genealogy) Major, and a Family History (Genealogy) Minor, as well as a range of other family history courses. They also host an annual Conference on Family History and Genealogy.[609]

The National Institute for Genealogical Studies[610] provides web-based courses for both family historians and professional genealogists. Their website states that, 'To support the needs of both amateur family historians and aspiring professional genealogists for *reliable and comprehensive education we have designed a series of courses (Basic, Intermediate, Advanced and Electives) leading to various Certificates in Genealogical Studies with specialization in various countries.'*

Having spent ages compiling this list, I have recently found a more comprehensive list on Cyndi's List, entitled, 'Education (Genealogical)'[611] with the following categories:
- Audio and Video from Conferences
- Awards, Competitions & Scholarships
- Conferences, Seminars & Workshops
- Correspondence, Independent, and Home Study Courses
- Credentials: Certification and Accreditation
- Discussion Groups & Study Groups
- General Resources
- Institutes, Campuses and Onsite Classrooms
- Online Courses & Webinars

People may not have obtained qualifications when they were younger and don't feel equipped to undertake academic study. Many genealogy courses are online, which can be a difficult method of study. Studying at home has many benefits, but also has inherent problems too, such as juggling home and academic life. Do any of the courses include practical as well as theoretical components? Some people may prefer to study through comprehensive books or introductory books, utilising archives, or private online research. Do the courses include philosophical enquiry and an investigation into ethical dilemmas as a component? Does studying a course make you a better genealogist?

A clear and succinct answer to a Facebook question (on a forum in The Genealogy Squad) was explained by Elizabeth Shown Mills: *'Did you mean a "certificate" or "certification"? One speaks to education. The other represents a professional credential that attests competency in research, analysis, and problem-solving. As an analogy to demonstrate the difference, one goes to school to get a law degree. Then the degree-holder takes the bar exam to prove s/he can competently apply what s/he was taught. Most genealogical education programs offer a "certificate" upon completion. A certificate could mean that you took one class, as with the NGS (National Genealogical Society) or BU (Boston University) options. It could mean that you took an intensive week-long institute on a specialized topic, such as those at GenFed (Genealogical Institute on Federal Records). It could mean that you enrolled in a years-long program of study requiring many courses to complete a degree-level certificate, as with NIGS (National Institute for Genealogical Studies) or the Family History–Genealogy degree at BYU (Brigham Young University). Linda Debe's blog post[612] … BU does not offer certification and taking the course is definitely not a guarantee that a student will pass independent certification/ credentialing exams administered in the U.S. by BCG (Board for Certification of Genealogists) and ICAPGen (International Commission for the Accreditation of Professional Genealogists).'*[613]

Code of Conduct or Ethics

Is there a need for a Code of Conduct or Ethics in genealogy, such as those devised by professions such as doctors, nurses, and lawyers? A Code of Conduct should be, '...*a central guide and reference to assist day-to-day decision making. It is meant to clarify an organization's mission, values and principles, linking them with standards of professional conduct... and can refer to a listing of required behaviours, the violation of which would result in disciplinary action. In practice, used interchangeably with Code of Ethics.*'[614]

As a comparison, the International Council of Nurses (ICN) Code of Ethics for Nurses, '...*is a guide for action based on social values and needs. The Code has served as the standard for nurses worldwide since 1953... The Code makes it clear that inherent in nursing is respect for human rights, including the right to life, to dignity and to be treated with respect. The ICN Code of Ethics guides nurses in everyday choices and it supports their refusal to participate in activities that conflict with caring and healing.*'[615]

This code is based on four ethical principles, which constitute the main domains of responsibility within which ethical issues are considered.

- respect
- competence
- responsibility
- integrity

Similarly, the UK's General Medical Council (GMC) state that 'Good Medical Practice'[616] describes what it means to be a good doctor, stating that doctors will:

- make the care of your patient your first concern
- be competent and keep your professional knowledge and skills up to date
- take prompt action if you think patient safety is being compromised
- establish and maintain good partnerships with your patients and colleagues
- maintain trust in you and the profession by being open, honest and acting with integrity

Doctors must make sure that their practice meets the standards expected of them, in four domains[617]

- knowledge, skills and performance
- safety and quality
- communication, partnership and teamwork
- maintaining trust

Does genealogy require a Code of Ethics? Can a genealogist have a philosophical debate about an issue, then reconcile their dilemmas on their own? Should they join with others to discuss these issues? Should genealogists have to undertake an academic course, then join a professional body and be accountable? What are the roles of professional bodies?

Professional Bodies

There are now a number of professional bodies that genealogists can potentially join. Some require qualifications, some require proven experience, some require a portfolio, and some require a mix of the three.

It appears that the first to be founded, in 1940, was The American Society of Genealogists (ASG), which is, *'an independent society of fellows, and is dedicated to serving the discipline of genealogy through promoting the highest standards of genealogical scholarship... Election as a Fellow of the ASG is dependent on nomination by current Fellows - external nominations are not considered.'*[618]

The ASG purposes are:

- to advance genealogical research standards and to encourage publication of the results
- to secure recognition of genealogy as a serious subject of research in the historical and social fields of learning

In 1968, AGRA (The Association of Genealogists and Researchers in Archives)[619] was founded in the UK, and their website states that it is, *'the professional organisation promoting high professional standards in the field of genealogy and historical research in England and Wales. AGRA is also prominent as a representative voice in matters relating to genealogy. All of our Members and Associates agree to abide by a stringent Code of Practice.'*[620] They also have a formal Complaints Procedure.[621] Find My Past explicitly recommend AGRA by stating on their website, *'If you're interested in commissioning an expert to do your family history research for you, Find My Past recommends the Association of Genealogists and Researchers in Archives. AGRA's members are experts in genealogy, heraldry and record searching and have high standards of expertise and professional conduct. Every member of AGRA has proved their competence and accepted AGRA's code of practice.'*[622] However, this is a dilemma, as many genealogists are a member of other professional bodies, but Find My Past explicitly recommend just one.

In August 1979, George Williams, on behalf of the Federation of Genealogical Societies (FGS), USA, developed the Genealogists' Code of Ethics. *'Asking legislatures to open vital records to genealogists deserved a commitment that the members of genealogical societies could use and care for these records in a professional manner. The first member society to adopt the Code was the Genealogical Society of Washtenaw County,*

Washington.'[623] One of the purposes of FGS shall be to 'promote ethical standards in genealogical research and practices.' (3.01D)[624]

In 1979, the Association of Professional Genealogists (APG) USA[625] was registered in the state of Utah, as, *'a non-profit corporation, to become a professional body capable of focusing the efforts of the professional genealogists worldwide... Membership is open to any person or institution willing to support the objectives and the APG Code of Ethics.'*[626] APG's home page states that it is, *'an international organization dedicated to supporting those engaged in the business of genealogy through advocacy, collaboration, education, and the promotion of high ethical standards.'*[627] The APG has devised Standards of Professionalism, whereby, *'a professional genealogist should always produce work that meets an acceptable professional standard.'*[628] The APG has a formal Complaints and Disciplinary Procedure.

The APG Code of Ethics and Professional Practices[629] serves to promote:

- a truthful approach to genealogy, family history, and local history
- the trust and security of genealogical consumers
- careful and respectful treatment of records, repositories and their staffs, other professionals, and genealogical organizations and associations

In 1981, The Association of Scottish Genealogists and Researchers in Archives (ASGRA) was founded under the patronage of the Lord Lyon King of Arms. *'ASGRA members are highly-qualified, and have many years' experience in carrying out research in Scottish archives, and assisting clients worldwide to discover their Scottish ancestry. Many members have individual expertise in particular regions, time periods or types of research, and several are published authors in the field of genealogy, social and local history. Members are required to prove their competence in using a wide variety of sources, and to adhere to a strict Code of Practice. Clients hiring an ASGRA member can be assured of receiving a professional, thorough and reliable service.'*[630] The ASGRA Code of Practice[631] was devised in partnership with Accredited Genealogists Ireland, and states that, *'It is expected of professional genealogists that they will adhere strictly to recognised research procedures, always seeking to maintain the highest standards of accuracy. Both in their research work and in their dealings, they will seek to uphold the integrity of the profession and to enhance its best interests...'* They have a formal Complaints Procedure (July 2006).

In 1986, Accredited Genealogists Ireland (AGI), (formerly the Association of Professional Genealogists in Ireland) was founded, which, *'...acts as a regulating body to maintain high standards amongst its members and to protect the interests of clients. Our members are drawn from every part of Ireland and represent a wide variety of interests and expertise. The ongoing involvement of individual members in lecturing and publishing maintains our position at the forefront of genealogical developments in Ireland.'*[632] The

AGI Code of Practice[633] was published 27 May, 2015. The AGI has a formal Complaints Investigation Procedure[634] and a Complaints Investigation Panel.[635]

In 1988, The International Association of Jewish Genealogical Societies (IAJGS) was formed, as, *'an organization of organizations to provide a common voice for issues of significance to its members, to advance our genealogical avocation, and to coordinate items such as the annual International Conference on Jewish Genealogy.'*[636] The Code of Conduct/ Ethics statement was approved by the IAJGS Board of Directors, 2 November, 2002, amended on 6 August 2016, and amended most recently on 13 June, 2017. The Code of Good Practices includes an updated version (in more modern English) of the late (died 5 January, 1994) Rabbi Malcolm Stern's 'Ten Commandments in Genealogy'[637] *'which remains as relevant today as when they were penned years ago.'*[638]

From 1997 to 2000, The Board for Certification of Genealogists (BCG) analysed, defined, and combined the best genealogy practices and created the Genealogical Proof Standard.[639] In 2000, BCG published The BCG Genealogical Standards Manual, which was updated in 2014.[640] Each individual seeking certification signs the Genealogist's Code, a pledge to act in every way to protect the public, clients (whether paying or pro bono), and the profession.[641] The Board of Certification states that, *'Both professional genealogists and casual family researchers need genealogy standards in order to get their genealogy right. Without standards, inaccuracies and myths can be created and perpetuated. Many of these errors can be avoided by working to genealogy standards. Each individual seeking certification signs the Genealogist's Code, a pledge to act in every way to protect the public, clients (whether paying or pro bono), and the profession.'*[642]

To reach a sound conclusion, genealogists need to meet all five components of The Genealogical Proof Standard[643] (GPS):

1. reasonably exhaustive research
2. complete and accurate source citations
3. thorough analysis and correlation
4. resolution of conflicting evidence
5. soundly written conclusion based on the strongest evidence

In 2000, The Accredited Genealogist® credential of the Genealogical Society of Utah (GSU) was transferred to the International Commission of the Accreditation of Professional Genealogists (ICAPGen[SM]).[644] The Mission Statement of ICAPGen explains that their aim is, *'to advance family history/ genealogy work around the world by accrediting and promoting genealogy professionals who are competent, ethical, and reliable, and to support the preservation of and access to genealogical materials.'*[645] AG professionals have demonstrated various knowledge and proficiencies[646] and are expected to adhere to high professional standards[647] at all times. They are required to sign a Professional Ethics Agreement when they first become accredited, and again every five years when they renew their credential(s). Members sign that they will adhere to

ICAPGen's Code of Ethics[648] which includes protection of the public, the consumer (client or colleague), and the profession.

The Register of Qualified Genealogists was founded in the UK, on 31 December, 2015, and, *'provides, and makes public, a record of those genealogists who hold a recognised qualification in the field of genealogy and associated practices, and who may be willing to provide professional services in that field... The purpose is therefore an enabling one on behalf of qualified genealogists, and is three-fold, serving the needs of customers for genealogical services, of individual practitioners and of the genealogical community.'*[649] The RQG has a Professional Code[650] which is an element of the Register to which Qualified Genealogists are expected to adhere.

The Code encompasses the following three core statements of values,[651] which underpin acceptable Genealogical Practice, which states that, as a Qualified Genealogist you are committed to striving for excellence and will:

- continue to develop and maintain your professional knowledge and competence, and remain committed to advancing your genealogical education and awareness of current genealogical issues
- carry out and deliver work to a competent standard to the best of your ability and capacity, through the use of close dialogue, robust research methods, clear written analyses and explanations of results and conclusions reached
- behave with integrity and uphold the reputation of the profession and the register

The RQG has a Resolution Procedure, which is overseen by a director. Durie stated that, *'There is no question that genealogy is heading towards becoming a mature, qualified profession, and a recognised academic discipline. The Register of Qualified Genealogists is a first step on a long path to bring this to fruition. Of course, it will take a generation, but genealogy is all about generations.'*[652]

Many people have come to genealogy through it being a hobby undertaken for many years; others have branched into genealogy from a discipline such as archiving, librarianship or lecturing, so they have many different backgrounds. The ASG notes that, professional genealogical work is not legally regulated at any level.[653] Different professional bodies have different requirements, some require experience, some require academic courses, some a mix. The word 'professional' has many implications. *'A person's work ethic is a representation of his character. A strong work ethic suggests that the person places a high value on doing a good job, as well as respecting others and functioning with integrity. Professionalism is a component of the concept of work ethic, which describes how a person comes to work and conducts himself on the job.'*[654] What can genealogists do, if asked to undertake what they consider is an unethical request? Some genealogical work crosses over with that of a Private Investigator. Solutions to specific ethical scenarios are not clearly defined anywhere.

The ethical genealogist

'Talking about professional ethics puts you on a high moral platform and encourages the other person to either join you or look up to you.'[655] We all think that we're a 'nice' person, and aren't involved in being unethical. As a relatively new discipline, however, ethical issues within genealogy are starting to become visible more, especially since DNA testing, and therefore many and varied ethical dilemmas will follow, some of which may be helped by studying accredited courses and/ or joining a professional body, but inevitably some of these ethical issues will have legal implications. So, what are the differences between ethical issues and moral issues in business? *'By definition, morals are values that we attribute to a system of beliefs, be they religious, political or philosophical, for example. Ethics are how business owners apply those beliefs in their short and long-term business decisions. As a result, these concepts inevitably are intertwined and must be applied carefully to maintain an image of professionalism and accountability.'*[656]

The ethical genealogist should ideally respect human rights, values, customs and spiritual beliefs of the individual, family and community. Ethical Decision-Making includes:[657]

- addressing the impact of the action or decision on others or relationships with them (altruistic considerations)
- determination of the 'right thing to do' - as defined by the values and principles which apply to this situation (idealistic considerations)
- potential consequences of the action or decision (individualistic considerations)
- business consequences of this action or decision (pragmatic considerations)

After You're Gone: Future Proofing Your Genealogy Research

My tree is on a couple of websites, with my password a coveted secret; my photographs are all in a huge box under the bed, and I will put names and dates on them at some stage, when I'm in my retirement home with my best friend; and my certificates are in a file in a completely different area of the house, next to my Psychology books and genealogy magazines. Any descendants interested in my family tree are going to have a struggle on their hands.

Thomas MacEntee expertly advised that, *'Try as we might, we really have little control over what will happen to our possessions, even our bodies, after we die. Yes, we can draw up legal documents, we can express our wishes to family members and more; however, there are no guarantees when it comes to these matters. The best we can do is prepare, plan and communicate now. When it comes to years of genealogy research and material that you have accumulated, what plans have you made to ensure that this legacy does not die with you? In 'After You're Gone: Future Proofing Your Genealogy Research,' you will find valuable advice on creating a realistic plan to get your "genealogy affairs" in order. Make sure that the next generation of researchers can benefit from your years of hard work and following your passion.'*[658]

MacEntee's informative book covers a wide range of topics including:

- the perils of inaction: lost genealogy
- action plan options
- getting organized
- taking inventory
- working with societies, libraries and archives
- technology to the rescue
- best practices for genealogy future proofing

The changing shape of family life

As family historians, we are used to established shapes and cultural norms for our society and the subsequent genealogical research. However, different practices are arising, and will change the future shape of society somewhat.

Transgender

When people change gender, what would you do about recording their name and sex in your tree? Feelings can run high, for example, singer and 'X Factor' programme judge Robbie Williams asked someone their name before their transition on the UK programme, which a number of viewers objected to. Shane Riley said: *'Speaking as a trans guy myself @robbiewilliams should've thought twice about asking Felix his dead name. It's invasive and just damn rude.'* And Alex Station said, *'...has No-one told Robbie Williams it's considered pretty darn rude to ask someone's birth name? That's quite an on-the-spot situation to be put in, having to explain oneself.'*[659]

A question recently posed on a website explained that, *'I know someone who is in transition. How should they be represented in a family tree? Do you change their gender but add a note documenting their transition? Do you change their gender and do nothing else? Also curious to know others opinions on people who decide to remain gender neutral.'*[660]

Replies included:

- *'I try to stress that my family tree work is apolitical; that means that I will show the facts... I would list the person as the gender they were born as, and include the change in that person's notes. It's too exhausting trying to tiptoe around every person's feelings.'*

- *'Consider the case of Bruce/ Caitlyn Jenner. Married three women at a time when same-sex marriages were illegal, and fathered six children. Putting Jenner as a woman in a family tree would be highly inaccurate from a genealogical perspective.'*
- *'Ask them! You can't guess what they'll say, and I argue you have no right to decide in their place.'*

IVF

In vitro fertilisation (IVF) is one of several techniques available to help people with fertility problems have a baby. During IVF, an egg is removed from the woman's ovaries and fertilised with sperm in a laboratory. The fertilised egg, called an embryo, is then returned to the woman's womb to grow and develop.[661] The first baby in the UK to be conceived by IVF was recently forty years old, in July 2018. *'For nine frustrating years, Lesley and John Brown tried to conceive a child but failed... On July 25, 1978, the Browns got what they had long wished for with the arrival of a daughter, Louise, a baby like no other the world had seen.'*[662] Brown and her long-term publicist, Martin Powell, of Empica PR, have written a book, *'My Life As the World's First Test-Tube Baby.'*[663] They explained that, *'At 11.47pm on July 25th 1978, Louise Brown was the first person ever to be born through science rather than as the result of two people having sex... For the first time Louise tells the story of her world changing birth and its impact on her life.'*

Permission to include given by (c) Martin Powell and Bristol Books
Photographer: Neil Phillips

There is a YouTube video, 'Louise Brown, My life as the world's first test-tube baby'[664] that can be viewed. Some comments posted in response to the video showing Louise's birth include[665]

- *how was this baby born in a test tube?⬚*
- *whoever is like this baby should be proud of who they are⬚*
- *she is in my science textbook⬚*
- *oh wow, they cut the mom fast and just ripped the baby out... And why are they posing with the baby like it's a prize and not handing it to the Mama?? Cool science, dubious about the practices*
- *fraud. the first test tube baby was one from India by a scientist named Subhas something*
- *why are you not satisfied with your children? Why do you splice their DNA to become something that will die in forty years? It's like you've taken their freedom. The freedom of life.*
- *the sacrament of Marriage was given for the union of man and woman in love and godliness. There is nothing godly about a man who sets himself up to play God. They must know that you cannot bring life in a test tube. This will not be accepted by Heaven. These children are not conceived by the Holy Ghost, the spirit within them at the moment of conception, because their conception is from a test tube, and an instrument of a so-called doctor upon earth. Your understanding of God is grossly mistaken⬚*
- *ok, up to this point, I'm fine with, but nowadays, they want to create a half-human, half-animal baby, that, I cannot stand to let happen⬚*
- *I thought they didn't clone a human yet⬚*

* huge range of comments there *

Bristol Museums has compiled 'The Lesley Brown Collection' because Lesley Brown was born in Bristol, UK. *'Many people from around the world sent cards and letters to the Brown family, including other women who had suffered fertility problems...The collection features photographs, films and mementoes from the Browns' travels to IVF events abroad. There are also letters from the scientists and doctors who treated Lesley Brown.'*[666] The catalogue for the papers of Lesley Brown (ref. 45827)[667] is available online, and available for research in their public search room during opening hours.

Is IVF a step towards the realm of 'designer babies'? The incorrect label 'test tube baby' can cause fear amongst people, and reportedly caused people to tease (and be very intrusive towards) Louise Brown. Grace MacDonald,[668] a Scottish woman, who gave birth to the second in vitro baby, in January 1979, didn't draw such a media circus. Louise's story is part of a much wider debate about IVF.[669] More modern developments in genetics have raised the moral, ethical and political stakes. What other methods can be used in the future to have a baby?

Donor conception

Donor conception is seldom a topic people think of when they think about genealogy.[670] It was common for recipients of donor gametes to be told there was little or no chance of the truth being revealed. Many were advised not to tell their children anything about their origins. Commercial DNA testing is causing problems regarding the industry's former standard of secrecy. Now, donor conceived adults are taking DNA tests and discovering that they were conceived using donor eggs, sperm, or embryo. Biological parents' relatives may be revealed through DNA testing, and wider family may be unaware that they have a relative who donated gametes.

Sperm donation is the provision (or donation) by a man of his sperm, principally for it to be used in the artificial insemination of a woman or women who are not his sexual partners for the purpose of achieving a pregnancy. Sperm may be donated privately and directly to the intended recipient, or through a sperm bank or fertility clinic.[671] Some people are now looking for their sperm donor father. This is portrayed in a reflective film, 'Thank You For Coming.'[672] Documentary filmmaker Sara Lamm, *'learned as an adult that she was conceived via sperm donor; it's taken eleven years, twelve DNA tests, five ancestry databases, one potential half-sister, and nine hundred sixth-cousins to (maybe) find her biological father. 'Thank You For Coming' is a genealogical detective story and a funny, bittersweet meditation on love, loss, and family.'[673]* Whilst the documentary is enlightening, one critic commented that, *'I felt somewhat repelled by her self-absorbed attachment to concepts involving blood and biology. It seemed gratuitous on her part to have to point out to her Dad that with her mom's death, and Sara's move to live with Dad and his new partner, she was an 'orphan' no longer related biologically to anyone in her household. 'What do we have in common?' she asks him. 'We share a life together,' he answers.'[674]* Also, Colin (the film maker's 'step' father) stated that *'Sara's mom would not be happy that this secret fact in the family history is being unearthed.'[675]*

People in this situation can consult the 'We Are Donor Conceived' website, which was launched in 2016, *'as a resource center for donor conceived people around the globe. It's also a place where donor conceived people can share their stories with each other and the general public in order to inspire greater understanding about the unique challenges we face'[676]* and they have a supportive Facebook group[677] created on 5 November 2016, with 1,133 members during April, 2019. Another Facebook group, DNA for the Donor Conceived[678] aims to give guidance in using DNA to locate biological family for individuals who are donor conceived and for donors searching for their biological children, and is a subgroup of The DNA Detectives. It was created on 1 August 2016, is a closed group, and had 1,855 members during April, 2019.

Many mothers may not inform the child that they were conceived through sperm donation, but it could be considered wrong not to reveal this information. Ethical dilemmas here include that some people may feel a genealogical void when told, and it could be argued that it is a human right for a person to know who their biological father is, and children conceived this way may want to trace their biological father. Is a sperm donor a father in the established sense of the word? Gordon commented that, *'When you know nothing about the biological background of one of your parents, it's easy to see how that search could become addictively all-consuming - and a suitable subject for a film.'*[679]

Some children whose parents had inheritable illnesses feel that they had worried needlessly throughout their lives, as they were not their biological child. Should the child over-ride their parent's wishes not to investigate their sperm donor father? Should sperm donors expect to be contacted years later by biological children? A sperm donor revealed on Facebook that he'd fathered one hundred and fifty children across America thanks to his 'super seed'[680] One mother summed up her dilemmas, writing that, *'My son looks a lot like me; but does he look like you? You were chosen because your profile matched my partner... You have no legal right over my son - you are not his parent... But I like the thought that he has another 'family' out there who share a bit of him. A family with a kind person in it whose act of generosity gave him life.'*[681]

Terms such as 'biological' or 'genetic' parent are used to refer to the parent(s) the donor conceived person is genetically related to. While 'legal' or 'social' parent is often used in reference to the non-biological parent(s) or the parent(s) that raised the child. Some people may argue that donor conceived people's social parents are their 'real' parents and that they should not care about their donor/ biological origin. A solution may be to use terms (being led by what the donor conceived person has said) to avoid confusion or upset.[682]

In the UK, the law changed in 2005 to give those conceived via donor eggs or sperm the right to their donor's contact information at the age of 18. Those born before 1991 are able to access the Donor Conceived Register[683] but this is dependent on both donor and child being on the register. In other countries, 'known,' 'open' or 'ID release' donors cost more than anonymous ones. Many countries around the world allow donation of gametes only on a completely anonymous basis and couples from all countries travel to these places to have treatment. There are two interesting radio programmes that can be listened to: 'Finding my real dad,'[684] which is a radio programme, whereby a listener describes how he learned he was conceived by sperm donation.' And 'I'm not looking to be a father,'[685] which is a programme about a sperm donor on what he expects from meeting his son.

Where (if at all) would a sperm donor father be represented on a family tree?

Artificial insemination

The first recorded experiment with artificial insemination in humans occurred in the late 1700s, when Scottish-born surgeon John Hunter[686] impregnated a women with her husband's sperm, resulting in a successful pregnancy.[687] In 1884, American physician

William Pancoast[688] performed a modified artificial insemination procedure when he injected sperm from a donor into a woman who was under anaesthesia. The woman, who was married, gave birth to a baby nine months later, but did not know that she had been impregnated with donor sperm.

Fertility doctor, Donald Cline, from Indiana, USA, who used his own sperm to artificially inseminate his patients without their consent, has been confirmed to be the father of at least fifty children, many of whom only recently discovered this information.[689] A number of the adult children connected through matching after doing a DNA test, and have formed a Facebook group. Zhang reviewed the ethical dilemmas that have arisen, including the scenarios arising from potentially finding one or two half siblings, however, these people found many half siblings. She reported that one child conceived this way said that she, *'struggled with what it meant, existentially, to have inherited the DNA of a man who would lie to his patients. Whatever made him do it, was that inside her, too?'*[690] One adult daughter, Ballard, reflected that, *'Here was her biological father, but he radiated no paternal warmth.'* When the half siblings met, they debated why Cline had used his own sperm, including whether he was just trying to keep his business running, or whether he wanted to implement a master race. Rudavsky reported that one of the mothers, Liz White, explained that Cline had told her that he would use sperm from a young donor doctor, and that he had promised that he would use that donor for no more than three pregnancies.[691] White explained that, *'Our goal is to establish Cline's egregious behavior as a criminal law... It began as a medical procedure.... It radically changed to a sexually deviant behavior.'*[692]

Surrogacy

In the UK, 'mother's rights' are explained as, *'The woman who gives birth is always treated as the legal mother and has the right to keep the child, even if they're not genetically related. Surrogacy contracts aren't enforced by UK law, even if a contract has been signed with the intended parents and they've paid for any expenses. It's illegal to pay a surrogate in the UK, except for their reasonable expenses.'*[693] Father's rights' are explained as, *'The child's legal father or 'second parent' is the surrogate's husband or civil partner unless: legal rights are given to someone else through a parental order or adoption, the surrogate's husband or civil partner didn't give their permission to their wife or partner. If a surrogate has no partner, or they're unmarried and not in a civil partnership, the child will have no legal father or second parent unless the partner actively consents.'* In the USA, it appears that the legal aspects of surrogacy in any particular jurisdiction are based on three key questions[694] and that, in conclusion, laws differ widely from one jurisdiction to another.[695]

An ethical dilemma here is whether to include the surrogate mother on a family tree? There is no one correct method, typology or visual display rule set for displaying these new types of complex relationships on a family tree, the new methods of creating genetic lineage: sperm, egg, uterus donors or surrogates, but, for health professionals, there are some conventions that are used when producing a genogram.[696]

'Designer' babies

The colloquial term 'designer baby' refers to, *'a baby whose genetic makeup has been artificially selected by genetic engineering combined with in vitro fertilization to ensure the presence or absence of particular genes or characteristics... In simpler terms, using biotechnology to choose what type of baby you want.'*[697] It has been argued that, *'In the era of post-genomic medicine, our DNA is likely to be spliced and edited so we can all enjoy life-long bliss, awesome peak experiences.'*[698]

Ethical dilemmas here include that potentially only the rich could afford it, which could create another gap in society. Designing babies feels feasible because there is a better understanding of genetics now, however, geneticists are not perfect, and errors could occur. Genes often have more than one use, and donors may not know about this. There may be a termination of some embryos, and there is the possibility of damage to the gene pool. It theoretically reduces the risks of genetic diseases and inherited medical conditions, and could prevent subsequent generations of family from getting specific characteristics or diseases. The procedure can give a child genes that the parents do not carry. The resultant baby has no choice in the matter, and other children in the family could be affected by parents' decision. If specific genetic make ups become more popular, even trends occurring, then there could be a loss of individuality; a potential extreme version is a *'rigid hierarchy of genetically-preordained castes.'*[699]

Brave New World

Babies whose genetic makeup has been artificially selected by genetic engineering to ensure the presence or absence of particular genes or characteristics could lead to the Darwinian order of natural selection being lost.[700] English writer, novelist and philosopher, Aldous Huxley (1894 - 1963),[701] author of *'Brave New World,'* warned about this kind of 'interference' in nature being taken over by those with more sinister motives. Themes in his novels included disenchanted social commentary, a dystopic (undesirable or frightening) view of the future, iconoclasm (the social belief in the importance of the destruction of icons and other images or monuments, most frequently for religious or political reasons). The Brave New World is, *'... an unsettling, loveless and even sinister place... Brave New World doesn't, and isn't intended by its author to, evoke just how wonderful our lives could be if the human genome were intelligently rewritten... Nor does Huxley's comparatively sympathetic account of the life of the Savage on the Reservation convey just how nasty the old regime of pain, disease and unhappiness can be.'*[702]

Aldous Huxley's grandfather was zoologist and comparative anatomist Thomas Henry Huxley (1825–1895), and his brothers were Julian Huxley[703] (an evolutionist, and the first director of UNESCO), and Nobel laureate physiologist Andrew Huxley.[704] Discussions amongst the family must have influenced all their thoughts and ideas. Aldous' father, Thomas Huxley, gave lectures and published papers which analysed the zoological position of man, including, *'Evidence as to Man's Place in Nature'* (1863), which contained two themes: firstly, that humans are related to the great apes; and, secondly, that the species has evolved in a similar manner to all other forms of life. The sketches are amazing. An online book[705] is available free of charge to download. Pearce warns us that, *'...how does Huxley turn a future where we're all notionally happy into the archetypal dystopia? ... The savage is eager to embrace a way of life he neither knows nor understands. And of course he comes unstuck.'*[706]

Gregor Mendel's seminal writings about inheritance patterns (in peas), which would later shape and inform DNA research, had been rediscovered in 1900, and the eugenics movement, based on artificial selection, was well established when Huxley was working on 'Brave New World.' Eugenics[707] is a movement that is aimed at improving the genetic composition of the human race. Historically, eugenicists advocated selective breeding to achieve these goals. Today, we have technologies that make it possible to more directly alter the genetic composition of an individual. However, people differ in their views on how to best (and ethically) use this technology.

Eugenics

Designing families and babies can lead to what could be considered more sinister extremes. Rivard explained that, *'Committees were convened to offer solutions to the problem of the growing number of 'undesirables' in the U.S. population... While at first sterilization efforts targeted mentally ill people exclusively, later the traits deemed serious enough to warrant sterilization included alcoholism, criminality, chronic poverty, blindness, deafness, feeble-mindedness, and promiscuity. It was also not uncommon for African American women to be sterilized during other medical procedures without consent.'*[708] The logo from the Second International Eugenics Congress, held in New York during September, 1921, featured a tree, with the words, *'eugenics is the self-direction of human evolution.'* Heeding Huxley's warnings, it should be noted that, *'Early efforts to breed better human beings have not been uniformly successful... However, eugenicists have not agreed upon which heritable traits should selected - nor by whom. Nor have they agreed on whether to use encouragement or coercion.'*[709]

Notions of designer babies, eugenics and an emerging Brave New World leads to a discussion of humans' relationships with A.I. (artificial intelligence).

Marrying a robot

Robots and Artificial Intelligence are increasingly becoming accessible. People who have become intimate with robots or humanoids, may feel the need to prove this fondness or love to the wider community. *'When the day arrives that robots look and act just like us, will marriage between humans and robots become acceptable? Is this the cure for those looking for love and companionship?'*[710] Clark felt that marrying your robot could benefit, '*shy people who are uncomfortable meeting others... the mentally ill and people who have unpleasant personalities.'*[711] People may not feel the need for human contact but still want a relationship. Marchant explains that, '*The era of love and sex with robots has begun and will continue to accelerate going forward, even if it remains a minority choice for the next couple of decades. But with sex and love will come calls for the right to marry. Indeed, there are already examples of people (OK, men) who want or claim to be married to their robot.'*[712]

David Levy, who won the 2009 Loebner prize (an annual competition based on the 'Turing test'[713] that, when communicating only via a keyboard, a judge should have trouble distinguishing the software responses from a human being's responses) has written the book, '*Love and Sex with Robots,'*[714] in which he claims that this practice will be routine by 2050. Prior to this, Levy's doctoral thesis researched sociology, sexology, robotics, artificial intelligence and other fields related to marriage, love and robots. Schofield concluded that all of the most important factors that cause humans to fall in love with one another could be programmed into robots.[715] Clark predicted that, '*...by 2050, robots and humans will be able to marry legally in the United States... Massachusetts will lead the way as it did in 2004, when it became the first state to allow same-sex marriages.'*[716] Murphy predicted that, '*... law makers will have to change legislation to allow robots to wed as society begins to view artificially intelligent machines in a different way... by the time there are no obstacles, the sex robots we are familiar with will become even more human-like and kind, protecting and loving. But one major obstacle in the UK will be the Church...'*[717]

However, Hanley argued that robot marriage is idiocy, '*Supposedly, marrying a robot is something 'the law must address.' But robots are programmed. Period. Can a robot ever have agency to give consent to sex or marriage? For that to happen, a human must program the cybernetics to appear to want to do that. If you think that this programming means that a robot has agency to marry, then you must believe that the same robot can decide to divorce. And if it can marry and divorce, then it must be able to get alimony/ palimony, child custody, and child support.'*[718] And Payton concluded that, '*marrying robots is a terrible idea.'*[719]

It appears that people can marry robots, and are doing so. Lah reported that, '*A 27-year-old Tokyo man 'married' Nene Anegasaki, a computer avatar... a videogame character in the Nintendo DS game called 'Love Plus.' The wedding was viewed live online by thousands in Japan... The wedding, while not legally binding, was Sal's way of expressing his devotion to his avatar girlfriend... Sal says Nene is better than a human girlfriend. She doesn't get angry if I'm late in replying to her. Well, she gets angry, but she forgives me quickly... With Nene, Sal doesn't feel the need to find a human girlfriend, he added.'*[720] Online dating could be seen as heading towards this situation, where you choose an ideal partner.

Marchant[721] observed that interracial marriage, equality between husband and wife, and same-sex marriage have now been legalised, and therefore robot marriage, polygamy or plural marriages may be legalised. Lynn quirkily commented that there are many potential benefits to marrying a robot,[722] including them having an off switch (and so would your parents in law), they last forever until the battery runs out, and can be a personal trainer for sex. Payton argued that marrying a robot may be legalised in the future, but the 'love' of a robot is, *'kept alive by delusion, but on its own it falls apart and rusts. To legalize robot-human nuptials would be to redefine marriage as a mechanism of self-gratification, and would perpetuate the delusion that self-love is real love.'*[723] But, has a robot any agency in these situations; compare to films 'Ex Machina'[724] (where a young programmer is selected to participate in a ground-breaking experiment in synthetic intelligence by evaluating the human qualities of a breath-taking humanoid A.I.); 'Lars and the Real Girl'[725] (where a delusional young man strikes up an unconventional relationship with a doll he finds on the Internet); and 'Human'[726] (which involves a collection of stories about and images of our world, offering an immersion to the core of what it means to be human).

A reporter, interviewing a married man who has a sexual relationship with his robot, asked whether it would be considered an affair if you are already married?[727] The husband said he would have a hard time choosing between his wife and the doll if he was forced to, and the wife pointed out that *'if he really wanted to he could have gone out and found someone else but he didn't do that, he was true to me…'* Computer scientist Noel Sharkey, who works for the Foundation of Responsible Robotics[728] (who also commentate about drones), has warned of the dangers of sex robots, claiming that the technology will make sex easier to obtain, and permanently change society. If there is a potential for robots to reproduce, would it be a robot child, or a host for a human child, or a mix? How would people annotate robots on a tree for example, date of birth, death dates? Who would the robot's parents and ancestors be?

Undertaking genealogy research in the future

It could be argued that people should decide who their children have children with, predicting the future, rather than recording and analysing the past. Some cultures rely on 'arranged marriages,' whereby the parents and wider family choose a marital family for their child. This can be a contentious issue within cultures that rely on marriage through love. With the availability of contraceptives, many people can now theoretically plan pregnancies, and have an element of control over the numbers of future children. Many women work outside the home, so have fewer children, as they have to juggle home and work. Same sex marriages may result in children from one of the partners at a time, or the couple could have a baby through surrogacy. These scenarios all have implications for the future of genealogy.

A 1988 episode of Star Trek[729] which is based in the 24th century, shows the crew in the year 2364 finding three frozen people from the past, who were then taken into the Star

Ship's sick bay and resuscitated, (see Series 1, Episode 26, from 8 minutes in), including 'Clare Raymond, 35, homemaker' (played by Gracie Harrison), who really missed her family.[730] The ship's counsellor showed her how her descendants were doing, in an automated collection of information about them (41 minutes in). She was shocked to see a photograph and information about a man who she assumed was her son, as he had the same name and surname, but he was, in fact, what would have been a very far distant descendent, although they were both now alive at the same time because of her having been frozen. When she was told she could visit him when they landed, she sadly thought she wouldn't, as she'd be *a relic*, but the counsellor remarked that she should get in touch with him, because *he was family.*

Whilst many genealogy sites provide matching hints that their computer program has found, it seems inevitable that much of the work will be done for us, in the future. A computerised chip on a grave headstone[731] could allow a visitor to look up the deceased and find a biography, pictures and other information. It may well be the case that all new babies will have DNA taken at birth, and that information will be stored, so we could immediately assess relationships. A father in the delivery suite would immediately know about paternity. You probably wouldn't have to draw up a family tree, as a hospital computer program will have already done that for you.

****

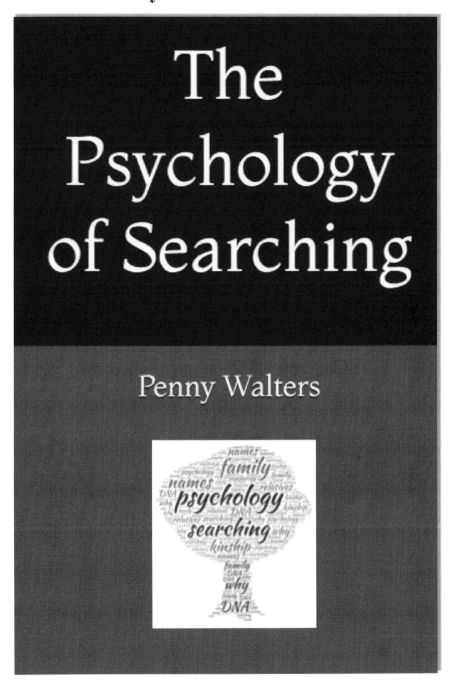

The Psychology of Searching

Penny Walters

ISBN: 9781687167262

Facebook review

Peggy Clemens Lauritzen, USA

I wish there had been a book like this when I first began doing serious genealogy research.

I received this book about 2-3 weeks ago, and really took my time perusing through its pages. The information we find in tracing our families and connecting with the living has taken on a completely different meaning than the world of scrolling through microfilms and visiting dusty courthouses that I grew up with.

Penny Walters has brought up several scenarios that causes some serious questioning about ethics that I personally feel are becoming even more and more important. Let me tell you about some things that really caught my attention in the book, and caused me to do some thinking:
1. The reasons people choose not to share a tree, or to make it public
2. Secrets and lies you may uncover in your tree, or others
3. DNA and misattributed paternity (MAP)
4. When and why do people want to find their birth family?
5. Names and surnames which become offensive
6. Code of conduct or ethics
7. Future proofing your genealogy

Penny has done an excellent job of providing 26 pages of references at the end of the book. I put checkmarks beside many of them that I want to remember; and they join the checkmarks that are sprinkled throughout the book. Yes, I mark up my books.

Penny has been a university lecturer for over 30 years, and earned her Doctorate and investigated "Ethical Dilemmas in Health Promotion". Being adopted at birth, she can certainly relate to many of the scenarios in her book.

There were several times that what she had written had me thinking so deeply, I went back and read it again. Will it help you in your research? Maybe. Will it help you be a better genealogist? Yes.

My own summation; it doesn't matter who's right. It matters what is right.

Great job, Penny! Really, really great job.

Thank you very much, Miss Peggy

Amazon Reviews of 'Ethical Dilemmas in Genealogy'

29 May 2019. Australia. 'Ethical Dilemmas in Genealogy' is a good book to read.
5***

This book actually made me stop and think about the relationship between ethics and genealogy. How do you handle the secrets of your family that you uncover with your research? This book also covers DNA and the surprises that you might uncover after you test members of your family. Whether you are just starting your family history or you have been researching for many years. Genealogy has changed because of DNA and what it is revealing.

31 May 2019. UK. Really interesting book
5***

This was a really interesting read, and gave many good insights into some of the problems that can arise from doing your tree. Would definitely recommend this book.

18 June 2019. UK. A must-read informative, fascinating and practical guide to researching your family history
5***

A great resource for anyone wanting to research their tree - or get DNA tested. What if you are not quite from the line you thought you were, you unintentionally upset family members with your search. ... think it couldn't happen to you? This book is a sensible and clear guide to the sorts of issues which can present themselves in researching family background - a reassuring guide that no matter what sensational finds you uncover (or not) you can search freely and how to talk to others around you so that you can all enjoy and learn from your own personal slice of history.

22 July 2019. USA. The "think" that should come first, not later
5***

Genealogy is fraught with tripping points. We get excited about each "find" and sometimes do not think ahead to what our research may lead to, for ourselves and for someone else. DNA has thrown us into the deep end, in many cases too much too soon; and the literature, research has not kept up. This book gives you a starting place to discuss ethics with fellow genealogists, family members who tend to overshare, and helping professionals who may want to take on softening the blow for folks with unexpected discoveries. Penny Walters brings personal experience to the areas of adoption and ethnic diversity. We can all be reminded of the many ways to do the right thing. An important book for all genealogists.

31 July 2019. USA. Covers a lot of topics - both genealogy and DNA-related
5*****

This was a great book that covers a broad range of ethical topics that should be considered by people who engage in genealogy, especially those who are considering or have already ordered DNA testing. It also covers special topics that commonly arise in genealogy, like adoptions.

10 August 2019. UK. A 'go to' resource
5*****

A really handy reference guide for anyone researching their own or the families of others or doing social research. The dilemma of whether to take a DNA test is becoming more prevalent and when you are dealing with the possibility of adoption or doubtful biological parenting in your results, this is a great resource. I liked the fact that you got to learn a little about the author and her own dilemmas whilst looking for blood relatives. As well as looking at the inferences and possible dilemmas with DNA testing, it also explains the science of it layman's terms. Lots of resources as well. Glad it's on my reference bookshelf.

13 August 2019. UK. Wise words and a thought-provoking read for genealogists
5*****

From the very start of her thought-provoking book, Dr Penny Walters asks probing questions about our favourite pastime; is genealogy a 'hobby' or a duty, and why do we feel so passionate about researching those who came before? Penny points out that we all have challenging decisions to make when investigating our family history, and choosing the best solution can become an ethical dilemma – especially in the modern era when the internet and DNA have revolutionised family history and made genealogy so accessible. From finding unverified online trees and new living relatives on social media, to discovering photo- or data-poaching or getting the bad feeling you may have coerced someone into taking a DNA test; there are a multitude of theoretical trap doors for modern-day family historians that can cause worry, upset and have unforeseen consequences.
Penny uses real-life examples to give the wisest researcher pause for thought and provides practical approaches and sage advice, including from knowledgeable genealogists working in the sector today. Whether you need to know how best to share or collaborate on your family history, trace adoptees or biological relatives, correct errors, choose a DNA test or deal with a new-found family secret that's too hot to handle, this is an absolute treasure of an ethical 'guide book' for the 21st-century family history researcher.
Also covering matters of identity and how to future-proof your research, it is a refreshing read that reminds us of the importance and value of being an ethical genealogist, enjoying our hobby while being mindful of the rights of others and the impact our actions may have on real lives. For passionate family history fans, it's well worth remembering that one man's meat is

another man's poison – even if those we are researching are in the past. A version of this review appeared in the August 2019 issue of the UK 'Family Tree' magazine.

6 January 2020. USA. This book is a check point for those researching in family history or genealogy!
5***

Overall this book is a very good guide for how we research in genealogy whether for our own families, for friends or clients. Penny does an excellent job of explaining what the ethical dilemmas can be and how to process carefully how we determine if we should share them privately or publicly. My yellow highlighters quickly ran out of ink as I tried to note the main points of the book. By reading the book I believe I will be more sensitive to how the material found may impact one person or many. Thank you Penny for coming forward and authoring such a needed book.

26 January, 2020, USA. Important book when studying genealogy and personal history
5***

As a 20+ year genealogist and 10+ year military research professional, I purchased Penny's book to explore the deeper layers of this work I do, that most of us do, that people are not as willing to discuss. As I move more into energy healing, ancestral lineage healing and helping families explore family patterns and go deeper than names, dates, places, battles, etc., Penny's book shed light on areas in which I have not worked or needed to consider, like Adoption.

Now working with adoptees through private facilitation sessions, I have more tools in my toolbox to help them navigate their journey. I have more questions to ask as they write their stories and explore their personal truths. The remainder of Penny's book also provides a lot of questions we can ask ourselves or our clients. Broader questions I think that should be discussed in the larger genealogy community also - something many are afraid to do because of taboo subjects and worries about offending someone. I think if we set those things aside and open up to these important questions, we can change and heal so much in our families and histories and the world.

Penny's book is one I will be recommending to my clients and using further in my many projects, classes, webinars, and research work. Highly recommend.

****

References

Chapter 1

[1] Quora. Chris MacDonald. What are some examples of ethical dilemmas? https://www.quora.com/What-are-some-examples-of-ethical-dilemmas : accessed 9 November, 2018

[2] The Ethics and Compliance Initiative. Glossary. http://www.ethics.org/resources/free-toolkit/toolkit-glossary : accessed 13 September, 2018

[3] Reference. Popular Hobbies. https://www.reference.com/world-view/popular-hobbies-america-2cf05a1805290f1 : accessed 13 June, 2018

[4] GenealogyInTime Magazine. How popular is genealogy? http://www.genealogyintime.com/articles/how-popular-is-genealogy-page01.html : accessed 30 December, 2018

[5] People's World. Eric A. Gordon 'Thank You for Coming': A sperm donor's daughter searches for identity. June 12, 2017. http://www.peoplesworld.org/article/thank-you-for-coming-a-sperm-donors-daughter-searches-for-identity/ : accessed 14 October, 2018

[6] International Association of Jewish Genealogical Societies. Blog. Code of Conduct. http://www.iajgs.org/blog/code-of-conduct/ : accessed 30 December, 2018

[7] The New Republic. The Mormon Church Is Building a Family Tree of the Entire Human Race. https://newrepublic.com/article/119785/extensive-mormon-genealogy-offers-limited-vision-history : accessed 8 July, 2018

[8] Jamaican Family Search. Patricia Jackson. http://www.jamaicanfamilysearch.com/Samples/Biograp.htm : accessed 21 May 2019

[9] NECN. Natasha Verma. Hundreds Gather for Cardinal O'Malley's Christmas Sermon in Boston. Posted 25 December, 2018. https://www.necn.com/news/new-england/Hundreds-Gather-for-Cardinal-OMalley-Sermon-in-Boston-503477251.html?fbclid=IwAR0miFrXedadIAZNek9YnWT7haSdAV7HxiKKyKFshPZgjTW41LKkUFYDu8E : accessed 1 January, 2019

[10] Vimeo. Gilad's Keynote Address - MyHeritage LIVE - November 2018. https://vimeo.com/299232829?from=outro-embed : accessed 21 May, 2019

[11] Genealogy's Star. Forgeries and False Family Trees. 13 October 2014. https://genealogysstar.blogspot.com/2014/10/forgeries-and-false-family-trees.html : accessed 28 November, 2018

[12] Daily Record. Davina McCall on the tears and cheers of her show Long Lost Family, TV husband Nicky Campbell and her love of home. https://www.dailyrecord.co.uk/entertainment/celebrity-interviews/davina-mccall-tears-cheers-show-3850104 : accessed 27 September, 2018

[13] Macdonald, I.G., 2018, Referencing for Genealogists: Sources and Citation. *The History Press* UK

[14] Ancestry. Boards. Topics. People downloading and re-uploading photos as their own. https://www.ancestry.com/boards/topics.methods.ethics/194/mb.ashx : accessed 19 September, 2018

[15] Dunaway D. K. and Baum, W. K., 2013, Oral History: An Interdisciplinary Anthology (American Association for State and Local History). Hareven, T., Ch. 14. The Search for Generational Memory. P.245. *Rowman & Littlefield Publishers.*

[16] Marketing Schools. Ethical Marketing. http://www.marketing-schools.org/types-of-marketing/ethical-marketing.html : accessed 29 January, 2019.

[17] Singer, P., 1994. Ethics. *Oxford University Press.*p.3.

[18] Diffen. Ethics vs. Morals. http://www.diffen.com/difference/Ethics_vs_Morals : accessed 15 April, 2018

[19] Stanford Encyclopedia of Philosophy. Gert, Bernard and Gert, Joshua. The Definition of Morality. First published 17 April, 2002; revised 8 February, 2016. https://plato.stanford.edu/entries/morality-definition/ : accessed 27 Oct, 2018

[20] English Oxford Living Dictionaries. Ethics. https://en.oxforddictionaries.com/definition/ethics : accessed 15 Apr, 2018

[21] Stanford Encyclopedia of Philosophy. Niiniluoto, Ilkka. The Definition of Morality. First published 17 April, 2002; substantive revision 8 February, 2016. https://plato.stanford.edu/entries/morality-definition/ : accessed 18 September, 2018

[22] Philosophy Basics. What is Philosophy? https://www.philosophybasics.com/general_whatis.html : accessed 11 August, 2018

[23] Google Dictionary. Philosophy. https://www.google.co.uk/search?q=Dictionary#dobs=philosophy :accessed 11 August, 2018

[24] Stanford Encyclopedia of Philosophy. Scientific Progress. First published 1, October, 2002; revised 15, June, 2015. https://plato.stanford.edu/entries/scientific-progress/ : accessed 27 October, 2018

[25] English Oxford Living Dictionaries. Ethics. https://en.oxforddictionaries.com/definition/ethics : accessed 15 Apr, 2018

[26] MacIntyre, A., 2002, 'A Short History of Ethics: A History of Moral Philosophy from the Homeric Age to the Twentieth Century', *Routledge*.

[27] Dewar, G., 2002, Advanced Religious Studies: AS & A Level Philosophy and Ethics Religion Through Diagrams. *Oxford Revision Guides*.

[28] Singer, P., 1994. Ethics. *Oxford University Press*.

[29] Robinson, D., Garratt C., 1999, 'Introducing Ethics.' *Totem Books, USA*

[30] Magee, B., 2001, 'The Story of Philosophy'. *Dorling Kindersley*.

[31] Florida State University. Department of Philosophy. What is Philosophy? https://philosophy.fsu.edu/undergraduate-study/why-philosophy/What-is-Philosophy : accessed 16 Sep., 2018

[32] The Ethics and Compliance Initiative. Mission statement. http://www.ethics.org/about/mission-statement : accessed 1 May, 2018

[33] Quora. Ravi Srivastava. https://www.quora.com/What-are-some-examples-of-ethical-dilemmas : accessed 9 November, 2018

[34] Quora. Chris MacDonald. What are some examples of ethical dilemmas? https://www.quora.com/What-are-some-examples-of-ethical-dilemmas : accessed 9 November, 2018

Chapter 2

[35] Bust of Plato, photograph taken by Penny Walters, Bristol University, November 2018

[36] Ancestry. Topic Boards. https://www.ancestry.com/boards/topics.methods.ethics/mb.ashx?cj=1&netid=cj&o_xid=0001029688&o_lid=0001029688&o_sch=Affiliate+External : accessed 19 December, 2018

[37] Burt, John R.F., Burtinshaw, Kathryn, 2018, Lunatics, Imbeciles and Idiots: A History of Insanity in Nineteenth Century Britain and Ireland, *Pen & Sword History*.

[38] Ancestry. Community Guidelines. https://www.ancestry.com/cs/legal/CommunityGuidelines : accessed 19 Feb, 2019

[39] Catudal Genealogy. Judy Schneider. Ethics and Genealogy. Posted 3 December 2013. http://www.catudals.com/2013/12/ethicsand-genealogy-i-once-belonged-to.html : accessed 28 December, 2018

[40] Roots Web. Smart Steps For Savy Genealogists. http://sites.rootsweb.com/~ncjohnst/begin.htm : accessed 28 December, 2018.

[41] Ancestry. Legal, privacy. http://ancestry.co.uk/cs/legal/PrivacyForYourFamilyTree : accessed 7 February, 2019

[42] Solove, Daniel J., 2004, The Digital Person: Technology And Privacy In The Information Age. p. 140. ISBN 978-0814798461.

[43] The International Association of Jewish Genealogical Societies. About. http://www.iajgs.org/blog/about/about-iajgs/ : accessed 2 April, 2019

[44] International Association of Jewish Genealogical Societies. Blog. Code of Conduct. http://www.iajgs.org/blog/code-of-conduct/ : accessed 30 December, 2018

[45] Andorno R The right not to know: an autonomy based approach. Journal of Medical Ethics 2004; 30:435-439. https://jme.bmj.com/content/30/5/435 : accessed 2 April, 2019

[46] Brin, D., 1998, The Transparent Society, *Perseus Books.* ISBN 0-7382-0144-8

[47] Byung-Chul Han, 2012, Transparenzgesellschaft, *Matthes & Seitz Verlag*

[48] Byung-Chul Han, 2015, The Transparency Society, *Stanford University Press*

[49] Byung-Chul Han, 2015, The Transparency Society, *Stanford University Press*

[50] Sanders, Todd & Harry G. West, 2003, *Powers revealed and concealed in the New World Order.* In H. G. West & T. Sanders (eds), Transparency and Conspiracy: Ethnographies of Suspicion in the New World Order. *Durham, NC: Duke University Press*, p. 16.

[51] Schneier, Bruce. 2015, Data and Goliath: The Hidden Battles to Collect Your Data and Control Your World, *W. W. Norton & Company,* ISBN 978-0-393-24481-6

[52] GEDmatch. https://www.gedmatch.com/ : accessed 2 April, 2019

[53] Association of Professional Genealogists Quarterly. Kerry Scott. DNA matches with no trees, not the dead-end you might think.. June 2018. P. 34. https://www.apgen.org/members/data/APGQPDF/APGQJun2018Online.pdf : accessed 26 October, 2018

[54] Ancestry. Boards. Topics. Users demanding help. 2 April, 2017. https://www.ancestry.com/boards/topics.methods.ethics/202/mb.ashx : accessed 19 September, 2018

[55] Catudal Genealogy. Judy Schneider. Ethics and Genealogy. Posted 3 December 2013. http://www.catudals.com/2013/12/ethicsand-genealogy-i-once-belonged-to.html : accessed 28 December, 2018

[56] Legacy Tree Blog. 13 secrets to getting replies from DNA cousins. https://www.legacytree.com/blog/13-secrets-to-getting-replies-from-dna-cousin-matches?utm_source=facebook&utm_medium=blog&utm_campaign=13-secrets-

getting-replies-dna-cousin-matches : accessed 2 April, 2019

[57] Family Tree Magazine. Rachel Fountain. 5 Ways to Use Your Genealogy Research (That Aren't More Research). August 22, 2018. https://www.familytreemagazine.com/premium/5-ways-genealogy-research/?k=H8Vg%2FXUOKbn%2BJKFA4fAzaNmeqNPEdjETA2F10HYRhXg%3D : accessed 24 August, 2018

[58] Eastman's Online Genealogy Newsletter. Dick Eastman. The Daily Online Genealogy Newsletter. https://blog.eogn.com/ : accessed 24 September, 2018

[59] Eastman's Online Genealogy Newsletter. Dick Eastman. Copyrights and other legal things. https://blog.eogn.com/copyrights-and-other-legal-things/ : accessed 24 September, 2018

[60] Dublin City Archives. http://www.dublincity.ie/main-menu-services-recreation-culture-dublin-city-public-libraries-and-archive-heritage-and-histo-39 : accessed 24 August, 2018

[61] Facebook. Dublin Historians. https://www.facebook.com/DubHistorians/ : accessed 24 August, 2018

[62] Facebook. Dublin Historians. About. https://www.facebook.com/pg/DubHistorians/about/?ref=page_internal : accessed 24 August, 2018

[63] NBC News. Kids learn cursive and connect with seniors through pen pal program. 21 May 2018. https://www.nbcnews.com/nightly-news/video/kids-learn-cursive-and-connect-with-seniors-through-pen-pal-program-1238054979864?v=railb& : accessed 25 September, 2018

[64] Blaine Bettinger, Paul Woodbury. DNA and the Next Generation. Posted 20 July, 2015. http://www.tnggn.org/dna-and-the-next-generation/ : accessed 20 December, 2018

[65] Dictionary. Tendril. https://www.dictionary.com/browse/tendril : accessed 28 February, 2019

[66] Who Do You Think You Are? Magazine. Letters to the editor. October, 2018. P. 8.

[67] Association of Professional Genealogists Quarterly. Kerry Scott. DNA matches with no trees, not the dead-end you might think.. June 2018. P. 33. https://www.apgen.org/members/data/APGQPDF/APGQJun2018Online.pdf : accessed 26 October, 2018

[68] My Heritage. Family Tree. Consistency Checker. https://www.myheritage.com : accessed 30 August, 2018

[69] Who Do You think You Are? Magazine. Celia Heritage. Which surname should I follow? P. 43. Issue 144. Oct, 2018.

[70] The Oxford Dictionary of Family Names in Britain and Ireland. 2016. Patrick Hanks, Richard Coates, and Peter McClure. http://www.oxfordreference.com/view/10.1093/acref/9780199677764.001.0001/acref-9780199677764?btog=chap&hide=true&page=2114&pageSize=10&skipEditions=true&sort=titlesort&source=%2F10.1093%2Facref%2F9780199677764.001.0001%2Facref-9780199677764 : accessed 24 September, 2018

[71] UK Census Online. The UK 1911 Census. https://www.ukcensusonline.com/census/1911.php : accessed 9 May 2018

[72] Find My Past. What is the 1939 Register? https://www.findmypast.co.uk/1939register/what-is-the-1939-register : accessed 9 May, 2018

[73] National Records of Scotland. National Health Service Central Register (NHSCR).History of the register. https://www.nrscotland.gov.uk/statistics-and-data/nhs-central-register/about-the-register/the-history-of-the-register : accessed 9 March, 2018

[74] National Records of Scotland. National Health Service Central Register (NHSCR). 1939 National Identity Register and How to Order an Official Extract. https://www.nrscotland.gov.uk/statistics-and-data/nhs-central-register/about-the-register/1939-national-identity-register-and-how-to-order-an-official-extract : accessed 9 March, 2019

[75] Find My Past. Announcing the release of the 1939 Register.https://blog.findmypast.co.uk/announcing-the-release-of-the-1939-register-1424355718.html : accessed 9 May, 2018

[76] My Heritage. 1939 Register. https://www.myheritage.com/research/collection-10678/1939-register-of-england-wales : accessed 11 May, 2018

[77] Ancestry. 1939 Register. https://search.ancestry.co.uk/search/db.aspx?dbid=61596&o_iid=87501&o_lid=87501&o_sch=Web+Property : accessed 11 May, 2018

[78] Who Do You Think You Are magazine. News. 1939 Register. http://www.whodoyouthinkyouaremagazine.com/news/ancestry-adds-1939-register-its-collections : accessed 9 March, 2019

[79] Who Do You Think You Are magazine. News. 1939 Register. http://www.whodoyouthinkyouaremagazine.com/news/ancestry-adds-1939-register-its-collections : accessed 9 March, 2019

[80] Who Do You Think You Are? Magazine. http://www.whodoyouthinkyouaremagazine.com/news/ancestry-adds-1939-register-its-collections : accessed 11 May, 2018

[81] Conversation between myself and Nathan Dylan Goodwin, 6 September, 2018.

[82] Psychology Today. Elizabeth Aura McClintock. Should Women Change Their Name When They Get Married? The antecedents and consequences of gender non-traditional surname choice. Posted Sep 06, 2018. https://www.psychologytoday.com/gb/blog/it-s-man-s-and-woman-s-world/201809/should-women-change-their-

name-when-they-get-married : accessed 24 March, 2019

[83] Britannica. Coverture. https://www.britannica.com/topic/coverture : accessed 2 April, 2019

[84] Southern Living. Darrisaw, Michelle. 2018. 16 common wedding traditions and the shocking history behind them. https://www.southernliving.com/weddings/history-wedding-traditions : accessed 24 March, 2019

[85] New York Times. Claire Cain Miller, Derek Willis. A question of identity. Maiden names on the rise again. https://www.nytimes.com/2015/06/28/upshot/maiden-names-on-the-rise-again.html : accessed 24 March, 2019

[86] Seattle Bride. Reid, Stephanie. 2018. The History Behind Maiden Vs. Married Names. https://seattlebridemag.com/expert-wedding-advice/history-behind-maiden-vs-married-names : accessed 24 March, 2019

[87] Grazia Daily. Everything You Should Know Before Getting A Double-Barrelled Surname. https://graziadaily.co.uk/life/real-life/double-barrelled-surnames/ : accessed 16 September, 2018

[88] Wikipedia. Double-barrelled name. https://en.wikipedia.org/wiki/Double-barrelled_name : accessed 16 Sep, 2018

[89] Stylist. Moya Crockett. How keeping your own surname changes the way people perceive your marriage. Posted 2018. https://www.stylist.co.uk/life/women-keeping-own-surname-maiden-name-after-marriage-psychology-politics-stats/178882 : accessed 24 March, 2019

[90] Victoria Clarke, Maree Burns, Carole Burgoyne. 2008. Who Would Take Whose Name? Accounts of Naming Practices in Same-sex Relationships. Journal of Community & Applied Social Psychology 18: 420–439.

[91] Statista. Women's celebrity weekly magazines ranked by print retail sales volume in the United Kingdom (UK) in 1st half 2018 (in copies sold). https://www.statista.com/statistics/321518/women-s-celebrity-weekly-magazines-ranked-by-sales-volume-uk/ : accessed 1 January, 2019

[92] GenealogyInTime Magazine. Why Genealogy Is Important. http://www.genealogyintime.com/articles/why-genealogy-is-important.html : accessed 21 May, 2019

[93] Facebook. Genealogy group. https://www.facebook.com/ : accessed 23 May, 2018

[94] Psychology Today. Nathan H. Lents. The Meaning and Meaninglessness of Genealogy. Posted Jan 29, 2018 https://www.psychologytoday.com/gb/blog/beastly-behavior/201801/the-meaning-and-meaninglessness-genealogy : accessed 30 September, 2018

[95] Psychology Today. Evan Imber-Black. The Power of Secrets., published July 1, 1998. https://www.psychologytoday.com/gb/articles/199807/the-power-secrets : accessed 5 December, 2018

[96] Catudal Genealogy. Judy Schneider. Ethics and Genealogy. Posted 3 December 2013. http://www.catudals.com/2013/12/ethicsand-genealogy-i-once-belonged-to.html : accessed 28 December, 2018

[97] Psychology Today. Evan Imber-Black. The Power of Secrets., published July 1, 1998. https://www.psychologytoday.com/gb/articles/199807/the-power-secrets : accessed 5 December, 2018

[98] Catudal Genealogy. Judy Schneider. Ethics and Genealogy. Posted 3 December 2013. http://www.catudals.com/2013/12/ethicsand-genealogy-i-once-belonged-to.html : accessed 28 December, 2018.

[99] Who Do You Think You Are? Magazine. Ancestry to fund The Secrets in My Family TV series. Rosemary Collins, 8 May 2017. http://www.whodoyouthinkyouaremagazine.com/news/ancestry-fund-secrets-my-family-tv-series : accessed 12 October, 2018

[100] Nikolay Zak. Jeanne Calment: the secret of longevity. Posted December, 2018. https://www.researchgate.net/publication/329773795_Jeanne_Calment_the_secret_of_longevity?fbclid=IwAR2UZllgsDWiyQD0x_gEOQVYaOLGxTy204xHXWE7JwwWGgQPtZ_wZ8GwA5g : accessed 20 January, 2019

[101] AOL News. The world's oldest person ever to have lived may have faked her age. https://www.aol.co.uk/news/2019/01/02/the-worlds-oldest-person-ever-to-have-lived-may-have-faked-her/?guccounter=1 : accessed 20 January, 2019

[102] Psychology Today. Everyone's a Criminal. How many do you know? More than you think. Jim Silver. 20 January, 2010. https://www.psychologytoday.com/gb/blog/crimes-courts-and-cops/201001/everyones-criminal : accessed 12 August, 2018

[103] The National Archives. Crime and Criminals. http://www.nationalarchives.gov.uk/help-with-your-research/research-guides-keywords/?show=keywords&keyword-letter=c&keyword=crime-and-criminals#step-three : accessed 9 March, 2019

[104] The National Archives. Trials in the Old Bailey and the Central Criminal Court. http://www.nationalarchives.gov.uk/help-with-your-research/research-guides/trials-old-bailey-central-criminal-court/ : accessed 9 March, 2019

[105] The National Archives. Coroners' Inquests. http://www.nationalarchives.gov.uk/help-with-your-research/research-guides/coroners-inquests/ : accessed 9 March, 2019

[106] The National Archives. Guides. Victorian Prisoners Photograph Albums 1872-1873. http://www.nationalarchives.gov.uk/help-with-your-research/research-guides/victorian-prisoners-photograph-albums-1872-1873/ : accessed 21 April, 2018

107 The National Archives. Prisoners: photograph album. http://discovery.nationalarchives.gov.uk/details/r/C1193588 : accessed 21 April, 2018

108 The National Archives. Prisoners: photograph album. http://discovery.nationalarchives.gov.uk/details/r/C1193589 : accessed 21 April, 2018

109 Science Museum. Alphonse Bertillon. http://broughttolife.sciencemuseum.org.uk/broughttolife/people/alphonebertillon : accessed 12 September, 2018

110 Wikipedia. Mug shot. https://en.wikipedia.org/wiki/Mug_shot : accessed 12 September, 2018

111 Daily Mirror. Chris Baynes. 19 January, 2017. Unusual crimes and odd punishments: Early 1900s mugshots show what life was like for convicts. https://www.mirror.co.uk/news/uk-news/unusual-crimes-odd-punishments-early-9655151 : accessed 27 August, 2018

112 West Glamorgan Archive Service. Swansea and Surrounding Area, Wales, Gaol Records, 1877-1922. https://www.swansea.gov.uk/westglamorganarchives : accessed 21 April, 2018

113 Fife FHS Shop. Fife Kalendar of Convicts, 1790 - 1880 (CD). https://shop.fifefhs.org/shop/cd-media/fife-kalendar-of-convicts-1790-1880-cd/ : accessed 3 May, 2018

114 Who Do You Think You Are? Magazine. Genealogy news roundup. Rosemary Collins. Fife Family History Society releases Kalendar of Convicts. 26 April 2018. http://www.whodoyouthinkyouaremagazine.com/news/genealogy-news-roundup-fife-family-history-society-releases-kalendar-convicts : accessed 3 May, 2018

115 Dictionary. Mugshot. https://www.dictionary.com/browse/mugshot : accessed 7 April, 2019

116 Wiktionary. Petty crime. https://en.wiktionary.org/wiki/petty_crime : accessed 7 April, 2019

117 Wikipedia. Convicts in Australia. https://en.wikipedia.org/wiki/Convicts_in_Australia : accessed 28 July, 2018

118 ABC News. Online records highlight Australia's convict past. Updated 25 Jul 2007. http://www.abc.net.au/news/2007-07-25/online-records-highlight-australias-convict-past/2512534 : accessed 28 July, 2018

119 Wikipedia. Al Qusais.https://en.wikipedia.org/wiki/Al_Qusais : accessed 13 September, 2018

120 Visit Dubai. Dubai Museum. https://www.visitdubai.com/en/pois/dubai-museum : accessed 12 September, 2018

121UiO. Research collections. Egyptian antiquities. https://www.khm.uio.no/english/research/collections/egyptian-antiquities/ : accessed 9 March, 2019

122 UiO. Research collections. Egyptian antiquities. https://www.khm.uio.no/english/research/collections/egyptian-antiquities/ : accessed 9 March, 2019

123 Ancient Egypt Online. Shabti, Shawabti and Ushabti. https://www.ancientegyptonline.co.uk/shabti.html : accessed 8 November, 2018

124 ATI. Joel Stice. Meet The Inca Ice Maiden, Perhaps The Best-Preserved Mummy In Human History. Posted September 7, 2017. https://allthatsinteresting.com/mummy-juanita-lady-of-ampato : accessed 2 April, 2019

125 Ranker. Lisa A Flowers. 'This Ancient Child Sacrifice Found Perfectly Preserved In Ice Is Fascinating.' https://www.ranker.com/list/facts-about-inca-ice-woman-juanita/lisa-a-flowers?var=9&utm_expid=16418821-398.XsB_bHIbRSSI3wZaZa7viw.2&utm_source=facebook&utm_medium=pd&pgid=1184675634928096&utm_campaign=Ancient_Child_Mummy_Add_On&asid=23842774447940455&psid=1714321368630184&utm_referrer=http%3A%2F%2Fm.facebook.com : accessed 27 August, 2018

126 UiO. Museum of Cultural History. The Gokstad man. https://www.khm.uio.no/english/visit-us/viking-ship-museum/exhibitions/gokstad/gokstad-grave.html : accessed 9 March, 2019

127 UiO. Museum of Cultural History. https://www.khm.uio.no/english/visit-us/viking-ship-museum/ : accessed 8 November, 2018

128 National Geographic. 9 Photos of Extraordinary Mummies, Ancient and Modern. https://news.nationalgeographic.com/2017/12/mummy-pictures-egypt-animals-bog-inca/ : accessed 3 September, 2018

129 The Independent. Tom Embury-Dennis. Mystery over identity of 4,000-year-old Egyptian mummy finally solved by FBI. Posted 07 April, 2018. https://uk.yahoo.com/news/mystery-over-identity-4-000-164019099.html : accessed 17 September, 2018

130 Bristol Museum & Art Gallery. Ancient Egypt: Life and Death https://www.bristolmuseums.org.uk/bristol-museum-and-art-gallery/whats-on/ancient-egypt-life-and-death/ : accessed 4 September, 2018

131 Wikipedia. William Blake. https://en.wikipedia.org/wiki/William_Blake : accessed 6 September, 2018

132 The Guardian. How amateur sleuths finally tracked down the burial place of William Blake. https://www.theguardian.com/culture/2018/aug/11/how-amateur-sleuths-finally-tracked-down-burial-place-william-blake : accessed 6 September, 2018

133 The Vintage News. Ian Harvey. People used to Picnic and Play Near their Deceased Loved Ones. Posted 24 September, 2018. https://www.thevintagenews.com/2018/09/24/picnic-in-the-cemetery/ : accessed 14 April, 2019

134 Fox News: Newspaper pulls woman's viral revenge obituary that says 'world is a better place without her.'

https://www.msn.com/en-gb/news/world/newspaper-pulls-womans-viral-revenge-obituary-that-says-world-is-a-better-place-without-her/ar-AAyjOzm?ocid=spartandhp : accessed 7 June, 2018

[135] The Guardian. Jeff Sparrow. How do we celebrate the virtues of dead loved ones in a secular age? Published 29 May, 2017. https://www.theguardian.com/commentisfree/2017/may/29/how-do-we-celebrate-the-virtues-of-dead-loved-ones-in-a-secular-age : accessed 2 April, 2019

[136] Family Search. World War I Records. https://www.familysearch.org/search/search/record/results?count=20&query=%2Bsurname%3Aname&collection_id={2125045%202126214%201921547%201878523%202761957%202489920%201807269%202568864%202202707%201858291%201968530%202513098}&et_cid=1078884&et_rid=113609315&linkid=CTA&cid=em-ww1-8001 : accessed 8 July, 2018

[137] Imperial War Museum. Margaret Brooks. 5 June 2018. Conscientious Objectors In Their Own Words. https://www.iwm.org.uk/history/conscientious-objectors-in-their-own-words : accessed 10 August, 2018

[138] Bristol Museums. Refusing to kill: Bristol's World War I conscientious objectors. 5 June - 14 July 2018 exhibition. https://www.bristolmuseums.org.uk/bristol-archives/whats-on/refusing-to-kill-bristols-conscientious-objectors/ : accessed 11 June, 2018

[139] Bristol Radical History Group. Home. https://www.brh.org.uk/site/ : accessed 10 August, 2018

[140] Bristol Radical History Group. Do You Have A Conchie In The Family? https://www.brh.org.uk/site/articles/do-you-have-a-conchie-in-the-family/ : accessed 4 September, 2018

[141] Find A Grave. Home. https://www.findagrave.com/ : accessed 4 September, 2018

[142] Find A Grave. About. https://www.findagrave.com/about : accessed 10 August, 2018

[143] The Romany & Traveller Family History Society. Home page. http://rtfhs.org.uk/ : accessed 8 May, 2018

[144] Warwick University. Danny Wilding The Educational Experiences of Gypsy Travellers: the Impact of Cultural Dissonance. https://warwick.ac.uk/fac/cross_fac/iatl/reinvention/issues/volume1issue1/wilding/ : accessed 31 October, 2018

[145] University of Manchester. Policy Blog. Yaron Matras. Counting Roma: the ethical dilemma. 20 May, 2015. http://blog.policy.manchester.ac.uk/featured/2015/05/counting-roma-the-ethical-dilemma/ : accessed 31 Oct, 2019

[146] Bristol Museums. First Floor. https://www.bristolmuseums.org.uk/bristol-museum-and-art-gallery/whats-at/first-floor/ : accessed 5 September, 2018

[147] Wikipedia. Longford Meeting House, Middlesex. https://en.wikipedia.org/wiki/Longford_Meeting_House,_Middlesex : accessed 25 September, 2018

[148] FFHS. Heathrow threat to Quaker burials. http://www.ffhs.org.uk/index.php : accessed 25 September, 2018

[149] Suffolk County Council Archives. National Lottery funding approved! https://www.suffolkarchives.co.uk/the_hold/news/national-lottery-funding-approved/ : accessed 25 September, 2018

[150] GenealogyBlog. Leland Meitzler. So the Parish Council Knocked the Headstones Over. http://www.genealogyblog.com/?p=27663 : accessed 20 May, 2018

[151] Huffington Post. Megan Smolenyak. Lost and Found for Humans. 17 June, 2013. https://www.huffingtonpost.com/megan-smolenyak-smolenyak/lost-and-found-for-humans_b_3447428.html : accessed 23 September, 2018

[152] BBC News. Sammy Woodhouse: Rotherham rapist access petition hits 200,000 mark. https://www.bbc.co.uk/news/uk-england-south-yorkshire-46382360 : accessed 29 November, 2019

[153] Transparency Project. Making family justice clearer. http://www.transparencyproject.org.uk/ : accessed 2 May 2019

[154] Ranker. Mariel Loveland Weird History. The Children Of Hitler's "Master Race" Experiment Are Still Alive, And Here's What They Look Like. https://www.ranker.com/list/children-of-nazi-lebensborn-breeding-program/mariel-loveland?var=9&utm_expid=16418821-398.XsB_bHIbRSSl3wZaZa7viw.2&utm_source=facebook&utm_medium=pd&pgid=642850749204637&utm_campaign=Children_of_Hitler_Add_On&asid=23842796350540195&psid=960856380737404&utm_referrer=http%3A%2F%2Fm.facebook.com : accessed 4 September, 2018

[155] Wikipedia. Dorothee Schmitz-Köster. https://de.wikipedia.org/wiki/Dorothee_Schmitz-Köster : accessed 5 September, 2018

[156] Dorothee Schmitz-Köster, Tristan Vankann. 2012. Lebenslang Lebensborn: Die Wunschkinder der SS und was aus ihnen wurde (German Edition). *Piper ebooks*.

[157] Antecedentia. www.antecedentia.com: accessed 24 January, 2019.

Chapter 3

[158] Wikimedia. DNA chemical structure. Madeleine Price Ball. https://commons.wikimedia.org/wiki/File:DNA_chemical_structure.svg : accessed 31 October, 2018

[159] Adapted from BBC. Bitesize articles. What is DNA? https://www.bbc.com/bitesize/articles/zvwbcj6 : accessed 31 October,2018

[160] DNA from the beginning. Concept 1. Children resemble their parents. http://www.dnaftb.org/1/bio.html : accessed 7 April, 2019

[161] DNA from the beginning. Concept 15. DNA and proteins are key molecules of the cell nucleus. http://www.dnaftb.org/15/bio.html : accessed 7 April, 2019

[162] DNA from the beginning. Concept 15. DNA and proteins are key molecules of the cell nucleus. http://www.dnaftb.org/15/bio-2.html : accessed 7 April, 2019

[163] Nature. Isolating Hereditary Material: Frederick Griffith, Oswald Avery, Alfred Hershey, and Martha Chase. https://www.nature.com/scitable/nated/article?action=showContentInPopup&contentPK=336 : accessed 7 April, 2019

[164] Hall, K., William Astbury and the biological significance of nucleic acids, 1938–1951. Studies in History and Philosophy of Biological and Biomedical Sciences, Volume 42, Issue 2, June 2011, Pages 119-128. https://www.astbury.leeds.ac.uk/about/Hall_paper.pdf : accessed 7 April, 2019

[165] Khan Academy. Classic experiments: DNA as the genetic material https://www.khanacademy.org/science/biology/dna-as-the-genetic-material/dna-discovery-and-structure/a/classic-experiments-dna-as-the-genetic-material : accessed 7 April, 2019

[166] Bio Ninja. Analysis of results of the Hershey and Chase experiment providing evidence that DNA is the genetic material. http://ib.bioninja.com.au/higher-level/topic-7-nucleic-acids/71-dna-structure-and-replic/hershey-and-chase.html : accessed 7 April, 2019

[167] Kings College London. A photo that changed the world. https://www.kcl.ac.uk/study/kings-in-time/a-photo-that-changed-the-world : accessed 7 April, 2019

[168] US National Library of Medicine. The Francis Crick Papers. The Discovery of the Double Helix, 1951-1953. https://profiles.nlm.nih.gov/SC/Views/Exhibit/narrative/doublehelix.html : accessed 7 April, 2019

[169] The Embryo Project Encyclopedia. Victoria Hernandez. The Meselson-Stahl Experiment (1957–1958). Published 18 April, 2017. https://embryo.asu.edu/pages/meselson-stahl-experiment-1957-1958-matthew-meselson-and-franklin-stahl : accessed 7 April, 2019

[170] The Nobel Prize in Physiology or Medicine 1962. https://www.nobelprize.org/prizes/medicine/1962/summary/ : accessed 7 April, 2019

[171] Explorable. Who discovered DNA. https://explorable.com/who-discovered-dna : accessed 9 March, 2019

[172] ISOGG. Introduction to DNA Testing. When did DNA testing come into use for genealogical purposes? https://isogg.org/wiki/Portal:DNA_testing : accessed 31 October, 2018

[173] MIT Technology Review. Antonio Regalado. 2017 was the year consumer DNA testing blew up. Posted 12 February, 2018. https://www.technologyreview.com/s/610233/2017-was-the-year-consumer-dna-testing-blew-up/ : accessed 13 September, 2018

[174] MIT Technology Review. Antonio Regalado. 2017 was the year consumer DNA testing blew up. Posted 12 February, 2018. https://www.technologyreview.com/s/610233/2017-was-the-year-consumer-dna-testing-blew-up/ : accessed 13 September, 2018

[175] The Guardian. Elle Hunt. 'Your father's not your father': when DNA tests reveal more than you bargained for. Posted 18 September, 2018. https://www.theguardian.com/lifeandstyle/2018/sep/18/your-fathers-not-your-father-when-dna-tests-reveal-more-than-you-bargained-for : accessed 24 September, 2018

[176] Tech Crunch. Frederic Lardinois. How MyHeritage found a new business in DNA. Posted 2018. https://techcrunch.com/2018/01/22/myheritage-says-it-sold-over-1m-dna-kits-last-year-annual-revenue-grew-to-133m/ : accessed 8 April, 2019

[177] The DNA Geek. How Fast Are the Databases Growing? https://thednageek.com/23andme-has-more-than-10-million-customers/ : accessed 14 April, 2019

[178] Blaine Bettinger and Paul Woodbury. DNA and the Next Generation: Part II. Posted 17 August, 2015. https://www.tnggn.org/dna-and-the-next-generation-part-ii/ : accessed 21 December, 2018

[179] High Definition Genealogy. https://hidefgen.com/ : accessed 11 April, 2019

[180] MacEntee, T. DNA Buying Guide: Are you sure you're buying the right DNA test? https://www.amazon.com/gp/product/B077NQXDQ2/ref=dbs_a_def_rwt_bibl_vppi_i2#customerReviews : accessed 23 October, 2018

[181] The DNA Geek. The Pros And Cons Of The Main Autosomal DNA Testing. 13 November, 2016. http://thednageek.com/the-pros-and-cons-of-the-main-autosomal-dna-testing-companies/ : accessed 17 Sep, 2018

[182] Top Ten Reviews. Ryan Brown. 30 June, 2018. https://www.toptenreviews.com/services/home/best-dna-testing-kits/ : accessed 17 September, 2018

[183] Gizmodo. Ed Cara. Don't Take the DNA Test You'll Probably Get for Christmas. Posted 19 December, 2018. https://gizmodo.com/dont-take-the-dna-test-youll-probably-get-for-christmas-1831068871 : accessed 22 December,

2019 : accessed 21 December, 2018

[184] FTDNA. 'Celebrate Mom genes.' https://www.familytreedna.com/ : accessed 30 April, 2018

[185] New York Times. Alyson Krueger. Are Genetic Testing Sites the New Social Networks? Like Facebook, but for fifth cousins, adoptive mothers and sperm-donor dads. June 16, 2018 https://www.nytimes.com/2018/06/16/style/23-and-me-ancestry-dna.html : accessed 26 August, 2018.

[186] The Mail On Sunday. Nicola Gill. Thousands of dads are left in shock as DIY paternity tests soar. Published 12 January, 2019. https://www.dailymail.co.uk/news/article-6585595/Thousands-dads-left-shock-DIY-paternity-tests-soar.html : accessed 9 March, 2019.

[187] Ancestry. Corporate. Company Overview. https://www.ancestry.com/corporate/about-ancestry/company-facts : accessed 12 April, 2019

[188] Ancestry. Company Overview. https://www.ancestry.com/corporate/about-ancestry/company-facts : accessed 12 April, 2019

[189] Abundant Genealogy. Thomas MacEntee. https://abundantgenealogy.com/genealogy-update-for-monday-october-29-2018/ : accessed 31 October, 2018

[190] Smarter Hobby. Best DNA Test for Ancestry. How to Choose the DNA Testing Kit That's Best for You. https://www.smarterhobby.com/genealogy/best-dna-test/ : accessed 20 April, 2019

[191] Family Tree DNA. https://www.familytreedna.com/ : accessed 20 April, 2019

[192] Family Tree DNA. About. https://www.familytreedna.com/about : accessed 20 April, 2019

[193] Jerusalem Post. Schelly Talalay Dardashti. When oral history meets genetics. Posted 30 March, 2008. https://www.jpost.com/Features/In-Thespotlight/When-oral-history-meets-genetics : accessed 20 April, 2019

[194] Wikipedia. Family Tree DNA. https://en.wikipedia.org/wiki/Family_Tree_DNA : accessed 20 April, 2019

[195] Smarter Hobby. Best DNA Test for Ancestry. How to Choose the DNA Testing Kit That's Best for You. https://www.smarterhobby.com/genealogy/best-dna-test/ : accessed 20 April, 2019

[196] MyHeritage. https://www.myheritage.com/ : accessed 11 September, 2018

[197] Wikipedia. Gilad Japhet. https://en.wikipedia.org/wiki/Gilad_Japhet : accessed 7 April, 2019

[198] Dash, J. (2003). Summoned to Jerusalem: The Life of Henrietta Szold. *Wipf & Stock Publishers.* p. 228. ISBN 9781592443055. Accessed 7 April, 2019

199 Jewish Women's Archive. Women of Valor. Henrietta Szold. https://jwa.org/womenofvalor/szold : accessed 9 April, 2019

[200] Wikipedia. MyHeritage. https://en.wikipedia.org/wiki/MyHeritage : accessed 11 September, 2018

[201] BBC Culture. What do our flags say about us? http://www.bbc.com/culture/story/20150714-what-do-our-flags-say-about-us : accessed 11 November, 2018

[202] MyHeritage Company Summary. Pro Bono Projects. https://cc.mhcache.com/wp-content/uploads/2018/10/Company-Summary-MyHeritage.pdf : accessed 12 April, 2019

[203] 23andMe. Questions page. https://www.23andme.com/ : accessed 14 April, 2019

[204] 23AndMe. FAQS. https://www.23andme.com/ : accessed 20 April, 2019.

[205] Smarter Hobby. Best DNA Test for Ancestry. How to Choose the DNA Testing Kit That's Best for You. https://www.smarterhobby.com/genealogy/best-dna-test/ : accessed 20 April, 2019

[206] GEDmatch. Tools for DNA & Genealogy Research. www.gedmatch.com : accessed 10 August, 2018

[207] GEDmatch. DNA for 'Dummies'. https://www.gedmatch.com/DNA_for_Dummies.php : accessed 13 Sep, 2018

[208] GEDmatch. Are Your Parents Related? https://www.gedmatch.com/compare_parents1.php : accessed 9 Sep, 2018

[209] GEDmatch. Home page. Posted 26 December, 2018. https://www.gedmatch.com/ : accessed 19 April, 2019.

[210] 23Mofang. https://23mofang.com/ : accessed 19 April, 2019

[211] GESEDNA. https://www.gesedna.com/ : accessed 19 April, 2019

[212] Currach. Tierney, J. Consanguinity Relationship Chart. https://app.box.com/s/puk9p04fj2hunma9ng5t : accessed 16 September, 2018

[213] Roberta Estes. Demystifying Ancestry's Relationship Predictions Inspires New Relationship Estimator Tool. Karin Corbeil. Posted 22 February, 2016. https://dna-explained.com/2016/02/22/demystifying-ancestrys-relationship-predictions-inspires-new-relationship-estimator-tool/ : accessed 24 September, 2018

[214] Nature. Maarten H. D. Larmuseau. Growth of ancestry DNA testing risks huge increase in paternity issues. Posted 3 December, 2018. https://www.nature.com/articles/s41562-018-0499-9.epdf?shared_access_token=uwp3dmj9rKYWxFZdAxkIudRgN0jAjWel9jnR3ZoTv0NhmB8hKWjXgzspv1F1lI2dLRxUk7nWXkqDcPnZi66ReLq7SonYzenYdufn3qprf082H5qsWoDrGp4XbRPm9jcZypiyDRYDqHWNAVwi1OcqXMGqM5PUk_lO53W_gI8oKf0%3D : accessed 2 January, 2019

[215] Psychology Today. Nathan H. Lents. The Meaning and Meaninglessness of Genealogy. Posted Jan 29, 2018 https://www.psychologytoday.com/gb/blog/beastly-behavior/201801/the-meaning-and-meaninglessness-genealogy : accessed 1 October, 2018

[216] BBC News. Hayley Compton and Caroline Lowbridge. How familial DNA trapped a murderer for the first time. Posted 23 September 2018. https://www.bbc.co.uk/news/uk-england-nottinghamshire-45561514 : accessed 14 April, 2019.

[217] Family Tree magazine. Police Use Genealogy DNA Site to Catch Golden State Killer. https://www.familytreemagazine.com/articles/news-blogs/genealogy_insider/dna-catches-golden-state-killer/?k=H8Vg%2FXUOKbn%2BJKFA4fAzaNmeqNPEdjETA2F10HYRhXg%3D : accessed 8 May, 2018

[218] GEDmatch. https://www.gedmatch.com/select.php : accessed 24 August, 2018

[219] PLOS Biology Journal. Guerrini CJ, Robinson JO, Petersen D, McGuire AL. 2 October, 2018. Should police have access to genetic genealogy databases? Capturing the Golden State Killer and other criminals using a controversial new forensic technique. https://journals.plos.org/plosbiology/article?id=10.1371/journal.pbio.2006906

[220] GEDmatch. Terms of Service and Privacy Policy. https://www.gedmatch.com/tos.htm : accessed 24 August, 2018

[221] GEDmatch. Terms of Service and Privacy Policy. GEDmatch purpose. https://www.gedmatch.com/tos.htm : accessed 13 April, 2019

[222] GEDmatch. Terms of Service and Privacy Policy. Use of results. https://www.gedmatch.com/tos.htm : accessed 13 April, 2019

[223] GEDmatch. https://www.gedmatch.com/select.php : accessed 24 August, 2018

[224] Gov.UK. Guide to the General Data Protection Regulation. https://www.gov.uk/government/publications/guide-to-the-general-data-protection-regulation : accessed 13 April, 2019

[225] Wired. What is GDPR? The summary guide to GDPR compliance in the UK. https://www.wired.co.uk/article/what-is-gdpr-uk-eu-legislation-compliance-summary-fines-2018 : accessed 13 April, 2019

[226] Crime Feed. DJ Freez Arrested As DNA From Gum & Bottle Links Him To 1992 Rape-Murder. http://crimefeed.com/2018/06/dj-freez-arrested-as-dna-from-gum-bottle-links-to-1992-rape-murder/?utm_source=facebook&utm_medium=social&utm_content=sf192680417&utm_campaign=investigationdiscovery&sf192680417=1 : accessed 1 July, 2018

[227] Washington Post. Eli Rosenburg. A serial rapist eluded police for years. Then they searched a genealogy site. https://www.msn.com/en-gb/news/crime/a-serial-rapist-eluded-police-for-years-then-they-searched-a-genealogy-site/ar-AAAyESy?ocid=spartanntp : accessed 24 September, 2018

[228] Who Do You Think You Are? Magazine. Rosemary Collins. What are the risks of using DNA websites in criminal investigations? 3 May, 2018. http://www.whodoyouthinkyouaremagazine.com/news/what-are-risks-using-dna-websites-criminal-investigations : accessed 19 September, 2018

[229] New York Times, Heather Murphy. 29 August, 2018. She Helped Crack the Golden State Killer Case. Here's What She's Going to Do Next. https://www.msn.com/en-gb/news/world/she-helped-crack-the-golden-state-killer-case-here's-what-she's-going-to-do-next/ar-BBMDp0m?ocid=spartanntp : accessed 30 August, 2018

[230] DNA and Family Tree Research. Gleeson, M. How do you feel about your DNA being used by the police? - the results of a survey. https://dnaandfamilytreeresearch.blogspot.com/2018/11/how-do-you-feel-about-your-dna-being.html : accessed 14 November, 2018

[231] Gizmodo. Ed Cara. Don't Take the DNA Test You'll Probably Get for Christmas. Posted 19 Dec, 2018. https://gizmodo.com/dont-take-the-dna-test-youll-probably-get-for-christmas-1831068871 : accessed 22 Dec, 2018

[232] Guerrini CJ, Robinson JO, Petersen D, McGuire AL. 2018. Should police have access to genetic genealogy databases? Capturing the Golden State Killer and other criminals using a controversial new forensic technique. 2 October, 2018. https://journals.plos.org/plosbiology/article?id=10.1371/journal.pbio.2006906 : accessed 14 November, 2018

[233] Wired. Molteni., M. The key to cracking cold cases might be genealogy sites. June, 2018. https://www.wired.com/story/police-will-crack-a-lot-more-cold-cases-with-dna/ : accessed 14 November, 2018.

[234] Guerrini CJ, Robinson JO, Petersen D, McGuire AL. 2018. Should police have access to genetic genealogy databases? Capturing the Golden State Killer and other criminals using a controversial new forensic technique. 2 October, 2018. https://journals.plos.org/plosbiology/article?id=10.1371/journal.pbio.2006906 : accessed 14 November, 2018

[235] Who Do You Think You Are? Magazine. Rosemary Collins. What are the risks of using DNA websites in criminal investigations? 3 May, 2018. http://www.whodoyouthinkyouaremagazine.com/news/what-are-risks-using-dna-websites-criminal-investigations : accessed 19 September, 2018

[236] Eastman's Online Genealogy Newsletter. Experts Outline Ethics Issues With Use of Genealogy DNA to Solve Crimes. https://blog.eogn.com/2018/06/01/experts-outline-ethics-issues-with-use-of-genealogy-dna-to-solve-crimes/ : accessed 19 June, 2018

[237] Yaniv Erlich, Tal Shor, Itsik Pe'er, Shai Carmi. Identity inference of genomic data using long-range familial searches. Science 09 Nov 2018: Vol. 362, Issue 6415, pp. 690-694. DOI: 10.1126/science.aau4832. Abstract http://science.sciencemag.org/content/362/6415/690 : accessed 22 December, 2018

[238] New York Times. China Uses DNA to Track Its People, With the Help of American Expertise. Sui-Lee Wee. Posted 21 February, 2019. https://www.nytimes.com/2019/02/21/business/china-xinjiang-uighur-dna-thermo-fisher.html : accessed 9 March, 2019

[239] Gizmodo. Melissa. During a Transplant Does the Donor's DNA Integrate Into the Host? 3 April, 2014.
https://gizmodo.com/during-a-transplant-does-the-donor-s-dna-integrate-into-1557455349 : accessed 13 April, 2019
[240] Ancestry. FAQ. 10. If I received a bone marrow transplant, should I use Ancestry DNA?
https://www.ancestry.co.uk/dna/legal/faq#about-2 : accessed 17 September, 2018
[241] U.S. Food and Drug Administration. https://www.fda.gov/ : accessed 20 April, 2019
[242] FDA allows marketing of first direct-to-consumer tests that provide genetic risk information for certain conditions. Posted: April 6, 2017. Page Last Updated: 28 March, 2018.
https://www.fda.gov/NewsEvents/Newsroom/PressAnnouncements/ucm551185.htm : accessed 21 Dec, 2018
[243] MSN. Simon Hattenstone. Rio Ferdinand: 'I used to drink 10 pints then move on to vodka.'
https://www.msn.com/en-gb/sport/spotlight/rio-ferdinand-'i-used-to-drink-10-pints-then-move-on-to-vodka'/ar-BBSzQnw?ocid=spartanntp : accessed 14 April, 2019
[244] Kristen V. Brown. 23andMe Is Selling Your Data, But Not How You Think. Posted 14 April, 2017.
https://gizmodo.com/23andme-is-selling-your-data-but-not-how-you-think-1794340474 : accessed 21 Dec, 2018
[245] Melissa Gymrek, Amy L. McGuire, David Golan, Eran Halperin, Yaniv Erlich. Identifying Personal Genomes by Surname Inference. Vol. 339, Issue 6117, pp. 321-324. http://science.sciencemag.org/content/339/6117/321 DOI: 10.1126/science.1229566
[246] CNBC. Christine Farr. Veritas is studying the DNA of people who live to 110, looking for clues to longevity. 19 Aug 2018. https://www.cnbc.com/2018/08/19/veritas-wants-to-sequence-dna-of-the-extremely-old-and-young.html : accessed 24 August, 2018
[247] The Legal Genealogist. Judy Russell, DNA: Life After Death. Jun 30, 2013.
https://www.legalgenealogist.com/2013/06/30/dna-life-after-death/ : accessed 20 May, 2018
[248] Medical Examiner. Cuyahoga County. Deceased Patient Custodian/ Next-of-Kin Consent for DNA Testing form.
http://medicalexaminer.cuyahogacounty.us/pdf_medicalexaminer/en-US/NOK-Consent-PT-ID-DNAtesting-v2.pdf : accessed 20 May, 2018
[249] DNA from the beginning. Concept 1. Children resemble their parents. http://www.dnaftb.org/1/bio.html : accessed 7 April, 2019
[250] US National Library of Medicine. The Francis Crick Papers. The Discovery of the Double Helix, 1951-1953.
https://profiles.nlm.nih.gov/SC/Views/Exhibit/narrative/doublehelix.html : accessed 7 April, 2019
[251] Ancestry DNA. See what your DNA reveals. https://www.ancestrydna.co.uk/kits : accessed 13 September, 2018
[252] Time. Gregory Rodriguez How Genealogy Became Almost as Popular as Porn. 30 May 2014.
http://time.com/133811/how-genealogy-became-almost-as-popular-as-porn/ : accessed 11 September, 2018
[253] ISOGG. Wiki. CentiMorgan. https://isogg.org/wiki/CentiMorgan : accessed 18 April, 2019
[254] My Heritage https://www.myheritage.com/ : accessed 19 June, 2018
[255] The Guardian. Elle Hunt. 'Your father's not your father': when DNA tests reveal more than you bargained for. 18 September, 2018. https://www.theguardian.com/lifeandstyle/2018/sep/18/your-fathers-not-your-father-when-dna-tests-reveal-more-than-you-bargained-for : accessed 24 September, 2018
[256] MIT Technology Review. Antonio Regalado. 2017 was the year consumer DNA testing blew up. 12 February, 2018
https://www.technologyreview.com/s/610233/2017-was-the-year-consumer-dna-testing-blew-up/ : accessed 13 September, 2018
[257] CBR Online. Ed Targett. Future Hackers Could Amend Stolen DNA. 6 June, 2018.
https://www.cbronline.com/news/myheritage-hack : accessed 31 October, 2018
[258] People's World. Eric A. Gordon 'Thank You for Coming': A sperm donor's daughter searches for identity. June 12, 2017. http://www.peoplesworld.org/article/thank-you-for-coming-a-sperm-donors-daughter-searches-for-identity/ : accessed 14 October, 2018
[259] Cambridge Dictionary. Riven. https://dictionary.cambridge.org/dictionary/english/riven : accessed 14 April, 2019
[260] Buzzfeed. News. Katie Notopoulos. Ancestry.com Is In Cahoots With Public Records Agencies, A Group Suspects. October 22, 2018. https://www.buzzfeednews.com/article/katienotopoulos/ancestry-com-reclaim-the-records-new-york-lawsuit?fbclid=IwAR37YwckxzY7qlyj6IzkTb6EHiOfZ17KI4Gy0bGsaScrWdCOV4bfjpRZ5uY : accessed 1 Nov, 2018
[261] NBC News. Alan Boyle. Who's keeping your genetic keys? Posted 16 January, 2002.
http://www.nbcnews.com/id/3077152/ns/technology_and_science-science/t/whos-keeping-your-genetic-keys/#.XBO-kvZ2vcv : accessed 20 December, 2018

Chapter 4

[262] Wikipedia Commons. Hitsuji Kinno. CC BY-SA 3.0. Adoption.
https://commons.wikimedia.org/w/index.php?curid=37832020 : accessed 17 October, 2018
[263] Dictionary. Baseborn. http://www.dictionary.com/browse/baseborn : accessed 1 July, 2018

264 Dictionary. Illegitimate. http://www.dictionary.com/browse/illegitimate?s=ts : accessed 26 September, 2018

265 Genuki. Virtual Reference Library. Poor Laws Bastardy Papers. http://www.genuki.org.uk/big/eng/LIN/poorbastard : accessed 4 July, 2018

266 Stack Exchange. Questions. https://history.stackexchange.com/questions/12521/which-bastards-became-kings : accessed 28 July, 2018

267 Ruth Paley, 2014, My Ancestor was a Bastard: A Family Historian's Guide to Sources for Illegitimacy in England and Wales. *Society of Genealogists Enterprises Ltd.*

268 SoG. Events. http://www.sog.org.uk/books-courses/events-courses/marriage-law-for-genealogists-illegitimacy-outside-the-law-1700-1 : accessed 12 August, 2018

269 Psychology Today. Nathan H. Lents. The Meaning and Meaninglessness of Genealogy. Posted 29 Jan, 2018 https://www.psychologytoday.com/gb/blog/beastly-behavior/201801/the-meaning-and-meaninglessness-genealogy : accessed 30 September, 2018

270 The Adoption History Project. Ellen Herman. https://pages.uoregon.edu/adoption/topics/transracialadoption.htm : accessed 27 August, 2018

271 The Adoption History Project. About. https://pages.uoregon.edu/adoption/about.html : accessed 27 August, 2018

272 American Adoptions. History of adoption. https://www.americanadoptions.com/adoption/history-of-adoption : accessed 27 August, 2018

273 People's World. Eric A. Gordon. World premiere play examines choice in reproductive justice. April 13, 2017. http://www.peoplesworld.org/article/world-premiere-play-examines-choice-in-reproductive-justice/ : accessed 17 October, 2017

274 The Irish Times. 16 September, 2008. 'Giving up a child for adoption has a lifetime impact'. A woman relieved to discover her son had turned out well after adoption. https://www.irishtimes.com/culture/giving-up-a-child-for-adoption-has-a-lifetime-impact-1.938812 : accessed 11 September, 2018

275 The Irish Times. 16 September, 2008. 'Giving up a child for adoption has a lifetime impact'. A woman who gave up her son 30 years ago. https://www.irishtimes.com/culture/giving-up-a-child-for-adoption-has-a-lifetime-impact-1.938812 : accessed 11 September, 2018

276 The Irish Times. 16 September, 2008. 'Giving up a child for adoption has a lifetime impact'. A man adopted 40 years ago, who feels shunned by his birth family. https://www.irishtimes.com/culture/giving-up-a-child-for-adoption-has-a-lifetime-impact-1.938812 : accessed 11 September, 2018

277 Adoptionland. Adoption Truth and Transparency Worldwide Network. Your baby is dead. https://adoptionland.org/p/2276/your-baby-is-dead-mothers-say-their-supposedly-stillborn-babies-were-stolen-from-them/ : accessed 21 April, 2018

278 CBC Radio. Indigenous women kept from seeing their newborn babies until agreeing to sterilization, says lawyer. Posted 13 November, 2018. https://www.cbc.ca/radio/thecurrent/the-current-for-november-13-2018-1.4902679/indigenous-women-kept-from-seeing-their-newborn-babies-until-agreeing-to-sterilization-says-lawyer-1.4902693 : accessed 22 December, 2018

279 Adoptionland. Your baby is dead. https://adoptionland.org/2015/11/30/your-baby-is-dead-mothers-say-their-supposedly-stillborn-babies-were-stolen-from-them/ : accessed 11 November, 2017

280 Baby Scoop Era Research Initiative. What was the "Baby Scoop Era"? http://babyscoopera.com/home/what-was-the-baby-scoop-era/?fbclid=IwAR3eAyBDgSsTzd5TSyeJsOTajvEgKc5S5IdxYiIvLCcEfuOLxriIs3rSfg8 : accessed 17 Oct 2018

281 Raidió Teilifís Éireann. News. Tuam Mother Baby. 3 March, 2017. https://www.rte.ie/news/2017/0303/856914-tuam-mother-baby/ : accessed 7 November, 2017

282 Mother And Baby Homes Commission Of Investigation. FAQ. http://www.mbhcoi.ie/MBH.nsf/page/Frequently%20Asked%20Questions-en : accessed 7 November, 2017

283 John Grenham. Blog. How to find other mother and baby home deaths. https://www.johngrenham.com/blog/2017/03/11/how-to-find-other-mother-and-baby-home-deaths/ : accessed 7 November, 2017

284 Verrier, N., (2015), The Primal Wound: Understanding the Adopted Child, *BAAF.* ISBN 9781905664764 Pg.xvi.

285 YouTube. Rod Stewart. The First Cut Is the Deepest. https://youtu.be/xoitegszoRc : accessed 12 August, 2018

286 Ludvigsen, A. & Parnham, J. (2004) Searching for siblings: The motivations and experiences of adults seeking contact with adopted siblings. Adoption and Fostering, 28(4), 56.

287 Feast, J. & Philpot, T. (2003). Searching questions: Identity, origins and adoption. London: British Association for Adoption and Fostering.

288 Powell, K.A. & Afifi, T.D. (2005). Uncertainty management and adoptees' ambiguous loss of their birth parents. Journal of Social and Personal Relationships, 22(1), 129–151.

289 Moran, R.A. (1994). Stages of emotion: An adult adoptee's post-reunion perspective. Child Welfare, 73(3), 249–260.

290 Feast, J. & Philpot, T. (2003). Searching questions: Identity, origins and adoption. London: British Association for

Adoption and Fostering.

[291] Ludvigsen, A. & Parnham, J. (2004) Searching for siblings: The motivations and experiences of adults seeking contact with adopted siblings. Adoption and Fostering, 28(4), 50–59.

[292] Ludvigsen, A. & Parnham, J. (2004) Searching for siblings: The motivations and experiences of adults seeking contact with adopted siblings. Adoption and Fostering, 28(4), 50–59.

[293] People's World. Eric A. Gordon 'Thank You for Coming': A sperm donor's daughter searches for identity. June 12, 2017. http://www.peoplesworld.org/article/thank-you-for-coming-a-sperm-donors-daughter-searches-for-identity/ : accessed 14 October, 2018

[294] The Adoption History Project. Massachusetts Adoption of Children Act, 1851. https://pages.uoregon.edu/adoption/archive/MassACA.htm : accessed 18 September, 2018

[295] Legislation UK Government. Adoption of Children Act 1926. https://www.legislation.gov.uk/ukpga/Geo5/16-17/29/resources : accessed 18 September, 2018

[296] GenGuide. Adoption Records. https://www.genguide.co.uk/source/adoption-records/137/ : accessed 19 April, 2019

[297] Adopted Children Register: GRO maintains the Adopted Children Register (ACR) which contains the particulars of adoptions authorised by order of a court in England or Wales on or after 1 January, 1927. The only information that is available from this register is a certified certificated copy of an entry, which is the equivalent of a birth certificate for an adopted person. Adoption Contact Register: GRO administers the Adoption Contact Register on behalf of the Department of Health. The register is a linking mechanism between an adopted person and their birth relatives, where both parties so wish. Abandoned Children Register: Since 1977, the births of abandoned babies, within England and Wales, whose parentage is unknown are recorded. Thomas Coram Register: A list held of children given into the care of the Foundling Hospital between the years 1853 and 1948

[298] HM Passport Office. Application for Birth Certificate Information Before Adoption. https://assets.publishing.service.gov.uk/government/uploads/system/uploads/attachment_data/file/349413/AdoptionsBIBAFormUK.pdf : accessed 15 April, 2018
Post or email the form to: adoptions@gro.gsi.gov.uk; Adoptions Section, Room C202, General Register Office, Trafalgar Rd., Southport, PR8 2HH

[299] Gov.UK https://www.gov.uk/ : accessed 16 July, 2018

[300] Child Welfare. Access to adoption records. P.1. https://www.childwelfare.gov/pubPDFs/infoaccessap.pdf : accessed 10 November, 2018

[301] Mental Help. Long-Term Issues For The Adopted Child. BH. 8 Dec. 2011. https://www.mentalhelp.net/articles/long-term-issues-for-the-adopted-child/ : accessed 12 August, 2018.

[302] Adopted Children Register Gov UK. Adoption records https://www.gov.uk/adoption-records : accessed 26 September, 2018

[303] NORCAP (2013, absorbed by BAAF). Adoption Services for Adults. http://www.adoptionservicesforadults.org.uk/ : accessed 26 September, 2018

[304] The Adoption Authority of Ireland. https://www.aai.gov.ie/ : accessed 12 August, 2018

[305] Scottish Adoption http://www.scottishadoption.org/ : accessed 12 August, 2018

[306] Facebook. NPN. https://www.facebook.com/NPNNaturalParentsNetwork/ : accessed 19 April, 2019

[307] Mental Help. Kathryn Patricelli, MA. Long-Term Issues For The Adopted Child. https://www.mentalhelp.net/articles/long-term-issues-for-the-adopted-child/ : accessed 12 August, 2018.

[308] Verrier, N., (2015), The Primal Wound: Understanding the Adopted Child, BAAF. ISBN 9781905664764

[309] BPS. The Psychologist. Darongkamas J., Lorenc, L. Going back to our roots. What factors drive a person to research a family tree, or an adoptee to search for their biological parents? Dec. 2008. Vol. 21. (1022-1025). https://thepsychologist.bps.org.uk/volume-21/edition-12/going-back-our-roots : accessed 26 October, 2018

[310] Family Tree Templates. https://www.familytreetemplates.net/category/bowtie : accessed 19 April, 2019

[311] Psychology Today. Nathan H. Lents. The Meaning and Meaninglessness of Genealogy. Posted Jan 29, 2018 https://www.psychologytoday.com/gb/blog/beastly-behavior/201801/the-meaning-and-meaninglessness-genealogy : accessed 30 September, 2018

[312] Argyle, M. 1981. The Psychology of Interpersonal Behaviour. P. 169. Pelican

[313] Ancestry. Support. Article. Listing Adopted Family in a Tree. https://support.ancestry.com/s/article/Listing-Adopted-Children-in-your-Ancestry-Member-Tree-1460091980271-3698?ui-force-components-controllers-recordGlobalValueProvider.RecordGvp.getRecord=1&r=8 : accessed 10 November, 2018

[314] Walters, Penny. 'Mixing DNA results with a paper trail.' Journal of the Bristol & Avon Family History Society, March, 2018, No. 171; The Name Event, London; Bath FHS; Gwent FHS; Brigham Young University, Provo, USA.

[315] Genesis GEDmatch. https://genesis.gedmatch.com/ : accessed 19 April, 2019

[316] Ancestry. Support. Finding Biological Family. https://support.ancestry.com/s/article/US-AncestryDNA-for-Adoptees-Search-Strategies : accessed 10 November, 2018

317 GEDmatch. Home page. Posted 26 December, 2018. https://www.gedmatch.com/ : accessed 19 April, 2019.

318 MyHeritage. DNA Quest. https://www.dnaquest.org/ : accessed 13 September, 2018

319 Facebook. DNA Detectives. https://www.facebook.com/groups/DNADetectives/ : accessed 12 August, 2018

320 Aust, K. Mirroring a Tree on Ancestry (for Adoptees). 16 May, 2016. http://knolaust.com/dnablog/mirroring-a-tree-on-ancestry/ accessed 12 August, 2018

321 Verrier, N., (2015), The Primal Wound: Understanding the Adopted Child, *BAAF*. P. 135. ISBN 9781905664764

322 Verrier, N., (2015), The Primal Wound: Understanding the Adopted Child, *BAAF*. P. 144. ISBN 9781905664764

323 Facebook PM. Pat Marley. 29 December, 2016

324 Harris, P., 2006, In Search of Belonging: Reflections of Transracially Adopted People. *BAAF*. ISBN 1903699770

325 Archive Org. W.H. Slingerland. 1919. Child-Placing in Families: A Manual for Students and Social Workers (New York: Russell Sage Foundation) P.125. https://archive.org/details/childplacinginfa00slin : accessed 27 August, 2018

326 The Adoption History Project. Herman, E. matching. https://pages.uoregon.edu/adoption/topics/matching.html : accessed 27 August, 2018

327 The Adoption History Project. Herman, E. Transracial Adoptions. https://pages.uoregon.edu/adoption/topics/transracialadoption.htm : accessed 27 August, 2018

328 Chung, N., 2018, All You Can Ever Know: A Memoir. *Catapult*

329 Guardian. Nicole Chung. Stories of transracial adoptees must be heard – even uncomfortable ones. Posted 4 April, 2019. https://www.theguardian.com/commentisfree/2019/apr/04/transracial-adoption-listen-understand?CMP=share_btn_fb&fbclid=IwAR2CVav5nH1yMkfpOzF8v6KtC2Sw1LJr4iWVyjxfwpQfz1KMHpE_YcfbVnQ : accessed 19 April, 2019

330 Mental Help. Long-Term Issues For The Adopted Child. JJ, Feb 18, 2010. https://www.mentalhelp.net/articles/long-term-issues-for-the-adopted-child/ : accessed 12 August, 2018.

331 Rebecca Compton. Psychology Today. Is Transracial Adoption Harmful to Kids? 11 May, 2016. https://www.psychologytoday.com/gb/blog/adopting-reason/201605/is-transracial-adoption-harmful-kids : accessed 12 August, 2018

332 Hamilton. E., *et al.* Adoption Quarterly, Volume 18, 2015 - Issue 3. Identity Development in a Transracial Environment: Racial/ Ethnic Minority Adoptees in Minnesota https://www.tandfonline.com/doi/abs/10.1080/10926755.2015.1013593 : accessed 12 August, 2018

333 ITV Press Centre. Long Lost Family. Series 8, Episode 2, Week 30. 24 July, 2018. https://www.itv.com/presscentre/ep2week30/long-lost-family-0 : accessed 25 July, 2018

334 One News Page. https://www.onenewspage.co.uk/n/Front+Page/1zj8wiik3y/First-transgender-searcher-on-ITV-Long-Lost.htm : accessed 25 July, 2018

335 Chris Creegan. How Long Lost Family reeled me in. 23 July, 2016. http://www.chriscreegan.com/blog/2016/07/23/how-long-lost-family-reeled-me-in/ : accessed 27 September, 2018

336 The Guild of One Name Studies. https://one-name.org/ : accessed 19 April, 2019

337 The Irish Post. News. Aidan Lonergan. Elderly Irish woman, 81, finally finds her 103-year-old mother after decades of searching. Posted January 25, 2019. https://www.irishpost.com/news/elderly-irish-woman-81-finally-finds-103-year-old-mother-decades-searching-163806 : accessed 26 January, 2019

338 Verrier, N., (2015), The Primal Wound: Understanding the Adopted Child, *BAAF*. ISBN 9781905664764

339 Verrier, N., (2010), Coming Home to Self: Healing the primal wound, *BAAF*. ISBN 9781905664818

340 Campbell, N., (2004), Blue-eyed Son: The Story of an Adoption. *Pan*. ISBN 0330433067

341 Adoption Society, Iredale, **S.**, Staples, M. (Editors). 1997. Reunions. *The Stationery Office*. ISBN 0117021504

342 WWF. Adopt an Animal. https://support.wwf.org.uk/adopt-an-animal/?_ga=2.251176453.2069514078.1535376318-708070169.1535376318 : accessed 27 August, 2018

343 Psychology Today. The Film 'Three Identical Strangers' The impact of an unethical adoption study. 11, Sep 2018. E. Kay Trimberger. https://www.psychologytoday.com/gb/blog/adoption-diaries/201809/the-film-three-identical-strangers : accessed 16 September, 2018

344 Vice. Kara Weisenstein. The Reason These Triplets Were Separated at Birth Is Beyond Messed Up. 10 July, 2018 https://www.vice.com/en_uk/article/594mek/the-conspiracy-behind-three-identical-strangers-is-beyond-messed-up : accessed 9 November, 2018

345 The Weekend Australian. Grace Collier. Hello, nice to finally meet you, this is my true identity. 17 November, 2018. https://www.theaustralian.com.au/news/inquirer/hello-nice-to-finally-meet-you-this-is-my-true-identity/news-story/30dff75640583185a62833492bebbf3b : accessed 17 November, 2018

Chapter 5

346 Wkimedia Commons. Augiasstallputzer. Globe. https://commons.wikimedia.org/wiki/File:Globe.svg : accessed 11

November, 2018
[347] Adapted from Dauntless Jaunter. Christian "Krzysiek" Eilers. Ethnicity, Nationality, Race, Identity, Culture & Heritage (E.N.R.I.C.H.) 2012. https://djaunter.com/enrich/ : accessed 11 November, 2018
[348] Wikipedia. Quadroon. https://en.wikipedia.org/wiki/Quadroon : accessed 1 February, 2019
[349] Wikipedia. Mulatto. https://simple.m.wikipedia.org/wiki/Mulatto : accessed 19 April, 2019
[350] Wikipedia. Dave. https://en.wikipedia.org/wiki/Dave_(rapper) : accessed 3 May, 2019
[351] YouTube. Dave. Black. https://www.youtube.com/watch?v=pDUPSNdmFew : accessed 6 April, 2019. Songwriter: David Orobosa Omoregie. Black lyrics © Tunecore Inc, Warner/Chappell Music, Inc, Kobalt Music Publishing Ltd.
[352] The Guardian. Miranda Sawyer. Black is confusing. Where does the line start and stop? Posted 3 March, 2019. https://www.theguardian.com/music/2019/mar/03/dave-psychodrama-interview-black-is-confusing : accessed 6 April, 2019
[353] Journal Edge. Blog. Vikas Acharya. https://vikasacharya.wordpress.com/2015/11/13/jamaica/ : accessed 28 May, 2017
[354] National Archives. Exhibitions, Citizenship, Brave New World. Postwar immigration. http://www.nationalarchives.gov.uk/pathways/citizenship/brave_new_world/immigration.htm : accessed 6 June, 2017
[355] National Archives. Bound For Britain, Experiences of Immigration To The UK. http://www.nationalarchives.gov.uk/education/resources/bound-for-britain/ :accessed 4 June 2017
[356] BBC. Mike Phillips. Windrush, The Passengers. Last updated 2011. http://www.bbc.co.uk/history/british/modern/windrush_01.shtml : accessed 4 June, 2017
[357] Phillips, M., Phillips, T. 1999. Windrush, The Irresistible Rise of Multi-Racial Britain. *Harper Collins.*
[358] IOM, International Organisation for Migration. Jamaica Mapping Exercise, July 2007. P. 8. https://web.archive.org/web/20110511105031/http://www.iomlondon.org/doc/mapping/IOM_JAMAICA.pdf : accessed 4 June 2017.
[359] Family Search. https://www.familysearch.org/ : accessed 23 July, 2018
[360] Family Search. Adella Allen. Jamaica, Church of England Parish Register Transcripts, 1664-1880Page 117; line number 92; GS film 1291708; Digital Folder 004620473; Image 00298. https://www.familysearch.org/ : accessed 19 April, 2019
[361] BBC. Nigel Pocock and Victoria Cook. The Business of Enslavement. William Beckford. http://www.bbc.co.uk/history/british/abolition/slavery_business_gallery_01.shtml#one : accessed 17 July, 2018
[362] Wikipedia. William Beckford of Somerley. https://en.wikipedia.org/wiki/William_Beckford_of_Somerley : accessed 17 July, 2018
[363] William Beckford, 1788. Remarks Upon the Situation of Negroes in Jamaica: Impartially Made from a Local Experience of Nearly Thirteen Years in that Island. T. and J. Egerton, Military Library, Whitehall. https://books.google.co.uk/books?id=Hr8NAAAAQAAJ&printsec=frontcover&source=gbs_ge_summary_r&cad=0#v=onepage&q&f=false : accessed 17 July, 2018
[364] John Carter Brown Library. Aestheticizing the landscape of sugar: George Robertson's views in the island of Jamaica. http://www.brown.edu/Facilities/John_Carter_Brown_Library/exhibitions/sugar/pages/aesthetics.html : accessed 17 July, 2018
[365] Geoff Quilley, Kay Dian Kriz, 2003. An Economy of Colour: Visual Culture and the North Atlantic World, 1660-1830. P.133. *Manchester University Press.* 203 pages
[366] Wikimedia Commons. Simon P. Triangle Trade. https://commons.wikimedia.org/wiki/File:Triangle_trade2.png : accessed 19 November, 2018
[367] Jamaican Family search. Slaves And Slavery In Jamaica. http://www.jamaicanfamilysearch.com/Samples2/slavery.htm : accessed 21 June, 2017
[368] Jamaican Family Search. Genealogy Research Library. *Slaves Imported and Exported 1702-1787.* http://www.jamaicanfamilysearch.com/Samples2/LongSlaveData.htm : accessed 22 June, 2017
[369] Wikipedia. Brookes (ship). https://en.wikipedia.org/wiki/Brookes_(ship) : accessed 13 July 2018
[370] Durham University. Palace Green transformed into a slave ship. https://www.dur.ac.uk/durham.first/winter07/slaveship/ : accessed 13 July 2018
[371] Discovering Bristol. Bristol and Transatlantic Slavery. http://www.discoveringbristol.org.uk/slavery/ : accessed 13 July, 2018
[372] The National Archives. Exhibitions. Black Presence. Abolition of the Slave Trade. http://www.nationalarchives.gov.uk/pathways/blackhistory/rights/abolition.htm : accessed 13 July, 2018
[373] Living Heritage. Parliament and the British Slave Trade. https://www.parliament.uk/slavetrade : accessed 13 July, 2018
[374] Grannum Guy. Researching African-Caribbean Family History. Last updated 17 February, 2011. http://www.bbc.co.uk/history/familyhistory/next_steps/genealogy_article_01.shtml : accessed 30 May, 2017

375 Ancestry. DNA, Genetic Ancestry. https://www.ancestry.co.uk/dna/origins/ : accessed 28 May, 2017

376 Jamaican Family Search. Genealogy Research Library. Jackson, Patricia. Last updated 2013. http://www.jamaicanfamilysearch.com/ : accessed 28 May, 2017

377 Wikipedia. Quadroon. https://en.wikipedia.org/wiki/Quadroon :accessed 19 April, 2019

378 Wikipedia. Hypodescent. https://en.wikipedia.org/wiki/Hypodescent : accessed 19 April, 2019

379 Wikipedia. Quadroon. https://en.wikipedia.org/wiki/Quadroon : accessed 3 February, 2019

380 Mitchell, Madeleine E., Jamaican Ancestry: How To Find Out More, p.1. https://www.amazon.co.uk/Jamaican-Ancestry-Find-More-Revised/dp/0788442821#reader_0788442821 : accessed 30 May, 2017

381 Family Search. Caribbean, Jamaica, Middlesex County, Saint Mary Parish. https://familysearch.org/wiki/en/Saint_Mary_Parish,_Jamaica#cite_note-1 : accessed 30 May, 2017

382 The Digital Library of the Caribbean (dLOC).http://dloc.com/ : accessed 9 September, 2018

383 'Jamaica Records, Caribbeana, Vol. 1 (1910):136. http://dloc.com/ : accessed 28 May, 2017

384 The Centre for the Study of the Legacies of British Slave-ownership, UCL. https://www.ucl.ac.uk/lbs/ : accessed 13 July, 2018

385 Grannum Guy. Researching African-Caribbean Family History. Last updated 17 February, 2011. http://www.bbc.co.uk/history/familyhistory/next_steps/genealogy_article_01.shtml : accessed 30 May, 2017

386 Discovering Bristol. Learning Journeys. The Georgian House. http://www.discoveringbristol.org.uk/slavery/learning-journeys/georgian-house/ : accessed 13 July, 2018

387 Bristol Museums. Georgian House Museum. https://www.bristolmuseums.org.uk/georgian-house-museum/ : accessed 9 September, 2018

388 Discovering Bristol. John Pinney: a plantation owner. http://www.discoveringbristol.org.uk/slavery/people-involved/traders-merchants-planters/caribbean-plantation-development/john-pinney-plantation-owner/ : accessed 9 September, 2018

389 Bristol Museums. Georgian House Museum. https://www.bristolmuseums.org.uk/georgian-house-museum/ : accessed 9 September, 2018

390 Visit Bristol. Pero's Bridge. https://visitbristol.co.uk/things-to-do/peros-bridge-p269523 : accessed 20 April, 2019

391 America's Black Holocaust Museum. https://abhmuseum.org/the-scourged-back-how-runaway-slave-and-soldier-private-gordon-changed-history/ : accessed 23 March, 2018

392 Wikimedia Commons. Scourged back by McPherson & Oliver, 1863, retouched.jpg https://commons.wikimedia.org/wiki/File:Scourged_back_by_McPherson_%26_Oliver,_1863,_retouched.jpg : accessed 15 October, 2018

393 Picture of a Slave. The Liberator. Boston, Massachusetts. 12 June 1863. p. 2. https://www.newspapers.com/clip/824572/the_liberator/? : accessed 12 November, 2012.

394 Wikipedia, Edward Colston. https://en.wikipedia.org/wiki/Edward_Colston : accessed 25 February, 2018

395 Wikipedia. John Cassidy. https://en.wikipedia.org/wiki/John_Cassidy_(artist) :accessed 7 September, 2018

396 Event Brite. Bristol slavery trail tickets.https://www.eventbrite.com/e/bristol-slavery-trail-tickets-38005512511# : accessed 9 September, 2018

397 Bristol Slave Trade Trail tour, facilitated by Dr. Edson Burton. burtonedson@gmail.com

398 Think baby names. Colston. http://www.thinkbabynames.com/meaning/1/Colston : accessed 20 April, 2019

399 Manchester & Lancashire Family History Society. http://www.mlfhs.org.uk/ : accessed 13 July, 2018

400 Parliament UK. Parliament and the British Slave Trade 1600-1833. Family History Research. https://www.parliament.uk/about/living-heritage/transformingsociety/tradeindustry/slavetrade/reflections-and-anecdotes/family-history-research/ : accessed 13 July, 2018

401 The Guardian. Opinion. Should Bristol's Colston Hall change its name – to distance itself from slavery? 21 Jun 2014 https://www.theguardian.com/commentisfree/2014/jun/21/should-colston-hall-change-name-slavery-bristol : accessed 21 April, 2019

402 ITV News. Breaking: Bristol's Colston Hall will change its name to escape 'toxic brand.' 26 April, 2017. http://www.itv.com/news/westcountry/2017-04-26/breaking-bristols-colston-hall-will-change-its-name-after-long-campaign/ : accessed 1 July, 2018

403 Bristol 24/7. Helen West. Colston Hall name change: what do you think? Apr 27, 2017. https://www.bristol247.com/news-and-features/news/colston-hall-name-change-think/ : accessed 1 July, 2018

404 Olawale Arts. About Me. http://olawalearts.org.uk/ : accessed 5 September, 2018

405 UWE. Staff Profiles. Dr Madge Dresser. https://people.uwe.ac.uk/Person/MadgeDresser : accessed 5 Sep, 2018

406 The Guardian. Opinion. Should Bristol's Colston Hall change its name – to distance itself from slavery? 21 Jun 2014 https://www.theguardian.com/commentisfree/2014/jun/21/should-colston-hall-change-name-slavery-bristol : accessed 1 July, 2018

407 ITV News. Bristol Music Trust: why we're changing the name of Colston Hall

http://www.itv.com/news/westcountry/update/2017-04-26/bristol-music-trust-why-were-changing-the-name-of-colston-hall/ : accessed 9 September, 2018.

[408] Colston hall. Vision and renaming. https://www.colstonhall.org/transform-the-hall/vision-and-renaming/ : accessed 20 April, 2019

[409] Google maps. Black Boys Hill https://www.google.co.uk/maps/search/black+boys+hill+bristol/@51.4698242,-2.6168814,17z/data=!3m1!4b1 : accessed 30 April, 2018

[410] Slavery Bath History. Bath and the Slave Trade. Elton House in Abbey Green and the Eltons of Clevedon Court, Bristol. Posted 24 February, 2016. https://slaverybathhistory.wordpress.com/2016/02/24/elton-house-in-abbey-green-and-the-eltons-of-clevedon-court-bristol/ : accessed 21 April, 2019

[411] Discovering Bristol. Blaise Castle House. http://discoveringbristol.org.uk/browse/slavery/blaise-castle-house/ : accessed 21 April, 2019

[412] Discovering Bristol. Estates within 2 miles of Bristol. http://www.discoveringbristol.org.uk/slavery/routes/america-to-bristol/profits/estates-2-miles-bristol/ : accessed 21 April, 2019

[413] The Free Dictionary. Lynching. https://www.thefreedictionary.com/lynching : accessed 14 November, 2018

[414] Grenham, J. Lynch Surname History. https://www.johngrenham.com/surnamescode/surnamehistory.php?surname=lynch&search_type=full : accessed 14 November, 2018

[415] House of Names. Lynch. https://www.houseofnames.com/lynch-family-crest : accesses 14 November, 2018

[416] Why Evolution is True. School named after Lynch family to be renamed because of racial connotations. https://whyevolutionistrue.wordpress.com/2017/07/26/school-named-after-lynch-family-to-be-renamed-because-of-racial-connotations/ : accessed 14 November, 2018

[417] Why Evolution is True. School named after Lynch family to be renamed because of racial connotations. https://whyevolutionistrue.wordpress.com/2017/07/26/school-named-after-lynch-family-to-be-renamed-because-of-racial-connotations/ : accessed 14 November, 2018

[418] Email discussion with D.P. Lindegaard, November, 2018

[419] Digital Library. Build A Book. Celebration of Women Writers. Narrative of Sojourner Truth, A Northern Slave Http://Digital.Library.Upenn.Edu/Women/Truth/1850/1850.Html : accessed 25 February, 2018

[420] University of Cambridge, Apollo. Mill, Mary. Edward & Eliza. https://www.repository.cam.ac.uk/handle/1810/262360 : Accessed 25 February, 2018

[421] Endangered Archives Programme, Manumission Liber: Volume 5 [1747-1838] https://eap.bl.uk/archive-file/EAP148-3-1-1 : accessed 25 February, 2018

[422] Lindegaard, D.P. Black Bristolians.

[423] John Jay College of Criminal Justice. New York Slavery Records Index. https://nyslavery.commons.gc.cuny.edu/ : accessed 25 February, 2018

[424] FMP. World Records. Naturalizations in Travel & Migration. https://search.findmypast.co.uk/search-world-records-in-travel-and-migration/and_naturalizations : accessed 9 September, 2018

[425] Sky News. Theresa May to hold 'Windrush' immigration summit after U-turn. 16 April, 2018. https://www.msn.com/en-gb/news/uknews/theresa-may-to-hold-windrush-immigration-summit-after-u-turn/ar-AAvWdhZ?ocid=spartandhp : accessed 27 August, 2018

[426] Metro. Joe Roberts. Thousands of Windrush Generation landing cards found in National Archives. 21 Apr 2018. http://metro.co.uk/2018/04/21/thousands-windrush-generation-landing-cards-found-national-archives-7485225/?ito=cbshare : accessed 3 May, 2018

[427] University College London. Legacies of British Slave-ownership https://www.ucl.ac.uk/lbs/ : accessed 12 Nov, 2018

[428] Bristol Museums. Georgian House Museum. https://www.bristolmuseums.org.uk/georgian-house-museum/ : accessed 9 September, 2018

[429] Wikipedia. Sojourner Truth. https://en.wikipedia.org/wiki/Sojourner_Truth : accessed 15 October, 2018

[430] Extract from 'Slavery As It Is,' Slavery A System of Inherent Cruelty, by Theodore D. Weld. Narrative Dictated by Sojourner Truth (ca.1797-1883); edited by Olive Gilbert; Appendix by Theodore D. Weld. Sojourner Truth, A Northern Slave, Emancipated From Bodily Servitude By The State Of New York, In 1828. With A Portrait. http://digital.library.upenn.edu/women/truth/1850/1850.html : accessed 13 July, 2018

[431] Wikimedia Commons. Sojourner Truth. https://commons.wikimedia.org/wiki/File:Sojourner_truth_c1870.jpg : accessed 15 October, 2018

[432] Time. Gregory Rodriguez How Genealogy Became Almost as Popular as Porn. 30 May 2014. http://time.com/133811/how-genealogy-became-almost-as-popular-as-porn/ : accessed 10 September, 2018

[433] Wikipedia. Stars on Sunday. https://en.wikipedia.org/wiki/Stars_on_Sunday_(TV_series) : accessed 3 February, 2019

[434] Hareven, T.K., The Search for Generational memory: Tribal Rites in Industrial society. file:///C:/Users/Lenovo/Documents/Genealogy/SearchMyPast%20business/BOOK/Ethics%20articles/generational%20

memory.pdf : accessed `18 September, 2018
[435] Barack Obama, 1995, Dreams from My Father (A Story of Race and Inheritance). P. vii. Times Books (1995), Three Rivers Press (2004)
[436] Obama, Barack. Memoir. 1995. Dreams from My Father: A Story of Race and Inheritance. https://en.wikipedia.org/wiki/Dreams_from_My_Father : accessed 10 September, 2018.
[437] Time. Gregory Rodriguez How Genealogy Became Almost as Popular as Porn. 30 May 2014. http://time.com/133811/how-genealogy-became-almost-as-popular-as-porn/ : accessed 11 September, 2018
[438] Library Aceondo. Adeyemi College of Education. History. Barack Obama. Dreams from my father. http://library.aceondo.net/ebooks/HISTORY/Dreams_from_My_Father-Barack_Obama.pdf : accessed 15 October, 2015
[439] Wikipedia. Sojourner. https://en.wikipedia.org/wiki/Sojourner : accessed 15 October, 2018
[440] Wikipedia. Sojourner. https://en.wikipedia.org/wiki/Sojourner_Truth : accessed 15 November, 2018
[441] Barack Obama, 1995, Dreams from My Father (A Story of Race and Inheritance). P. xi. Times Books (1995), Three Rivers Press (2004)
[442] University of London. School of Advanced Study. What's Happening in Black British History III. https://www.sas.ac.uk/videos-and-podcasts/philosophy/what-s-happening-black-british-history-iii-session-1-david-killingray : accessed 13 July, 2018
[443] Mitchell, Madeleine E. 2008. Jamaican Ancestry: How To Find Out More. p. xiv. https://www.amazon.co.uk/Jamaican-Ancestry-Find-More-Revised/dp/0788442821#reader_0788442821 : accessed 30 May, 2017
[444] Wikipedia. Sankofa. https://en.wikipedia.org/wiki/Sankofa : accessed 23 July, 2018
[445] Internet Archive. WayBack Machine. African Tradition, Proverbs and Sankofa. https://web.archive.org/web/20110420131901/http://ctl.du.edu/spirituals/literature/sankofa.cfm : accessed 23 July, 2018
[446] Adrian Stone. Going back to his roots: How a Bristol man traced his family back to his enslaved African ancestor. https://social.shorthand.com/bristol247/u2sfRkleqc/going-back-to-his-roots : accessed 13 July, 2018
[447] The National Archives. Research Guides. Slavery or slave owners. http://www.nationalarchives.gov.uk/help-with-your-research/research-guides/slavery-or-slave-owners/ : accessed 13 July, 2018
[448] Ancestry. Search. Census & Electoral Rolls Slave Registers of former British Colonial Dependencies, 1813-1834. https://search.ancestry.co.uk/search/db.aspx?htx=List&dbid=1129&offerid=0%3a7858%3a0 : accessed 13 July, 2018
[449] Voice online. Going Back To His Roots. http://www.voice-online.co.uk/article/going-back-his-roots-0 : accessed 13 July, 2018
[450] IMDb. Noel Clarke. https://www.imdb.com/name/nm0164929/ : accessed 9 September, 2018
[451] The Genealogist. Noel Clarke. 30 August 2017. https://www.thegenealogist.co.uk/featuredarticles/2017/who-do-you-think-you-are/noel-clarke-626/ : accessed 23 July, 2018
[452] BBC. WDYTYA. Noel Clarke. https://www.bbc.co.uk/programmes/p05d0zqm : accessed 26 December, 2019
[453] BBC. WDYTYA. Noel Clarke, Series 14. 14 September, 2017. From slave to landowner. http://www.bbc.co.uk/programmes/p05g29xp : accessed 23 July, 2018
[454] WDYTYA. Shirley Ballas. Series 15. Episode 5. https://www.bbc.co.uk/programmes/b0bdlqnh : accessed 23 Jul, 2018
[455] Daily Mail online. Shirley Ballas. http://www.dailymail.co.uk/news/article-5980695/Strictly-Come-Dancing-Shirley-Ballas-finds-ancestors-slaves-BBC-Think-Are.html : accessed 23 July, 2018
[456] Wikipedia. Madagascar. https://en.wikipedia.org/wiki/Madagascar : accessed 9 September, 2018
[457] WDYTYA? Magazine. http://www.whodoyouthinkyouaremagazine.com/episode/marvin-humes : accessed 9 September, 2018
[458] WDYTYA? Magazine. Where does Marvin Humes visit in his episode of WDYTYA? http://www.whodoyouthinkyouaremagazine.com/blog/where-does-marvin-humes-visit-his-episode-wdytya : accessed 9 September, 2018
[459] WDYTYA? Magazine. Johnathon Scott. 6 websites for tracing Caribbean ancestors. http://www.whodoyouthinkyouaremagazine.com/blog/6-websites-tracing-caribbean-ancestors : accessed 9 September, 2018
[460] Guild of One Name Studies. Allen. https://one-name.org/name_profile/allen/ : accessed 1 February, 2019
[461] FTDNA. Allan. https://www.familytreedna.com/groups/allan/about/background : accessed 1 February, 2019
[462] Facebook. UK Jamaica Family Roots. https://www.facebook.com/groups/1117612944938263/?ref=br_rs : accessed 1 February, 2019
[463] University of Birmingham. https://www.birmingham.ac.uk/research/activity/cwmh/research/history-detectives.aspx : accessed 21 April, 2019
[464] Anti Slavery. History Detectives: Black People in the West Midlands, 1650-1918.

http://www.antislavery.ac.uk/items/show/416 : accessed 5 May, 2019

[465] Ancestry. What is a reference panel? https://www.ancestry.com/cs/dna-help/ethnicity/estimates : accessed 9 September, 2018

[466] Ancestry. Welcome to Your Ethnicity Estimate. 2m 21s. https://www.ancestry.com/cs/dna-help/ethnicity/intro : accessed 17 September, 2018

[467] Voice online. Going Back To His Roots. Adrian Stone. http://www.voice-online.co.uk/article/going-back-his-roots-0 : accessed 13 July, 2018

[468] Ancestry. Genetic Communities. African Caribbeans. https://www.ancestry.co.uk/dna/origins/59CF2F77-B456-4620-B4DF-3ED7AC7B700F/view-all/11.24/story : accessed 6 May, 2017

[469] Estes, R. DNAeXplained – Genetic Genealogy. Discovering Your Ancestors – One Gene at a Time. Ethnicity Testing – A Conundrum. Posted February 10, 2016. https://dna-explained.com/2016/02/10/ethnicity-testing-a-conundrum/ : accessed 9 September, 2018

[470] Andre Kearns. Tracing African Ancestry using DNA. Posted Aug 5, 2018. https://medium.com/@andrekearns/tracing-african-ancestry-using-dna-52065e19632e?fbclid=IwAR3cHSWyAJ1DEVGSeGw--w5XvGOQhtA-GRtx5yafhPfqJ29Nev-KbM978rc : accessed 3 January, 2018

[471] Andre Kearns. Tracing African Ancestry using DNA. Posted Aug 5, 2018. https://medium.com/@andrekearns/tracing-african-ancestry-using-dna-52065e19632e?fbclid=IwAR3cHSWyAJ1DEVGSeGw--w5XvGOQhtA-GRtx5yafhPfqJ29Nev-KbM978rc : accessed 3 January, 2018

[472] AncestryDNA. Understanding Patterns of Inheritance: Where Did My DNA Come From? (And Why It Matters). Anna Swayne. March 5, 2014. https://blogs.ancestry.com/ancestry/2014/03/05/understanding-patterns-of-inheirtance-where-did-my-dna-come-from-and-why-it-matters/?o_xid=85757&o_lid=85757&o_sch=Email+Programs : accessed 24 August, 2018

[473] Genetics. The Tech. Barry Starr. Shouldn't my sister and I have the same ancestry results for our DNA? We have the same parents. https://genetics.thetech.org/ask-a-geneticist/same-parents-different-ancestry : accessed 13 Sep, 2018

[474] Ancestry. Ethnicity FAQ. https://www.ancestry.co.uk/cs/dna-help/ethnicity/faq#timechange : accessed 17 September, 2018

[475] Ancestry. Ball, C.A. et al. Ethnicity Estimate White Paper. https://www.ancestry.com/cs/dna-help/ethnicity/whitepaper : accessed 9 September, 2018

[476] Kitty Cooper. Finally, Ancestry's New Ethnicity Estimates. 12 September, 2018. http://blog.kittycooper.com/2018/09/finally-ancestrys-new-ethnicity-estimates/ : accessed 17 September, 2018

[477] GEdmatch. https://www.gedmatch.com : accessed 21 April, 2019

[478] Ancestry. DNA origins. https://www.ancestry.co.uk/dna/origins/35E039C4-DB9C-406B-BCDE-F3E72F081B5B?o_iid=90600&o_lid=90600&o_sch=Web%20Property : accessed 25 September, 2018

[479] Kaitlyn Wylde. Spotify & AncestryDNA users can now generate personalized playlists based on their DNA heritage results. 20 September, 2018. https://www.bustle.com/p/spotify-ancestrydna-users-can-now-generate-personalized-playlists-based-on-their-dna-heritage-results-11957587 : accessed 24 September, 2018

[480] Philosophy Talk. What is Cultural Appropriation? https://www.philosophytalk.org/blog/what-cultural-appropriation : accessed 23 September, 2018

[481] Luther Chips College. Cultural appropriation vs. cultural appreciation. https://www.lutherchips.com/4405/features/cultural-appropriation-vs-cultural-appreciation/ : accessed 21 April, 2019

[482] Ancestry. DNA Playllist. https://ancestrydnaplaylist.withspotify.com/1584986/your-playlist : accessed 25 September, 2018

[483] Wikipedia. Sinéad O'Connor. https://en.wikipedia.org/wiki/Sinéad_O%27Connor : accessed 25 September, 2018

[484] Foy Vance. http://foyvance.com/ : accessed 25 September, 2018

[485] Saint Sister. http://www.saintsisterband.com/ : accessed 25 September, 2018

[486] African Grooves. Les Sympathics de Porto Novo. http://africangrooves.blogspot.com/2015/10/les-sympathics-de-porto-novo-benin-to.html : accessed 25 September, 2018

[487] Walters, Penny. 'So where are you from? Being diaspora.' British Connections, International Society for British Genealogy and Family History Volume 18, Issue 3 July – September 2017, pp. 51-52

[488] Taylor, S., 2003, Narratives of Identity and Place. The Meanings of place and identity. P. 13. https://books.google.co.uk/books?id=VGqLAgAAQBAJ&pg=PA14&lpg=PA14&dq=nostalgia+(%E2%80%98when+place,+identity,+culture+and+ancestry+coincided%E2%80%99&source=bl&ots=zwto5p_7Z4&sig=FRHJNunzOLotrtidD0ktWlqUV6g&hl=en&sa=X&ved=2ahUKEwj808bwmNTdAhVMKMAKHXKkAD0Q6AEwAHoECAIQAQ#v=onepage&q=nostalgia%20(%E2%80%98when%20place%2C%20identity%2C%20culture%20and%20ancestry%20coincided%E2%80%99&f=false : accessed 24 September, 2018

[489] Oxford Dictionaries online. Diaspora. https://www.oxforddictionaries.com/ : accessed 4 August, 2017.

[490] Oxford Reference. Diaspora. http://www.oxfordreference.com/view/10.1093/oi/authority.20110803095716263 :

accessed 21 April, 2019

[491] BBC News. The Irish exodus: In search of a brighter future. 17 March, 1998.
http://news.bbc.co.uk/1/hi/uk/1224611.stm : accessed 4 August, 2017.

[492] Family Tree magazine USA. German Genealogy 101 Online Course.
https://www.familytreemagazine.com/store/university/german-genealogy-101-r8300-september-24?k=H8Vg%2FXUOKbn%2BJKFA4fAzaNmeqNPEdjETA2F10HYRhXg%3D&utm_medium=email&utm_source=course&utm_campaign=ftu-vlw-nl-180924-german : accessed 24 September, 2018

[493] BBC News. The Irish exodus: In search of a brighter future. 17 March, 1998.
http://news.bbc.co.uk/1/hi/uk/1224611.stm : accessed 4 August, 2017.

[493] BBC News. One in four Britons claim Irish roots. 16 March, 2001. http://news.bbc.co.uk/1/hi/uk/1224611.stm :
accessed 4 August, 2017.

[493] Statistics Canada. 2006 Census Topic-based tabulations. Ethnic Origin. http://www12.statcan.gc.ca/census-recensement/2006/dp-pd/tbt/Av-
eng.cfm?LANG=E&APATH=3&DETAIL=0&DIM=1&FL=A&FREE=0&GC=0&GID=0&GK=0&GRP=1&PID=97614&PRID=0&PTYPE=88971,97154&S=0&SHOWALL=0&SUB=801&Temporal=2006&THEME=80&VID=17526&VNAMEE=&VNAMEF= :
accessed 6 August, 2017

[493] Australian Bureau of Statistics. Media Fact Sheet. 27, June, 2007.
http://www.abs.gov.au/Ausstats/abs@.nsf/7d12b0f6763c78caca257061001cc588/5a47791aa683b719ca257306000d536c!OpenDocument : accessed 6 August, 2017

[493] Bowden, Noreen. Global Irish. http://www.globalirish.ie/ : accessed 4 August, 2017.

[493] A Letter From Ireland. Irish surnames update. http://www.aletterfromireland.com/irish-surnames-update-march-2016/ accessed 31 July, 2017.

[494] Statistics Canada. 2006 Census Topic-based tabulations. Ethnic Origin. http://www12.statcan.gc.ca/census-recensement/2006/dp-pd/tbt/Av-
eng.cfm?LANG=E&APATH=3&DETAIL=0&DIM=1&FL=A&FREE=0&GC=0&GID=0&GK=0&GRP=1&PID=97614&PRID=0&PTYPE=88971,97154&S=0&SHOWALL=0&SUB=801&Temporal=2006&THEME=80&VID=17526&VNAMEE=&VNAMEF= :
accessed 6 August, 2017

[495] Australian Bureau of Statistics. Media Fact Sheet. 27, June, 2007.
http://www.abs.gov.au/Ausstats/abs@.nsf/7d12b0f6763c78caca257061001cc588/5a47791aa683b719ca257306000d536c!OpenDocument : accessed 6 August, 2017

[496] Bowden, Noreen. Global Irish. http://www.globalirish.ie/ : accessed 4 August, 2017.

[497] A Letter From Ireland. Surnames Update. http://www.aletterfromireland.com/irish-surnames-update-march-2016/
accessed 31 July, 2017.

[498] Taylor, S., 2003, Narratives of Identity and Place. The Meanings of place and identity. Nash, C. P. 14.
https://books.google.co.uk/books?id=VGqLAgAAQBAJ&pg=PA14&lpg=PA14&dq=nostalgia+(%E2%80%98when+place,+identity,+culture+and+ancestry+coincided%E2%80%99&source=bl&ots=zwto5p_7Z4&sig=FRHJNunzOLotrtidD0ktWIqUV6g&hl=en&sa=X&ved=2ahUKEwj808bwmNTdAhVMKMAKHXKkAD0Q6AEwAHoECAIQAQ#v=onepage&q=nostalgia%20(%E2%80%98when%20place%2C%20identity%2C%20culture%20and%20ancestry%20coincided%E2%80%99&f=false :
accessed 24 September, 2018.

[499] Next Gen. Genealogy Network. DNA and the Next Generation: Part II. Posted 17 August, 2015.
https://www.tnggn.org/dna-and-the-next-generation-part-ii/ : accessed 22 Dec., 2018.

[500] John Grenham, 2004, 'Tracing Your Irish Ancestors', (pp10-11), *Gill & Macmillan.*

[501] Walters, Penny. 'Being From a Diaspora. A Journey to where My Ancestors Were From.' Journal of the Bristol &
Avon Family History Society, Dec. 2017, No. 170, pp.30-31.

[502] Google Maps. Drimoleague.
https://www.google.co.uk/maps/place/Baurnahulla,+Drimoleague,+Co.+Cork,+Ireland/@51.6599482,-9.2700001,15z/data=!3m1!4b1!4m5!3m4!1s0x484507f75d3a9c35:0xa00c7a99731bc80!8m2!3d51.6599357!4d-9.2612453 : accessed 18 September, 2018

[503] Explore West Cork. Drimoleague. http://explorewestcork.ie/villages/drimoleague/ : accessed 18 September, 2018

[504] Walters, Penny. 'Visiting Where Your Ancestors Came From.' Irish Lives Remembered, Issue 39, Winter 2017, pp. 47-49 https://www.irishfamilyhistorycentre.com/store/854 : accessed 18 September, 2018

[505] Kearney, T, O'Regan, P., 2015, Skibbereen, The Famine Story. *Macalla Publishing.*

[506] Mizen Head.http://www.mizenhead.net/ : accessed 21 April, 2019

[507] Wikipedia. Sneem. https://en.wikipedia.org/wiki/Sneem : accessed 21 April, 2019

[508] Valentia Island. Grotto and slate quarry. http://www.valentiaisland.ie/life-business/history-culture/grotto-slate-quarry/ : accessed 21 April, 2019

[509] Wiktionary. Race Memory. https://en.wiktionary.org/wiki/race_memory : accessed 21 April, 2019

[510] Psychology Today. Berit Brogaard. Remembering Things From Before You Were Born. Can memories be innate? 24 February, 2013. https://www.psychologytoday.com/us/blog/the-superhuman-mind/201302/remembering-things-you-were-born : accessed 13 November, 2018

[511] Psychology Today. Nathan H. Lents. The Meaning and Meaninglessness of Genealogy. Posted Jan 29, 2018 https://www.psychologytoday.com/gb/blog/beastly-behavior/201801/the-meaning-and-meaninglessness-genealogy : accessed 30 September, 2018

[512] Strokestown Park. History. http://www.strokestownpark.ie/the-history-of-strokestown-park/ : accessed 18 September, 2018

[513] Strokestown Park. http://www.strokestownpark.ie/ : accessed 5 May, 2019

[514] 2018 Irish Famine Summer School. Irish Journeys: Famine Legacies and Reconnecting Communities. 20-24 June, 2018. Penny Walters. 'Genealogy Tourism: a new niche market.'

[515] Bristol Museum. Fabric Africa - Fashion Show. https://www.facebook.com/events/2064713050487271/?notif_t=event_calendar_create&notif_id=1536571997742309 :accessed 10 September, 2018

[516] Toma´s R., Jime´nez. Affiliative ethnic identity: a more elastic link between ethnic ancestry and culture. Ethnic and Racial Studies Vol. 33 No. 10 November 2010. pp. 1756-1775. https://pdfs.semanticscholar.org/8c42/d53fc43d32c560388a9a74661c0e904665ed.pdf : accessed 21 September, 2018

[517] Cork Foundation. About. https://corkfoundation.com/about/ : accessed 18 September, 2018

[518] Wikipedia. Native Americans in the United States. https://en.wikipedia.org/wiki/Native_Americans_in_the_United_States : accessed 13 September, 2018

[519] Henry Louis Gates, Jr. and Lisa Arnold. Huffington Post. Joining Your Family's Native American Tribe. 5 January, 2016, updated 6 December, 2017 https://www.huffingtonpost.com/henry-louis-gates-jr/joining-your-familys-nati_b_8917854.html : accessed 9 September, 2018

[520] Ancestry. Native American Records. https://search.ancestry.com/search/group/nativeamerican : accessed 10 July, 2018

[521] Amie Bowser Tennant. My Kith & Kin. Southeastern Native American Research. https://mykithnkin.blogspot.com/2014/06/southeastern-native-american-research.html : accessed July 10, 2018

[522] Oklahoma Historical Society. Andrew K. Frank, Trail of Tears (term), The Encyclopaedia of Oklahoma History and Culture. www.okhistory.org : accessed July 10, 2018

[523] Oklahoma Historical Society. Andrew K. Frank. Five Civilized Tribes. The Encyclopaedia of Oklahoma History and Culture, http://www.okhistory.org/publications/enc/entry.php?entry=FI011 : accessed 10 July, 2018

[524] Oklahoma Historical Society. Andrew K. Frank. Five Civilized Tribes. The Encyclopaedia of Oklahoma History and Culture, http://www.okhistory.org/publications/enc/entry.php?entry=FI011 : accessed 10 July, 2018

[525] Wikipedia. Dawes Commission. https://en.wikipedia.org/wiki/Dawes_Commission : accessed 13 September, 2018

[526] HuffPost. Elizabeth Warren Releases DNA Test Results. 15, October 2018. https://www.yahoo.com/news/elizabeth-warren-releases-dna-test-104435317.html : accessed 15 October, 2018.

[527] Carlos D. Bustamante. Executive summary report. Elizabeth Warren. https://mk0elizabethwarh5ore.kinstacdn.com/wp-content/uploads/2018/10/Bustamante_Report_2018.pdf : accessed 15 October, 2018.

[528] Daily Mail newspaper. http://www.dailymail.co.uk/femail/article-5111715/Meghans-family-members-Harrys-laws.html#ixzz4zdKLcG3d : accessed 27 November, 2017.

[529] The Guardian. Meghan Markle's wedding was a rousing celebration of blackness. Afua Hirsch. 20 May 2018. https://www.theguardian.com/uk-news/2018/may/19/meghan-markles-wedding-was-a-celebration-of-blackness : accessed 27 July, 2018

[530] Wikipedia. Reverend Michael Curry. https://en.wikipedia.org/wiki/Michael_Curry_(bishop) : accessed 10 September, 2018

[531] Hello Magazine. Reverend Michael Curry. https://www.hellomagazine.com/royalty/2018052248818/reverend-michael-curry-royal-wedding-invite-april-fools/ : accessed 10 September, 2018

[532] Wikipedia. Oprah Winfrey. https://en.wikipedia.org/wiki/Oprah_Winfrey : accessed 10 September, 2018

[533] Serena Williams. https://www.serenawilliams.com/ : accessed 10 September, 2018

[534] Alexis Ohanian. https://en.wikipedia.org/wiki/Alexis_Ohanian : accessed 10 September, 2018

[535] IMDb. Idris Elba https://www.imdb.com/name/nm0252961/ : accessed 10 September, 2018

[536] IMDb. Gina Torres. https://www.imdb.com/name/nm0868659/ : accessed 10 September, 2018

[537] Buzz Feed Video. Ethnically Ambiguous People Take A DNA Test. 6 October, 2018. https://www.youtube.com/watch?v=5171eGo13hs : accessed 17 October, 2018

[538] Ancestry. Ethnicity FAQ. https://www.ancestry.co.uk/cs/dna-help/ethnicity/faq#timechange : accessed 17 September, 2018

[539] Ancestry. Why is my percentage for a region higher (or lower) than my family tree suggests it should be? https://www.ancestry.com/cs/dna-help/ethnicity/expectations : accessed 9 September, 2018

[540] The DNA Geek. Major Enhancement to AncestryDNA's Ethnicity Estimates. 12 September, 2018. http://thednageek.com/major-enhancement-to-ancestrydnas-ethnicity-estimates/ : accessed 17 September, 2018

[541] GEDmatch. 'One to many' matches. https://www.gedmatch.com/select.php : accessed 9 September, 2018

[542] Huffington Post. Christine Michel Carter. I Celebrated Black History Month … By Finding Out I Was White. https://www.huffingtonpost.com/entry/i-celebrated-black-history-month-by-finding-out-i_us_58b1ce17e4b0e5fdf61972bb : accessed 13 November, 2018

[543] DNA Explained. Roberta Estes. Liv Tyler - Who Do You Think You Are - Drummer Boy. https://dna-explained.com/2017/04/23/liv-tyler-who-do-you-think-you-are-drummer-boy/ : accessed 9 May 2018

[544] DNA Explained. Roberta Estes. RBM reply. 28 April, 2017 https://dna-explained.com/2017/04/23/liv-tyler-who-do-you-think-you-are-drummer-boy/ : accessed 10 September, 2018

Chapter 6

[545] Wikipedia. Genealogy. https://en.wikipedia.org/wiki/Genealogy : accessed 15 November, 2018

[546] Hareven, T.K., The Search for Generational memory: Tribal Rites in Industrial society. In Harold Marcuse, Department Of History, University Of California. http://www.history.ucsb.edu/faculty/marcuse/classes/201/articles/78HarevenSearchGenerationalDaedalus0001.pdf : accessed 27 October, 2018

[547] Time. Gregory Rodriguez How Genealogy Became Almost as Popular as Porn. 30 May 2014. http://time.com/133811/how-genealogy-became-almost-as-popular-as-porn/ : accessed 10 September, 2018

[548] Time. Gregory Rodriguez How Genealogy Became Almost as Popular as Porn. 30 May 2014. http://time.com/133811/how-genealogy-became-almost-as-popular-as-porn/ : accessed 10 September, 2018

[549] The Internet Archive. Collins, Arthur. (1741) The English baronetage, vol. 1. P. 8. London: Printed for Tho. Wotton. Tichborne. http://archive.org/details/englishbaroneta00unkngoog : accessed 15 March, 2017

[550] Funding Universe. Her Majesty's Stationery Office History. http://www.fundinguniverse.com/company-histories/her-majesty-s-stationery-office-history/ : accessed 26 October, 2018

[551] Wikipedia. The American Antiquarian Society. https://en.wikipedia.org/wiki/American_Antiquarian_Society : accessed 15 November, 2018

[552] Wikipedia. John Farmer. https://en.wikipedia.org/wiki/John_Farmer_(author) : accessed 15 November, 2018

[553] Burkes Peerage. Home page. http://burkespeerage.com/ : accessed 21 April, 2018

[554] National Archives. History of the Public Records Acts. http://www.nationalarchives.gov.uk/information-management/legislation/public-records-act/history-of-pra/ : accessed 19 June, 2018

[555] University of California. Southern Regional Library facility. Microfiche. http://www.srlf.ucla.edu/exhibit/text/BriefHistory.htm : accessed 1 May, 2018

[556] Pearl Scan Group. Microfiche Scanning. https://www.microfiche-microfilm-scanning.co.uk/microfiche-scanning : accessed 26 October, 2018

[557] DNA from the beginning. Concept 1. Children resemble their parents. http://www.dnaftb.org/1/bio.html : accessed 7 April, 2019

[558] Cokayne, George E., ed. (1887-1898) The complete peerage of England, Scotland, Ireland … London: G. Bell & Sons. https://archive.org/details/completepeerage02cokahrish (vol. 2, Bra-C) : accessed 14 March, 2017

[559] George Edward Cokayne. https://en.wikipedia.org/wiki/George_Edward_Cokayne : accessed 21 April, 2018

[560] Wikipedia. William Phillimore. https://en.wikipedia.org/wiki/William_Phillimore_Watts_Phillimore : accessed 21 April, 2018

[561] UK Genealogy Archives. William Phillimore. https://ukga.org/cgi-bin/search.cgi?action=ViewRec&DB=11&recid=23317 : accessed 21 April, 2018

[562] Wikisource. 1922 Encyclopædia Britannica/ Round, John Horace. https://en.wikisource.org/wiki/1922_Encyclopædia_Britannica/Round,_John_Horace : accessed 21 April, 2018

[563] FamilySearch. About. https://www.familysearch.org/ : accessed 8 December, 2019

[564] Geni. Percival Boyd. https://www.geni.com/people/Percival-Boyd/6000000040393499089 : accessed 1 May, 2018

[565] Society of Genealogists. George Frederick Tudor Sherwood. http://www.societyofgenealogists.com/love-in-the-archives-the-love-letters-of-george-and-sophia-sherwood-and-a-genealogical-romance/ : accessed 21 April, 2018

[566] NGS. History. Condensed by Shirley Langdon Wilcox, from articles in the National Genealogical Society Quarterly, December 1953-March 1955. https://www.ngsgenealogy.org/cs/history : accessed 26 August, 2018

[567] NGS. Shirley Langdon Wilcox. 'The National Genealogical Society: A Look at Its First One Hundred Years.' https://www.ngsgenealogy.org/galleries/aboutngs/history_of_ngs_4.0.pdf : accessed 26 August, 2018

[568] Society of Genealogists. G. W. Marshall. http://www.sog.org.uk/news/article/g-w-marshalls-the-genealogist-guide-1903-is-now-available-online-for-societ : accessed 22 April, 2018

[569] Internet Archive. American and English Genealogies. https://archive.org/details/americanenglishg00usliuoft : accessed 22 April, 2018

[570] Internet Archive. About. https://archive.org/about/ : accessed 26 August, 2018

[571] George Cokayne. 1900. The Complete Baronetage. https://archive.org/stream/cu31924092524374#page/n7/mode/2up : accessed 21 April, 2018

[572] The Society of Genealogists. About the Society. http://www.sog.org.uk/about/history-of-the-society/ : accessed 21 April, 2018

[573] Pine, L. G., ed. (1949) *Burke's genealogical and heraldic history of the peerage, baronetage and knightage, Privy Council & order of precedence.* 99th ed. London: Burke's Peerage. https://archive.org/stream/burkesgenealogic1949unse#page/n0/mode/2up : accessed 15 March, 2017

[574] US National Library of Medicine. The Francis Crick Papers. The Discovery of the Double Helix, 1951-1953. https://profiles.nlm.nih.gov/SC/Views/Exhibit/narrative/doublehelix.html : accessed 7 April, 2019

[575] Locke Books. Free download. Rabbi Malcolm H. Stern. Americans of Jewish Descent: 600 Genealogies (1654-1988).http://www.lockebooks.com/post.php?q=First%20American%20Jewish%20Families%20600%20Genealogies%20 1654%201988 : accessed 30 December, 2018

[576] The National Archives. History of the Public Records Acts. http://www.nationalarchives.gov.uk/information-management/legislation/public-records-act/history-of-pra/ : accessed 19 June, 2018

[577] The Federation of Family History Societies. http://www.ffhs.org.uk/ : accessed 26 October, 2018

[578] Federation of Genealogical Societies. About. Our History. https://fgs.org/about/our-history/ : accessed 30 December, 2018

[579] Federation of Genealogical Societies. Home page. https://fgs.org/ : accessed 30 December, 2018

[580] Guild of One Name Studies. Home. https://one-name.org/about-the-guild/ : accessed 21 November, 2018

[581] Guild of One Name Studies. Benefits of Joining. https://one-name.org/about-the-guild/benefits-of-joining-the-guild/ : accessed 21 November, 2018

[582] Association of Professional Genealogists. About Us. https://www.apgen.org/about/index.html : accessed 11 September, 2018

[583] APG. About. https://www.apgen.org/about/ : accessed 14 April, 2019

[584] JewishGen. Who we are. https://www.jewishgen.org/JewishGen/Who.html : accessed 14 April, 2019

[585] Ancestry. Blog. Family Tree Maker: 20-Year Anniversary. https://blogs.ancestry.com/ancestry/2009/12/11/family-tree-maker-20-year-anniversary/ : accessed 22 April, 2019

[586] The Genealogical Speakers Guild. About Us. https://www.genealogicalspeakersguild.org/aboutus.php : accessed 29 December, 2018

[587] The Peerage. http://www.thepeerage.com/index.htm : accessed 13 June, 2018

[588] The Peerage, Darryl Lundy. http://www.thepeerage.com/p10106.htm#i101053 : accessed 22 April, 2018

[589] The National Archives. http://www.nationalarchives.gov.uk/about/our-role/what-we-do/our-history/ : accessed 1 May, 2018

[590] The National Archives. http://www.nationalarchives.gov.uk/ : accessed 1 May, 2018

[591] ISOGG. What is ISOGG? https://isogg.org/wiki/Wiki_Welcome_Page : accessed 31 October, 2018

[592] ISOGG Wiki. 23AndMe. https://isogg.org/wiki/23andMe : accessed 22 April, 2019

[593] GenealogyInTime Magazine. About Us. http://www.genealogyintime.com/about-us.html : accessed 30 December, 2018

[594] Burkes Peerage Foundation. https://burkespeerage.com/foundation_foundation.php : accessed 22 April, 2018

[595] FFHS. Rebranding. http://www.ffhs.org.uk/rebranding.php : accessed 23 April, 2019

[596] Chron. 10 Characteristics of Professionalism. Chris Joseph; Updated June 27, 2018. https://smallbusiness.chron.com/10-characteristics-professionalism-708.html : accessed 19 September, 2018

[597] Irish Times. John Grenham. Irish Roots: Professional genealogy lives on despite internet. 15 June, 2015. https://www.irishtimes.com/culture/heritage/irish-roots-professional-genealogy-lives-on-despite-internet-1.2243031 : accessed 5 May, 2019

[598] FutureLearn. Courses. Genealogy. https://www.futurelearn.com/courses/genealogy : accessed 11 September, 2018

[599] The University of Strathclyde. Centre for lifelong learning. Genealogy. https://www.strath.ac.uk/studywithus/centreforlifelonglearning/genealogy/ : accessed 11 September, 2018

[600] YouTube. Genealogy: Researching Your Family Tree - Further Study. 28m50s. https://www.youtube.com/watch?v=tYheAfm-F_Y : accessed 11 September, 2018

[601] The University of Dundee. Centre for Archive and Information Studies. Family and Local History. https://www.dundee.ac.uk/cais/programmes/familylocalhistory/ : accessed 11 September, 2018

[602] Pharos Tutors. Online Genealogy Courses. https://www.pharostutors.com/ : accessed 11 September, 2018

[603] NCC Resources Ltd. Genealogy Diploma . https://www.ncchomelearning.co.uk/genealogy-diploma.html : accessed 19 September, 2018

[604] The Institute of Heraldic and Genealogical Studies. IHGS. Correspondence Course in Genealogy. http://www.ihgs.ac.uk/courses-correspondence : accessed 11 September, 2018

[605] The Society of Genealogists. Events and courses. http://www.sog.org.uk/books-courses/events-courses/ : accessed 19 September, 2018

[606] The Federation of Family History Societies. http://www.ffhs.org.uk/events/courses.php : accessed 15 April, 2018

[607] National Archives. http://media.nationalarchives.gov.uk/index.php/category/family-history/ : accessed 15 April, 2018

[608] Brigham Young University, Utah. Center for Family History and Genealogy, https://cfhg.byu.edu/Pages/Home.aspx : accessed 11 September, 2018

[609] BYU. Family History Conferences. https://familyhistoryconferences.byu.edu/ : accessed 22 April, 2019

[610] The National Institute for Genealogical Studies. https://www.genealogicalstudies.com/?fbclid=IwAR01Sf_K3xewgvlwBYZ6cldlHTL_hTP8HuJICGRvACZIl3vYFJdedDLeSgg : accessed 10 November, 2019

[611] Cindi's List. Education (Genealogical). https://www.cyndislist.com/education/?fbclid=IwAR3HBu-Ncd9gyHbmtuQTKBUprGNXmiMl5OvijhybX-KnsjqkxsNhC3hq_YE : accessed 10 November, 2019

[612] Linda's Family of Nutz. Blog Spot. Linda Debe. Furthering your genealogical education. Updated 12 June, 2019. https://lindasfamilyofnutz.blogspot.com/?fbclid=IwAR0b77hpxRJw_e_amMR5iDJDdKuumE4mUTuvVr-YYoQFuiSJsci6wJ9m6uc : accessed 10 November, 2019

[613] Facebook. Genealogy Squad. Elizabeth Shown Mills answers a member's question about courses. https://www.facebook.com/groups/genealogysquad/?multi_permalinks=2473063702937514&notif_id=1573407557636163&notif_t=group_activity : accessed 10 November, 2019

[614] The Ethics and Compliance Initiative. Glossary. http://www.ethics.org/resources/free-toolkit/toolkit-glossary : accessed 13 September, 2018

[615] The International Council of Nurses. Code of Ethics for Nurses. https://www.icn.ch/sites/default/files/inline-files/2012_ICN_Codeofethicsfornurses_%20eng.pdf : accessed 13 September, 2018

[616] GMC UK. Good medical practice.https://www.gmc-uk.org/ethical-guidance/ethical-guidance-for-doctors/good-medical-practice : accessed 19 September, 2018

[617] GMC UK. The duties of a doctor registered with the General Medical Council https://www.gmc-uk.org/ethical-guidance/ethical-guidance-for-doctors/good-medical-practice/duties-of-a-doctor : accessed 19 September, 2018

[618] The American Society of Genealogists. http://fasg.org/about/ : accessed 19 September 2018

[619] AGRA. Welcome to AGRA. http://www.agra.org.uk/ accessed 13 April, 2018

[620] AGRA. Code of Practice. http://www.agra.org.uk/about-code-of-practice : accessed 13 April, 2018

[621] AGRA. Complaints Procedure. http://www.agra.org.uk/about-complaints-procedure : accessed 13 April, 2018

[622] Find My Past. https://www.findmypast.co.uk/articles/partner-page-agra accessed 13 April, 2018

[623] FGS. Sandra Hargreaves Lubeking and Loretto Dennis Szucs. FGS history 1975–2000. https://fgs.org/about/our-history/ : accessed 30 December, 2018

[624] Federation of Genealogical Societies. Bylaws. https://fgs.org/about/bylaws/ : accessed 30 December, 2018

[625] Association of Professional Genealogists. About Us. https://www.apgen.org/about/index.html : accessed 11 September, 2018

[626] Association of Professional Genealogists. History. https://www.apgen.org/history/index.html : accessed 11 September, 2018. (From the 20th Anniversary Issue of APG Quarterly, August 1999. Compiled by Tanya Kelley, with contributions from Robert C. Anderson, CG, FASG, Roger D. Joslyn, CG, FUGA, FASG, Suzanne McVetty, CG, Eileen Polakoff, Shirley Langdon Wilcox, CG, Kay Germain Ingalls, CGRS).

[627] APG. Home page. https://www.apgen.org/ : accessed 27 October, 2018

[628] Association of Professional Genealogists. https://www.apgen.org/ : accessed 13 September, 2018

[629] Association of Professional Genealogists. Code of Ethics and Professional Practices. www.apgen.org/ethics : accessed 15 April, 2018

[630] The Association of Scottish Genealogists & Researchers in Archives, ASGRA. History. http://www.asgra.co.uk/history.php accessed 13 April, 2018

[631] The Association of Scottish Genealogists & Researchers in Archives, ASGRA. Code of Practice. http://www.asgra.co.uk/codeofpractice.php accessed 13 April, 2018

[632] Accredited Genealogists Ireland. http://accreditedgenealogists.ie/ : accessed 13 April, 2018

[633] Accredited Genealogists Ireland. Constitution. http://accreditedgenealogists.ie/constitution/#constit_rules : accessed 15 April, 2018

[634] AGI. Complaints Investigation Procedure. http://accreditedgenealogists.ie/constitution/ accessed 13 April, 2018

[635] AGI. Complaints Investigation Panel http://accreditedgenealogists.ie/constitution/ accessed 13 April, 2018

[636] The International Association of Jewish Genealogical Societies. Blog. About. http://www.iajgs.org/blog/about/about-iajgs/ : accessed 30 December, 2018

[637] JewishGen InfoFile. Rabbi Malcolm Stern's 'Ten Commandments in Genealogy.' https://www.jewishgen.org/InfoFiles/mstern.txt : accessed 30 December, 2018

[638] International Association of Jewish Genealogical Societies. Blog. Code of Conduct. http://www.iajgs.org/blog/code-of-conduct/ : accessed 30 December, 2018

[639] BCG. Ethics and Standards. https://bcgcertification.org/ethics-standards/ : accessed 5 May, 2019

[640] BCG. Genealogy Standards, fiftieth-anniversary edition (2014). https://bcgcertification.org/product/bcg-genealogy-standards/ : accessed 19 September, 2018

[641] The Board for Certification of Genealogists. Genealogist's Code of Ethics. https://bcgcertification.org/ethics-standards/code/ : accessed 15 November, 2018

[642] The Board for Certification of Genealogists. Ethics and Standards. https://bcgcertification.org/ethics-standards/ : accessed 19 September, 2018

[643] BCG Certification. Genealogical Proof Standard. https://bcgcertification.org/ethics-standards/ : accessed 5 May, 2019

[644] International Commission for the Accreditation of Professional Genealogists. https://www.icapgen.org/ : accessed 23 December, 2018

[645] International Commission for the Accreditation of Professional Genealogists. Mission statement. https://www.icapgen.org/about-icapgen/mission-statement/ : accessed 23 December, 2018

[646] International Commission for the Accreditation of Professional Genealogists. Did you know? https://www.icapgen.org/wp-content/uploads/2018/07/Did-you-know-ICAPGen-facts.pdf : accessed 23 December, 2018

[647] International Commission for the Accreditation of Professional Genealogists. Professional Standards. https://www.icapgen.org/professional-ethics/ : accessed 23 December, 2018

[648] International Commission for the Accreditation of Professional Genealogists. Code of Ethics. https://www.icapgen.org/professional-ethics/code-of-ethics/ : accessed 23 December, 2018

[649] Register of Qualified Genealogists, RQG. http://www.qualifiedgenealogists.org/ : accessed 19 September, 2018

[650] RQG. The Professional Code. http://www.qualifiedgenealogists.org/the-professional-code : accessed 19 Nov, 2018

[651] Qualified Genealogists. The Professional Code. https://www.qualifiedgenealogists.org/the-professional-code : accessed 23 April, 2019

[652] Register of Qualified Genealogists. Homepage. http://www.qualifiedgenealogists.org/ : accessed 19 Nov, 2018

[653] FASG. Resources. Accreditation. https://fasg.org/resources/accreditation/ : accessed 19 September, 2018

[654] Chron. Small Business. Meaning of Professionalism and Work Ethic. Kimberlee Leonard. Updated June 30, 2018. https://smallbusiness.chron.com/meaning-professionalism-work-ethic-746.html : accessed 19 September, 2018

[655] Changing Minds. Values, morals and ethics. http://changingminds.org/explanations/values/values_morals_ethics.htm : accessed 17 September, 2018

[656] Chron. Small Business. What Are the Differences Between Ethical Issues & Moral Issues in Business? https://smallbusiness.chron.com/differences-between-ethical-issues-moral-issues-business-48134.html : accessed 16 September, 2018

[657] The Ethics and Compliance Initiative. Glossary. http://www.ethics.org/resources/free-toolkit/toolkit-glossary : accessed 13 September, 2018

[658] Amazon products. Thomas MacEntee. After You're Gone: Future Proofing Your Genealogy Research. https://www.amazon.com/gp/product/B00X8QDQEA/ref=dbs_a_def_rwt_bibl_vppi_i9 : accessed 8 November, 2018

[659] MSN. Robbie Williams called 'disrespectful' by X Factor fans for asking transgender contestant his name before transition. https://www.msn.com/en-gb/entertainment/celebrity/robbie-williams-called-disrespectful-by-x-factor-fans-for-asking-transgender-contestant-his-name-before-transition/ar-BBN3N5o?ocid=spartandhp : accessed 9 September, 2018

[660] Reddit. Genealogy Comments. Documenting transgender in a family tree. https://www.reddit.com/r/Genealogy/comments/74fop7/documenting_transgender_in_family_tree/ : accessed 15 November, 2018

[661] NHS UK. IVF. https://www.nhs.uk/conditions/ivf/ : accessed 15 November, 2018

[662] New York Times. Clyde Haberman. 10 June, 2018. Scientists Can Design 'Better' Babies. Should They? https://www.nytimes.com/2018/06/10/us/11retro-baby-genetics.html : accessed 17 September, 2018

[663] Brown, L., Powell, M., 2015. Louise Brown: My Life As the World's First Test-Tube Baby. Bristol Books. https://books.google.co.uk/books/about/Louise_Brown.html?id=puIBSQAACAAJ&source=kp_book_description&redir

esc=y : accessed 27 August, 2018

[664] YouTube. Louise Brown, My life as the world's first test-tube baby'. 2015. 4 minutes, 51 seconds. https://www.youtube.com/watch?v=uoRhVmX8krM : accessed 5 September, 2018

[665] YouTube. First test tube baby Louise Brown (1978). 2 minutes, 18 seconds. https://www.youtube.com/watch?v=pqu8Y4XGFK4&app=desktop : accessed 5 September, 2018.

[666] Bristol Museums. Allie Dillon and Nicky Sugar. The first IVF mother: the Lesley Brown collection. Posted on May 30, 2018 by Lauren MacCarthy. https://www.bristolmuseums.org.uk/blog/first-ivf-mother-lesley-brown-collection/ : accessed 11 June, 2018

[667] Bristol Archives. Papers of Lesley Brown, the first woman to conceive through IVF. http://archives.bristol.gov.uk/Record.aspx?src=CalmView.Catalog&id=45827 : accessed 23 April, 2019

[668] BBC News. Martin Hutchinson Beating the odds: IVF's first boy. Last updated 23 July, 2003. http://news.bbc.co.uk/1/hi/health/3052688.stm : accessed 23 April, 2019

[669] Personal conversation with Nathan Dylan Goodwin. August, 2018

[670] Advice given, with thanks, by a genetic genealogist in collaboration with donor conceived adults (DCA) via social media support groups. May 2019

[671] Wikipedia. Sperm donation. https://en.wikipedia.org/wiki/Sperm_donation#Private_or_.22directed.22_donors : accessed 16 October, 2018

[672] IMDb. 2017. Thank you for coming. https://www.imdb.com/title/tt5932420/ : accessed 14 October, 2018

[673] IMDb. 2017. Thank you for coming. https://www.imdb.com/title/tt5932420/ : accessed 14 October, 2018

[674] People's World. Eric A. Gordon 'Thank You for Coming': A sperm donor's daughter searches for identity. June 12, 2017. http://www.peoplesworld.org/article/thank-you-for-coming-a-sperm-donors-daughter-searches-for-identity/ : accessed 14 October, 2018

[675] People's World. Eric A. Gordon 'Thank You for Coming': A sperm donor's daughter searches for identity. June 12, 2017. http://www.peoplesworld.org/article/thank-you-for-coming-a-sperm-donors-daughter-searches-for-identity/ : accessed 14 October, 2018

[676] We Are Donor Conceived. https://www.wearedonorconceived.com/ : accessed 22 April, 2019

[677] Facebook. We Are Donor Conceived. https://www.facebook.com/groups/wearedonorconceived/ : accessed 22 April, 2019

[678] Facebook. DNA for the Donor Conceived. https://www.facebook.com/groups/1623033431359526/ : accessed 22 April, 2019

[679] People's World. Eric A. Gordon 'Thank You for Coming': A sperm donor's daughter searches for identity. June 12, 2017. http://www.peoplesworld.org/article/thank-you-for-coming-a-sperm-donors-daughter-searches-for-identity/ : accessed 14 October, 2018

[680] The Mirror Newspaper. Sperm donor who advertises on Facebook says he's fathered 150 children across America thanks to 'super' seed https://www.mirror.co.uk/news/us-news/sperm-donor-who-advertises-facebook-12889072 : accessed 15 November, 2018

[681] The Guardian. The letter you always wanted to write. A letter to … my son's sperm donor. 2 Apr 2011. https://www.theguardian.com/lifeandstyle/2011/apr/02/letter-to-sons-sperm-donor : accessed 14 October, 2018

[682] Advice given, with thanks, by a genetic genealogist in collaboration with donor conceived adults (DCA) via social media support groups. May 2019

[683] Donor Conceived Register. http://donorconceivedregister.org.uk/ : accessed 5 May, 2019

[684] BBC. iPM. Finding My Real Dad. 24 minutes. https://www.bbc.co.uk/programmes/b0bgbhk3 : accessed 28 April, 2019

[685] BBC. iPM I'm not looking to be a father. 24 minutes. https://www.bbc.co.uk/programmes/b0bgp8kd : accessed 28 April, 2019

[686] Royal College of Surgeons. John Hunter. https://www.rcseng.ac.uk/museums-and-archives/hunterian-museum/about-us/john-hunter/ : accessed 22 April, 2019

[687] Britannica. Artificial insemination in humans. https://www.britannica.com/science/artificial-insemination#ref1125363 : accessed 22 April, 2019

[688] Fertstert. Gregoire, A.T., Mayer, R.C., The Impregnators. Pp. 130-135. https://www.fertstert.org/article/S0015-0282(16)35476-0/pdf : accessed 22 April, 2019

[689] Daily Mail. https://www.dailymail.co.uk/news/article-6823737/48-children-discover-fertility-doctor-used-sperm-WITHOUT-patients-consent-dad.html : accessed 22 April, 2019

[690] The Atlantic. Sarah Zhang. Posted April, 2019. https://www.theatlantic.com/magazine/archive/2019/04/fertility-doctor-donald-cline-secret-children/583249/?fbclid=IwAR3AlRQVOs5hGBaxDyT6Hx6KywGkaSJuY7DAXc1hEeSVdtmqNAioUEAOhEM : accessed 22 April, 2019

[691] Indy Star. Shari Rudavsky. 'I was raped 15 times and didn't even know it': Fertility fraud bill advances. Posted 25 January, 2019. https://eu.indystar.com/story/news/2019/01/23/donald-cline-aftermath-fertility-fraud-bill-advances-indiana-senate/2656610002/ : accessed 22 April, 2019

[692] Indy Star. Shari Rudavsky. 'I was raped 15 times and didn't even know it': Fertility fraud bill advances. Posted 25 January, 2019. https://eu.indystar.com/story/news/2019/01/23/donald-cline-aftermath-fertility-fraud-bill-advances-indiana-senate/2656610002/ : accessed 22 April, 2019

[693] Gov. UK. Rights for surrogate mothers. https://www.gov.uk/rights-for-surrogate-mothers : accessed 9 Sep, 2018.

[694] Wikipedia. Surrogacy laws by country. https://en.wikipedia.org/wiki/Surrogacy_laws_by_country : accessed 9 September, 2018

[695] Wikipedia. Surrogacy laws by country. https://en.wikipedia.org/wiki/Surrogacy_laws_by_country : accessed 9 September, 2018

[696] Genealogy Stack Exchange. Reply. How to display sperm/egg donors or surrogates on a family tree? https://genealogy.stackexchange.com/questions/10177/how-to-display-sperm-egg-donors-or-surrogates-on-a-family-tree : accessed 9 September, 2018

[697] Future for All. Designer Babies. https://www.futureforall.org/bioengineering/designer-babies.html : accessed 17 September, 2017

[698] Huxley.Net https://www.huxley.net/ : accessed 9 September, 2018

[699] Huxley.Net https://www.huxley.net/ : accessed 9 September, 2018

[700] Huxley.Net https://www.huxley.net/ : accessed 9 September, 2018

[701] Wikipedia. Aldous Huxley. https://en.wikipedia.org/wiki/Aldous_Huxley : accessed 9 September, 2018

[702] Huxley.Net. https://www.huxley.net/ : accessed 9 September, 2018

[703] Wikipedia. Julian Huxley. https://en.wikipedia.org/wiki/Julian_Huxley : accessed 23 April, 2019

[704] Wikipedia. Andrew Huxley. https://en.wikipedia.org/wiki/Andrew_Huxley : accessed 23 April, 2019

[705] Gutenburg. Amy E. Zelmer, and David Widger. Project Gutenberg's Evidence as to Man's Place in Nature, by Thomas H. Huxley. Last Updated 22, January 2013 https://www.gutenberg.org/files/2931/2931-h/2931-h.htm : accessed 17 September, 2018

[706] Huxley.Net. Pearce, D. Brave New World? A Defence Of Paradise-Engineering. https://www.huxley.net/ : accessed 15 November, 2018

[707] Know Genetics. Introduction to Eugenics. http://knowgenetics.org/history-of-eugenics/ : accessed 23 April, 2019

[708] Wikipedia. International Eugenics Conference. https://en.wikipedia.org/wiki/International_Eugenics_Conference : accessed 23 April, 2019

[709] Huxley.Net. Sir Francis Galton (1822-1911). https://www.huxley.net/contexts/index.html : accessed 9 Sep, 2018

[710] Super Cool Robots. Marriage to Robots Ok in the Future? 14 February, 2015. http://www.supercoolrobots.com/marriage-to-robots-ok-in-the-future/ : accessed 17 September, 2018

[711] Science. How Stuff Works. Josh Clark. Will robots get married? https://science.howstuffworks.com/robot-wedding.htm : accessed 17 September, 2018

[712] Slate. Gary Marchant. A.I. Thee Wed. Humans should be able to marry robots. http://www.slate.com/articles/technology/future_tense/2015/08/humans_should_be_able_to_marry_robots.html?via=gdpr-consent : accessed 17 September, 2018

[713] University of Toronto. Department of Psychology. Eyal Reingold and Johnathan Nightingale. Eyal Reingold and Johnathan Nightingale. PSY371. Artificial Intelligence Tutorial Review. http://www.psych.utoronto.ca/users/reingold/courses/ai/turing.html : accessed 17 September, 2018

[714] Harper Collins. 2008. Love and Sex with Robots. https://www.harpercollins.com/9780061359804/love-and-sex-with-robots/ : accessed 17 September, 2018

[715] The Guardian. Interview. Let's talk about sex... with robots. Jack Schofield. 16 September, 2009. https://www.theguardian.com/technology/2009/sep/16/sex-robots-david-levy-loebner : accessed 17 Sep, 2018

[716] Science. How Stuff Works. Josh Clark. Will robots get married? https://science.howstuffworks.com/robot-wedding.htm : accessed 17 September, 2018

[717] The Sun newspaper. Margi Murphy. Cyber ceremonies. British law WILL bend to allow humans and robots to marry sooner than you think. Posted 20 December, 2016. https://www.thesun.co.uk/news/2447039/british-law-will-bend-to-allow-humans-and-robots-to-marry-sooner-than-you-think/ : accessed 17 September, 2018

[718] Medium. Brian Hanley. Robot marriage is idiocy—Let me prove it to you. Reductio ad absurdum. https://medium.com/@brianhanley/robot-marriage-is-idiocy-let-me-prove-it-to-you-reductio-ad-absurdum-b977ea53c78b : accessed 17 September, 2018

[719] The Federalist. Bre Payton. 12 August, 2015. http://thefederalist.com/2015/08/12/marrying-robots-terrible-idea/ : accessed 17 September, 2018

[720] CNN. Kyung Lah. Tokyo man marries video game character. 17 December, 2009.

http://edition.cnn.com/2009/WORLD/asiapcf/12/16/japan.virtual.wedding/ : accessed 17 September, 2018

[721] Slate. Gary Marchant. A.I. Thee Wed. Humans should be able to marry robots. http://www.slate.com/articles/technology/future_tense/2015/08/humans_should_be_able_to_marry_robots.html?via=gdpr-consent : accessed 17 September, 2018

[722] Wired. Regina Lynn. 10 reasons I'd rather marry a robot. https://www.wired.com/2007/11/sexdrive-1130/ : accessed 17 September, 2018

[723] The Federalist. Bre Payton. 12 August, 2015. http://thefederalist.com/2015/08/12/marrying-robots-terrible-idea/ : accessed 17 September, 2018

[724] IMDb. 2014. Ex Machina. https://www.imdb.com/title/tt0470752/ : accessed 17 September, 2018

[725] IMDb. 2007. Lars and The Real Girl. https://www.imdb.com/title/tt0805564/ : accessed 17 September, 2018

[726] IMDb. 2015. Human. https://www.imdb.com/title/tt3327994/ : accessed 17 September, 2018

[727] News Hub. Doco explores married man's 'relationship' with sex doll. November, 2017. https://www.newshub.co.nz/home/world/2017/11/doco-explores-married-man-s-relationship-with-sex-doll.html : accessed 17 September, 2018

[728] Responsible Robotics. https://responsiblerobotics.org/ : accessed 23 April, 2019

[729] TV.Com. Star Trek: The Next Generation. Series 1, Episode 26 - The Neutral Zone. Aired 16 May, 1988. http://www.tv.com/shows/star-trek-the-next-generation/the-neutral-zone-19013/ : accessed 17 September, 2019

[730] Fandom. The Neutral Zone episode. https://memory-alpha.fandom.com/wiki/The_Neutral_Zone_(episode) : accessed 30 September, 2019

[731] The Vintage News. Ian Harvey. People used to Picnic and Play Near their Deceased Loved Ones. Posted 24 September, 2018. https://www.thevintagenews.com/2018/09/24/picnic-in-the-cemetery/ : accessed 14 April, 2019

****

Made in the USA
Coppell, TX
13 November 2020

41235281R10102